THE
REAL ESTATE
FAST TRACK

THE
REAL ESTATE
FAST TRACK

HOW TO CREATE A

$5,000 TO $50,000 PER MONTH

REAL ESTATE CASH FLOW

David Finkel

WILEY

John Wiley & Sons, Inc.

Library of Congress Cataloging-in-Publication Data:

Finkel, David.
    The Real Estate Fast Track : How to Create a $5,000 to $50,000 Per Month Real Estate Cash Flow / David Finkel.
        p.   cm.
    ISBN-13: 978-0-471-72830-6 (pbk.)
    ISBN-10: 0-471-72830-6 (pbk.)
    1. Real estate investment.   2. Real estate business.   3. Cash flow.   I. Title.
    HD1382.5.F565 2006
    332.63'24—dc22

                                                                                        2005031914

Printed in the United States of America.

10   9   8   7   6   5   4   3   2   1

To my lifelong partner, love, and best friend—Heather.
You are my forever.

CONTENTS

PART ONE
The Advanced Investor Workshop

Section I: EARLY STAGE LEVEL TWO INVESTING—DEVELOPING THE FIVE CORE INVESTOR SKILLS

PART TWO
The Real World—12 Months
Building Your Investing Business

PART THREE
Your Turn—Turning This Book into Cash Flow

How Two Escapees from Corporate America Built a Highly Profitable Real Estate Business (and How You Can, Too!)

I can't begin to tell you how proud and excited I was when David asked me to share my story as the Foreword to this book. You see, over the past five years David has been a very important friend and mentor to me and my wife Susan. In fact, David has been one of the most important wealth mentors we've had and we're living proof that the ideas and strategies contained in the pages of this book work. They worked for my wife and me, and I know that they will work for you, too.

When we first met David and Peter at a real estate workshop almost five years ago, my wife Susan and I were trapped in the rat race of corporate America. Susan was a CPA and I was a sales executive for a large corporation. Don't get me wrong—we were grateful for the comfortable living we were earning; but we felt trapped all the same.

You see, Susan had always dreamed of balancing her career with the flexibility and freedom to be fully engaged and raise our kids. She wanted to volunteer at the school, watch all the soccer games, and be home when they got home from school. And I—well, let's just say I dreamed of having the time to be there to watch my kids grow up, instead of being off working long hours for a large company.

So there we were, both working more than we wanted, and at the same time wishing that we could spend more time at home, focused on our growing family.

That's when we made the decision that for things to be different, we need to *make* them different. So we took the plunge and joined David and Peter's Mentorship Program. And what a ride it has been!

The first year of our investing we completed 18 deals. While we made a healthy profit from those deals, by far the greatest payoff was the learning we accumulated. By the end of our second year we had established profitable referral relationships with several of the local banks, which to this day still continue to send deals our way on bank-owned real estate that they want to sell quickly.

Over time our business developed into three areas. First, there is the foreclosure business that we have created. This business is almost entirely systematized right now, just like David teaches you how to do in this book. It generates an average of two to three houses a month that we buy and then fix up or flip. Our second business is our rental portfolio of houses and small to medium-sized apartment buildings. This is our freedom fund that generates a six-figure rental cash flow for our family. And finally, there is the real estate development business that we have, doing small to medium-sized developments in two states.

How did we accomplish all this in less than five years? Simple. We listened to the best. And make no mistake about it, David is one of the best I've ever worked with. When you master the strategies and techniques he has laid out in the pages of this book you'll literally propel your investing business to the next level. Over the years I've read every book he has written and attended every course he has taught; they have made me millions of dollars, and he can help you do the same thing.

But there is a catch here. You're going to have to be the one putting in the work turning the ideas in this book into cash in your bank account. No one can do the work for you. All I can say is that I am so thankful that I listened and took action. And I urge you to do the same. Read this book cover to cover. Devour it! Then get out there and get to work. You can and will succeed, if you listen to the ideas David so clearly lays out in the pages of this book.

STEPHEN WILKLOW
Past Mentorship Graduate and
Current Mentorship Coach

Creating real wealth is never a solo job; it always requires the combined efforts of many people. I want to thank the people who have made my life richer and fuller, and without whom the *Creating Cash Flow* series would never have come to be.

First, I want to thank those people in my business life who have been instrumental in helping me to fulfill my mission to help generations of investors become massively wealthy and to use that wealth to bless the world.

To the entire team at John Wiley & Sons, Inc. and Cape Cod Compositors—you are great to work with, balancing your professional skill with a deep commitment to produce meaningful projects that touch people's lives. I am proud to be associated with you.

To my Maui Mastermind friends and team: Diane, Scott, Amy, Monica, Gabe, Meagan, Morgan, Aaron, Elizabeth, Michael, Beverly, Blake, the other Michael, Stephen, Susan, and the very special Maui participants. You inspire me to be more of who I truly am. Thank you.

Thank you to my friends at Mentor Financial Group (MFG): Peter, Paige, Amy, Gayla, Beth, Dennis, Marilyn, Angela, Jeff, Christina, Kim, Laura, Alex, Brian, Thomas, the other Thomas, Elizabeth, Deb, Bob, Lourdes, Larry, Aubrey, Michelle, Stephen, Cheryl, Scott, John, Rob, Emily, and Nate. You will always be family to me. My deepest appreciation also to all the clients and students of MFG—past, present, and future. You have let me into your lives, and while you may never know this, you have given me more than I can ever repay by taking action and living the ideas in this book.

Thank you also to the other business friends who have contributed so much over the years: Lee, Robert, J.P., Terry, Chris, the other Lee, Clay, Bill, Ann, the other Bill, and Todd.

Finally, to those people who have made me truly wealthy—my friends and family—thank you for your presence in my life: Heather, Alex, Laurie, Stacey, Mom and Bill, Dad and Karen, my grandparents—Morey and Gerry, Arthur and Jillian, Daniel, Miranda, Gail, Mark and Trish, Darcy, Eric and Luz, Karimjeet, Jean and Phillip, Daryl and Dara, Margie, Martin, Jonathon and Kirsten, Gratia and Bill, Lydia, Jillian, Ethan and Jen, Edson, Sharon, Grant and Jana, Nancy and Ysa, Madeleine and Claira, Ted, and the list goes on.

What if there was a way for you to create $5,000 to $50,000 per month of real estate cash flow? And what if, instead of having to work 40, 60, 80 hours each week to earn this money you could build your investing business so that in five to seven years you could go passive in your investing and enjoy the cash flow without the day-to-day work? And finally, what if you could do it in a way that would make your cash flow *secure*—so that no matter what some bigwig at some large corporation decided, your income streams still flowed to you month after month, year after year?

That probably seems impossible, or maybe too good to be true. But just for a brief moment, imagine it were truly available to you.

How would it feel to know that you have the freedom to do what you want, when you want, with whom you want, the way you want? Imagine you are in total control of your financial life with a myriad of choices laid out before you each and every day. The freedom can make you light-headed, giddy, perhaps a little dizzy!

Welcome, my friend, to the world of real estate investing. When done the right way, investing in real estate can create for you an inflation-proof cash flow that will take care of you and your family forever.

Before I begin, I want to make one thing abundantly clear—this is going to take work. If you think you can just get started with your investing and wake up tomorrow morning a multimillionaire, you need to think again. Using the ideas I am going to share with you, working part-time, it may take you as long as 10 years to build your real estate cash flow to the point where you can retire and live comfortably on that cash flow for the rest of your life. If you are a full-time investor, it may take you five to seven years to achieve this degree of financial freedom. But wouldn't it be worth it to work hard and smart for five to seven years and at the end of that time be in a position to comfortably retire with your income stream secure? Think about it. Most people spend 40-plus years working to build *other* people's businesses, and in the end over 95 percent of them end up either dead or dead broke, depending on the government or other people for their financial survival. These aren't my numbers, they're the federal government's! Does spending 40 years of your life for a 5 percent chance of success seem like a good bet to you? It's probably clear to you where I stand on the matter!

Instead I suggest that you take a fraction of that same energy and effort and redirect it into yourself—building your own investing business so that you can take care of yourself and your family the way that, in your heart of hearts, you know you deserve. The road will be harder than you ever imagined, but the rewards will be sweeter than you could ever have anticipated. And the best thing of all is that once you build your profitable investing business the right way, it's a straightforward process to turn that business into a hands-off moneymaker for you.

That's the real power of real estate—it's a business in which an average person can earn extraordinary income because of the nature of the business.

My Story

Indulge me for a moment, if you will, as I give you a quick snapshot of how I got started with my investing and what I've been able to accomplish. You deserve to know more about the person who will be mentoring you in building your investing business. In fact, later in the book I talk about why you should never listen to someone's advice unless that person has what you want in the area of life that he or she is talking about.

I started out as an athlete, training to play in the Olympics. My sport was field hockey and I played on the United States National Team for about seven years. As I was gearing up to play in the Olympics, I started having severe back pain and nerve problems in my left leg. By the time the doctors and I finally figured out what was going on over a year later, it was too late for me to play in the Olympics. (It turned out that I had a small tumor—benign—in my hip, growing on my sciatic nerve. The surgeon removed the tumor and I am fully healed, although too late to play in the Olympics.)

As you can imagine, I was deeply saddened by that lost opportunity. But out of the darkest of events equivalent or greater good fortune comes. In my case it was in the form of my real estate mentor and business partner for many years—Peter Conti.

When we met at a wealth workshop we were both attending, we hit it off from the start. Peter had been very successful investing in Colorado, and he wanted to start teaching investing to others. The problem was that while he was a savvy investor, he wasn't much for teaching. I, on the other hand, had supported myself through my playing career by teaching and coaching. He had the real estate know-how, and I had the ability to break skills down and teach them in a way that transferred that knowledge fast. Within 12 months of working together I had put together dozens of deals and was on my way to building a sizable real estate portfolio of my own.

Over the years, I've built investing businesses that invested in single family houses, condos, and apartment buildings. I've bought everything from small, one-bedroom condos to huge apartment complexes.

But by far the biggest thing I have learned is exactly how to help new and seasoned investors alike make a ton more money with less time and effort. Over the past decade, my clients have literally bought and sold over a *billion* dollars of real estate. Again, I'm not sharing this to impress you, but rather to impress upon you how doable real estate really is. I started out as a 26-year-old athlete, with no real business experience and no knowledge of real estate, and within six years I was a multimillionaire. If I can do it, you can too. In fact, it's my belief that there is no better vehicle for creating and enjoying your wealth than real estate. It is just such a simple, yet powerful wealth-creating force that the average person can become incredibly successful investing.

The Eight Major Business Success Factors

Real estate lets you automatically harness the eight biggest business success factors in a way to consistently produce big cash profits. Let's look at all eight now.

Business Success Factor One: Leverage

Real estate lets you leverage yourself into the property using other people's money. Over the years that I have mentored several thousand students in launching their investing businesses, my students typically have less than 5 percent of the value of the property in the deal as their cash and over 95 percent of the funding coming from outside sources. That means they have a leverage multiplier of over twenty-fold! The best part of real estate leverage is that you can use what's called *upside leverage* to get the benefits of the magnifying return of leverage without the downside risk that's normally associated with it.

Business Success Factor Two: Appreciation

In very few businesses do the assets of that business appreciate in value year after year. In fact, in most businesses, the capital assets *depreciate* every year—that is, go down in value. Real estate is one of the few capital assets that a business can own that goes up in value over time. What this means is that at the same time your real estate business is generating cash flow month in and month out, the underlying assets, the real estate itself, are going up in value and adding to your net worth.

Business Success Factor Three: Tax Savings

In almost no other business are your profits so potentially shielded from the wealth-diminishing effects of taxes as they are when investing in real estate. The government wants investors to provide housing and commercial real estate, and it incentivizes them with powerful tax advantages that even the smallest of investors can tap into.

Business Success Factor Four: Simple to Sell or Rent

The biggest challenge for most businesses is to find their customers. In fact, for many businesses this is the single greatest challenge they'll ever face—to establish the customer base to generate the cash flow to support their business.

But with real estate, this is much easier. Take the case of an average rental house that rents for $1,500 per month. When you find one renter for that house who lives there for a year, your real estate business will generate $18,000 of gross income from the rents that year. And what if you are able to keep that tenant happily living in that property for three years? That means that one tenant will generate $54,000 of gross income for your business. All that income from leasing out one property!

Now multiply that by 10 houses and you have a simple part-time rental business that generates $180,000 per year of gross income, or over $1.8 million of gross income over 10 years. In very few other business can the average person generate that type of sales volume without an expensive and highly skilled sales team. But with real estate it's a simple and straightforward process. Why? Because there is always a ready market for quality real estate. And this is true whether your goal is to rent out a property, sell it to a retail buyer, or put a tenant buyer in your property on a rent-to-own basis.

Or, if you prefer the route of buying low and selling high, in what other business can you so easily make a $400,000 sale like selling a house? Or have highly skilled sales agents fighting to get the rights to sell your house for you for such a small sales commission? I think you get the idea.

Business Success Factor Five: Inflation-Proofed

By its very definition, inflation means that the purchasing power of a dollar is diminished because the cost for staples like food, shelter, and clothing has increased. Built into the very formula by which inflation is measured is the assumption that as the cost of living increases, with it goes the cost, whether it be sales price or rental amount, of real estate. This means that as you build your cash flow–generating investing business, your profits are inflation hedged because your real estate will rise with the tide of inflation. While over the short term this may not seem to matter, over 20 to 30 years it will make a huge difference to your quality of life because your cash flow will have more than doubled as it keeps pace with inflation. Plus, the underlying equity you have, which is a large component of your net worth, will have also gone dramatically higher.

Business Success Factor Six: Forced Appreciation

One of the best things about real estate is that it exists in an imperfect marketplace. There is no absolute determiner of value because personal circumstances, market conditions, and individual skill and expertise have a dramatic influence on the price and terms with which you can acquire a property. This means you can buy a $400,000 property for 30 to 40 percent below value, and the very moment you buy the property, because your circumstances are different, that property is instantly worth $120,000 to $160,000 more! Remember, value does not exist independently of the owner's context. This makes real estate one of the fastest pathways to building great wealth.

When I look at all the ways my students have literally made hundreds of millions of dollars, the simple truth is that forced appreciation was the single most important profit generator for them in the early years of their investing. Over time, the appreciation and cash flow from their portfolios outpaced forced appreciation in importance, but never underestimate the power of personal circumstances and the specialized skills and knowledge you are acquiring to help you make hundreds of thousands of dollars in the early years of your investing.

Business Success Factor Seven: Easy to Autopilot

Real estate is one of the easiest businesses to put on autopilot. By building your investing business the right way, you are able to transition out of the day-to-day oversight of your investing company, and into the passive role of a hands-off investor who works a few hours a day or less overseeing his or her investing business.

Business Success Factor Eight: Cash Flow

By far the biggest benefit that the typical investor craves from real estate is the cash flow it can generate because this cash flow means freedom. Freedom from working for a boss or company that doesn't value you. Freedom to be in control of your own life.

There are essentially **four types of real estate cash flow.** First, there is the **monthly cash flow** that is derived from the spread between the monthly income a property generates and the monthly expense of owning it. This positive cash flow is what most investors think of when they talk about real estate cash flow. But it is only one of the four sources of income from a property.

Second, you have **up-front cash flow** that comes from the larger chunks of up-front payments your buyers or tenant buyers pay you for the property. For example, if you put a new tenant buyer in one of your homes on a rent-to-own basis*

---

*To gain immediate access to a FREE ebook on how to sell your property on a rent-to-own basis, go to **www.InvestorFasttrack.com.**

and they give you a $10,000 nonrefundable option payment, this money in essence is a form of up-front cash flow. In many ways this type of cash flow is even better than monthly cash flow because you get it all up front instead of having to wait every month for it. Another example of up-front cash flow is a student of mine who found a motivated seller with a property he wanted to unload fast. My student locked up the property using my standard "Agreement to Buy Real Estate" contract, and within three weeks he had sold his contract (i.e., the right to buy that property for such a discounted cash price) to another investor for $15,000 cash! Not bad for a month's work—part-time!

The third type of cash flow is **re-fi cash flow**, which comes when you refinance a property that you own that has gone up in value, in order to tap into the equity and pull out money from it. This type of cash flow is tax-free since it's a "loan" and not actual "profit"; still, it is spendable and investable. The key to intelligently using this type of cash flow is to make sure the property still rents out comfortably for more than the real cost of maintaining it, which includes the new mortgage payments from the refinance, so that you have a safety buffer built into the deal in case the rental market cools. In my opinion, the very best reason to tap into re-fi cash flow is to invest the money into another property. This way you get the profits from two properties instead of only the one you had before!

And the final type of cash flow is the **back-end cash flow** that comes when you resell a property. For example, I have many students who buy 6 to 12 new properties every year, and sell 2 to 4 of their existing portfolio. They earn a few thousand dollars a month or more from the monthly cash flow, but they earn another $150,000 or more each year from the back-end cash flow they get from selling a few of their properties each year. One other benefit of this type of cash flow is that this income is often taxed as *long-term capital gain* versus ordinary earned income. This saves you about 60 percent on your tax bill! I strongly urge you to hang on to all of your real estate that you can over the long term, but there is nothing wrong with pruning your real estate portfolio and selling off some of your properties each year for cash flow, provided you are acquiring even more properties than you are selling each year. In a way, this lets you upgrade your portfolio as you sell off the trouble properties and keep the very best of the best over time.

If the other seven Business Success Factors form a solid foundation upon which you can build your real estate fortune, then factor eight—cash flow—is the fuel that you'll need to reach your destination. Ultimately you will want your real estate business to generate all four types of real estate cash flow to fuel your journey on the Real Estate Fast Track.

The Three Investor Levels—
Your Proven Pathway to Real Estate Success

Over the years of working with thousands of investors I created a model to explain the progression every investor must make on his or her path from launching an investing business to becoming financially free. I call this powerful model the Three Investor Levels.

Level One

Level One investing is about belief. It's about proving to yourself that not only does real estate work for other people, but it works for *you*! How do you prove this to yourself? By *doing* a few deals and making a significant profit. As a Level One investor you have the certainty that real estate will be your proven path to financial success. Yes, you know you still have a lot to learn, but you've seen for yourself how lucrative and possible it really is. The key for Level One is getting yourself into action.

Level Two

Level Two is all about mastering the five core skills of real estate investing and building an investing business to support your real estate portfolio. At first Level Two is about building your knowledge base of investing strategies, tools, and techniques, but later it's about building a real estate investing *business*.

Why is this so important for you? Because ultimately, if you don't learn how to leverage yourself through building a strong business infrastructure of systems and people, you will be limited in two critical ways. First, you will be limited in the scale of projects and profits you can earn. You just can't do big deals without the infrastructure there to make the deal stand. Second, unless you build an investing business, you'll be limited in your potential to create the time and freedom you truly want. That's why it's so important to learn to build an investing business.

In the end, it's this investing business that will help you step into Level Three investing and enjoy a Level Three lifestyle. While Level Two investors create healthy cash flows for themselves and increase their net worth significantly every year, they are still actively tied to their investing business. They are the heart and engine that drives that investing business forward. Without them, their investing businesses will fizzle and die.

Level Three

Level Three is about mastering the art of building an investing business that works so you don't have to. If Level Two investors are the heart, pumping the business forward, Level Three investors are the brain, directing the big picture of the business and enjoying the consistent profits from that business, *without* getting caught up in any of the day-to-day activities for the business. Imagine having built your real estate mini empire in such a way that you earn massive income without having to be involved in the day-to-day oversight of the business. Level Three investors earn at least as much as Level Two investors, but they do it passively. This means Level Three investors work less than 10 hours per *month*. Their property portfolio and real estate business works without them needing to be there to run things.

Level Three investors know how to do *big* real estate deals on commercial real estate, how to convert excess cash into passive streams of income through joint venturing and lending, and how to build a stand-alone business to support their real estate empire in a way that creates time freedom.

The bottom line is that Level Three investors have learned to put their investing on autopilot so they don't just make money, but they create *passive* streams of income.

In the beginning, you'll have to front-load your effort as you develop as an investor. It will take you hundreds of units of effort to succeed as a Level One investor and get your first few paydays. Later, as a Level Two investor, it will take you 10 to 20 units of effort to get your paydays. And finally, as a Level Three investor, it may only take one or two units of effort to enjoy a lifetime of paydays. But you've got to pay your dues at the start.

The Unvarnished Truth about Creating a $5,000 to $50,000 per Month Real Estate Cash Flow

Imagine what it would mean for you if you were able to build your investing business to the point where it generated $5,000 to $50,000 per month, every month. Now take it one step further. What if it only took you 20 hours or less per week to run your investing business? How would it impact your family now that you have this freedom and control over your time? What would you be able to do with your time now that you have the security of knowing that each month $5,000 to $50,000 of cash flow will be streaming into your bank account—month after month, year after year, decade after decade?

Let's be candid here, the average investor never reaches this degree of freedom. The average real estate investor gets wealthy very slowly, and over 30 or 40 years creates a large net worth. They do this by buying 5 or 10 rental properties that they care for and nurture over their lifetime, and in the end these rental properties are their retirement security. This is a solid plan, and it works for hundreds of thousands of mom-and-pop investors around the world.

But what if you don't want to wait 30 years or longer? What if you want it to happen *faster*?

Accelerating the Process—Building Wealth *Fast*

So just how fast can you make it happen? How long will it take you to reach your real estate dreams? Well, years back when Peter first got started with his investing he didn't know anything about real estate. In fact, he started out as an auto mechanic because that's what he had always been good at. He came from a family of seven kids, and he was the one who was expected to struggle all his life. For many years he lived up to this expectation. Yet even during those times there was a part of him that hungered for something more.

All the time he was working for five dollars an hour as a mechanic, he paid close attention and studied what wealthy people were doing. Again and again he watched how so many of those who had started out with nothing had been able to create great wealth investing in real estate.

Sometimes you need to hit rock bottom before you decide to make a change.

For Peter this day came when he was working in an auto repair shop. It was wintertime and the owner was trying to save money by turning off the heat in the garage. It was so cold that his fingers were turning numb as he worked on the cars lined up around him.

He saw the shop owner walk out of the heated office with a steaming mug of coffee. It looked so good he rummaged through his tool box for his mug and went into the office to pour himself a cup, more to wrap his hands around for warmth than anything really.

Just as he was walking out of the office to go back to work, the owner stopped him and said, "Peter! That coffee is for customers only!" As you can imagine, Peter felt about two inches tall as he turned and went back to work. It was at that moment, right then, that he made the decision that he would take the leap and start his investing. He vowed that never again would he or his family be financially dependent on anyone else. He would create the financial freedom to take care of his family and live the life he always knew waited for him.

I wish I could tell you that it was easy, that he made his millions overnight. But he didn't. It was plain hard work. Back when Peter got started, there weren't any structured Mentorship Programs he could join to take him by the hand and show him exactly how to do his investing. He had to figure most of it out by himself. He did invest heavily on home study courses and real estate workshops—to the tune of over $20,000 his first few years in the business—but he said that since he never went to college, he just called that "tuition" for his "Real Estate Degree." And after all, he did earn it all back in his very first year of investing, on his first two real estate deals. Isn't that the way all education should be, paying for itself in 12 months or less?

His next real hurdle came as his real estate portfolio grew so big that he was completely wrapped up in managing it. In fact, at its peak he was so busy dealing with tenants and toilets that he went for a two-year stretch without picking up even one more property. You see, he hadn't learned the difference between being a real estate investor and building a real estate investing business. He was stuck at that point in his life in the landlord trap of tenants and toilets, struggling to keep his head above water. Yes, he was making a lot of money, but he had to work long hours to keep the properties going.

In the end it took Peter close to 10 years to figure out how to build a real estate investing business that worked hard so he didn't have to, which allowed him to enjoy Level Three success. It's pretty remarkable that he was able to do it at all, since no one knew how to teach him this progression. Sure, there were plenty of people teaching techniques for structuring deals or finding motivated sellers, but no one who could show him how to structure his investing business so it worked better without him in it. He had to figure this out all on his own.

Now I on the other hand had it much easier. Not because I was smarter or had a background in real estate, neither of which was the case. Remember, I was the ex-jock who had to give up on my dreams of playing in the Olympics because of a serious injury. I started with no money, no credit, and no business experience of any real kind. Heck, when I met Peter I was living in the attic of a converted garage because that was all I could afford!

But I did have one powerful factor in my favor. When I first started learning how to invest, I had Peter as my personal mentor. In essence, I was Peter's first Mentorship student and I got the benefit of Peter's years of experience. It only took me five years to reach Level Three success with my investing. What was the difference? I had Peter as my mentor and reached Level Three 100 percent faster!

Over the past decade of mentoring new investors to succeed building a profitable real estate business, we've gotten better and better with every generation of students we trained. We've had students blaze through the program and reach Level Three success in less than three years (the current record is 22 months), although the average time it takes for most Level Three students to get there is closer to five to seven years.

So how long will it take you? The answer depends on you. Are you going to listen and follow my instructions? Are you going to get yourself to work consistently to build your investing business, even when you hit moments of frustration where you just want to throw in the towel? Then I think you can do it in five years or less. I believe this is truly possible for you. But let's get real here. What if it took you twice as long? Wouldn't it be worth investing 10 years to create financial freedom for yourself and your family for the rest of your lives? Most people work at jobs for over 40 years and *never* reach financial freedom. I've *never* had a student who stayed the course who didn't succeed in a quarter of that time! And most did it much faster than that.

That's exactly what this book is going to help you do—to get on the Real Estate Fast Track to building a profitable investing business so that you can create a $5,000 to $50,000 per month real estate cash flow, and do it in five years or less.

The road won't always be easy. If it was, then it would be congested and you'd get stuck in the traffic jam of the scared and lazy masses. At times it will seem like the slope is just too steep and the surface just too rocky. But if you persevere, and listen to the coaching and guidance of those who have traveled that road already, I guarantee you can make it to the end. And I know the end is completely worth it for you. Remember, I've made the journey myself and have helped thousands of clients do it too.

In fact, for the first time ever I'll be sharing my advanced real estate business building system with the masses. Normally clients pay me tens of thousands of dollars for this information, and they consistently tell me it was worth every penny. And why not? They've turned the information I'm about to share with you in this book into a cash flow–creating investing business that yields them and their families hundreds of thousands of dollars every year! And you can do the same thing yourself.

This means you won't have the guesswork and months of wasted effort of struggling to figure out the big picture of how to build your investing business. You'll be empowered with technique after technique, strategy after strategy, shortcut after shortcut, to help you build your real estate cash flow as fast as possible.

In essence, the Real Estate Fast Track will allow you to tap into the two most powerful wealth-creation forces on this planet—OPE and OPS.

Tapping into the Power of OPE— Other People's Experiences

OPE stands for "other people's experiences." I want to be clear here that the experiences that matter most to you are those of people who have built what you want to build and who enjoy what you want to enjoy. You need to make sure that the people you listen to concerning real estate investing have done it themselves.

The simple test is to ask yourself, has this person successfully done what I want to do in the area they are advising me in? If they have, then and only then do they have something of value to share with you.

And when you find these people—hang on their every word! Their wisdom is more precious than gold because it will save you *years* of effort and struggle. Remember how I was able to succeed in my investing in half the time that Peter did, because he was my mentor? That's the power of tapping into OPE.

Leveraging OPS—Other People's Systems

The second great wealth accelerator is OPS—other people's systems. A system is simply an organized process that you can apply to generate consistent results in a specific area of your investing business. Build the right systems for your investing business, and not only will you make a fortune, but you'll be able to free yourself from the day-to-day operation of your investing business. Learn the right systems from other people, and you'll save *years* of effort and struggle.

In this book you'll learn all kinds of real estate systems to successfully build your profitable investing business from the start. In addition, you'll learn the master system of building business systems that autopilot specific parts of your investing business so that they consistently generate excellent results. In truth, you are leveraging your investing by letting me hand you all these powerful business systems upon which to build your profitable investing business. That's how you'll be able to build your investing business to generate a $5,000 to $50,000 real estate cash flow so quickly.

By tapping into OPE and OPS, you will quickly earn the financial freedom and security you've always dreamed of having. What's more, right from the start you'll *know* that you're on the right track—the fast track—to creating wealth.

So what exactly is this "Real Estate Fast Track" we keep talking about?

The Real Estate Fast Track is the proven path that leads new investors from their beginning at the start of Level One, and takes them all the way to Level Three success. It's what I've been helping investors do for years, and now it's your turn. Are you ready to make this journey?

I'll be giving you a detailed road map of where your investing business will need to go, both in the beginning and as you grow it, so that you have a clear and accurate picture of the end towards which you are working, and the milestones and markers along the way.

Not only will you get the Fast Track Map™, but you'll also get to watch six "Early Stage Level Two" investors work to follow that map in the real world as they apply the very same strategies, techniques, and lessons you'll be learning in this book to reach Level Three success.

You'll see where they get stuck so you can safely sidestep those pitfalls. And you'll learn how they troubleshoot problems as they come up, to make your profits and success assured.

The *Creating Cash Flow* Series

This book is the second in the three-book *Creating Cash Flow* series. This series is designed to teach you everything you need to know, not just to make money investing in real estate—that part is easy—but to put your investing business on autopilot and create passive cash flow so that you can enjoy the freedom and lifestyle of a truly wealthy investor. This progression of residualizing your real estate income is one that most investors miss. They never learn how to take themselves out of the "doing" and, as a consequence, they are always working hard to care for and manage their real estate portfolio. Hence they either fall into the landlord trap of tenants and toilets, or they are constantly scrambling to find their next great deal so that they can sell it for a fast profit. Or they give up all together, saying real estate takes just too much work.

What they don't know, in fact aren't even aware is possible, is that there's a better way. There is a way to invest in real estate so that over the course of several years you build your investing business into an independent entity that can not only look after itself but, better still, can produce consistent cash flow and equity buildup—month after month, year after year. That's what the *Creating Cash Flow* series will be teaching you. This three-book series will take you through each of the three levels of investing success.

In the first book of the *Creating Cash Flow* series, *Buying Real Estate without Cash or Credit*, you learned everything you needed to know to get started investing and do your first deal in 90 days or less.

Here in book two, you'll learn how to build a $5,000 to $50,000 per month cash flow as you succeed as a Level Two investor. You'll learn how to master the five core investor skills:

1. Marketing—Finding great deals in any market.
2. Structuring—How to structure win-win real estate deals.
3. Negotiation—How to get the other party to say yes to the deal you want.
4. Analysis—How to determine if a deal is good in five minutes or less.
5. Contracts—How to write up moneymaking real estate deals.

Plus you'll learn how to build a profitable investing business that consistently grows your profits and free time.

Read the Series in Any Order—Each Book Stands Alone

Now you may be wondering whether you need to read the series in order. You don't. Each of these books has been carefully designed to stand on its own. I do recommend that you ultimately read all three books because the strategies and techniques they share complement each other, but you can do it in any order.

Quick Overview of the *Creating Cash Flow* Series

Book One: *Buying Real Estate without Cash or Credit*
Focus: On giving beginning investors the critical information they need to get started making money investing in real estate in the next 60 to 90 days. The book takes you by the hand and shows you step-by-step, action-by-action, strategy-by-strategy the fastest way for you to successfully get started with your investing.

Investor Level: Primarily for Level One investors who are just getting started with their investing, it's also designed for Level Two and Three investors who want to cherry-pick powerful investing strategies and techniques to immediately put to work in their investing businesses.

Book Two: *The Real Estate Fast Track: How to Create a $5,000 to $50,000 per Month Real Estate Cash Flow*
Focus: On giving you a clear, proven pathway from where you are to Level Three success as an investor. You'll learn the five core investor skills and how to leverage yourself to make more money with your investing with less time and effort. You'll also learn about the difference between merely being a real estate investor and building a successful real estate investing *business*. You'll also get the clear action steps you need to take to build your own profitable investing business.

Investor Level: Designed for all three investor levels. Level One investors will learn more strategies and techniques to help them get started with their investing. Level Two investors will get the all important Fast Track Map™ to follow to enjoy the real success they are after. And finally, Level Three investors will again get powerful concepts and techniques that they can pick and choose from to immediately upgrade their already thriving investing businesses.

(continued)

Quick Overview of the *Creating Cash Flow* Series *(continued)*

Book Three: *Advance Secrets to Building Your Real Estate Cash Flow*
Focus: To show you how to put your investing business on autopilot and create passive cash flow so that you can enjoy the freedom and lifestyle of a truly wealthy investor. This book is designed to help you take that final step up into Level Three success where you transition yourself out of the day-to-day operation of your real estate business so that you can truly enjoy the freedom and security you have worked so hard to earn. The book will focus on how you can take your new time and freedom and invest it in larger deals on commercial real estate, and how to take the profits your real estate is generating and convert them into passive streams of income.

Investor Level: While Level Two and Level Three investors will get the most from the solid how-to part of the book, Level One investors may get even more from the book as it inspires them with exactly what is possible and clearly lays out the end toward which they are working, in vivid and totally practical detail.

A Brief Review of *Buying Real Estate without Cash or Credit*

For those of you who have already read *Buying Real Estate without Cash or Credit*, use the following review to remind yourself of some of the key lessons of that book. For those of you who are starting the *Creating Cash Flow* series with this book, *The Real Estate Fast Track*, you can use this review as a summary of the critical lessons you will learn later when you eventually read it.

The 16 Key Concepts from *Buying Real Estate without Cash or Credit*

Key Concept 1: The Paradox of Playing It Safe

In today's world of a globalized economy and rapidly changing business environment, the most dangerous thing you can do is to "play it safe." Playing it safe is tantamount to choosing known failure. Instead, if you want things to be different for you and your family, *you* are the one who is going to have to make it different. The days of depending on a benign corporation or government to take care of you are over. That's why real estate investing is so exciting. It gives you a simple vehicle to build financial security and freedom for yourself. But to take advantage of this financial vehicle, you've got to take some calculated risks. Considering that your alternative is known failure, the odds when you take that leap are considerably in your favor!

The thing that scares most people back into playing it safe is information overload. When people get confused they tend to freeze, just like a deer in the headlights of an 18-wheeler! That's why *Buying Real Estate without Cash or Credit* was all about cutting through the blizzard of data and leaving you with the essential core you needed to know to get started with your investing and successfully complete your first deal in 90 days or less.

Key Concept 2: The Foundation of All Winning Real Estate Deals

Every profitable real estate deal has as its foundation a motivated seller. One of the best parts of real estate is that it exists in an imperfect market where personal circumstances dramatically affect the value of any piece of property at any given moment. One owner with a specific circumstance may value a property at $400,000; another owner with that same property but a different set of circumstances may value it at $500,000.

This is important to you because as a real estate investor you are getting paid to bring value to the table, and one of the biggest ways you create value is by solving a motivated seller's real estate problems. You build value into the deal on your side by helping the seller deal with challenging times, and you earn a fair and healthy profit to the degree you are able to accomplish this. The key is that all great real estate deals start with a motivated seller. Which brings us to the next key concept.

Key Concept 3: The Winning Deal Formula

The general wisdom that real estate is all about location, location, location is flat out wrong. In the real world of investing, real estate is first and foremost about the motivation of the seller; secondly, it's about the price and terms with which you can acquire a property; and then and only then about the location of the property.

In fact, the **Winning Deal Formula** goes on to define the exact proportion of these three key ingredients for all winning real estate deals.

- Sixty percent of the deal is dependent on the seller's motivation.
- Thirty percent of the deal is dependent on the financing.
- Ten percent of the deal is dependent on the location and property itself.

When you really let this key lesson sink in it changes the way you structure your investing business. No longer do you look for the perfect property in the perfect location. Instead, you focus your early efforts on finding motivated sellers, the more the better—which brings us to the next key concept.

Key Concept 4: How to Find Motivated Sellers Over the Phone in Two Minutes or Less

Once you understand how every profitable deal starts with finding a motivated seller, the next critical lesson is how exactly to find and qualify sellers over the telephone. This is where the "Quick Check Scripts" came into play. These simple scripts showed you exactly what to say and, more importantly, how to say it, so that you could easily qualify any seller over the telephone in two minutes or less.

You also learned about how to preempt the two most common objections when talking with sellers over the phone, and how to avoid the three most common mistakes new investors make when dialing for deals.

The bottom line is that, used properly, the telephone is one of your most powerful deal-finding tools available. And since nearly every method you have to generate leads will ultimately require you to talk with the seller over the phone, to qualify them as to their motivation and situation, the faster you can get fluent with this critical investor skill the better.

Key Concept 5: The Five Fastest Ways to Find Your First (or Next) Deal

While there are literally over 100 different marketing techniques to find motivated sellers and profitable real estate deals, there are five that are the most important for you to test out first.

1. **Do your dials.** Outbound calls you make to "for sale" and "for rent" classified ads in your local paper are the first and most important early

technique for finding motivated sellers. Not only is this the fastest way to get lots of practice talking with owners of properties, but it is also one of the cheapest ways!

2. **Place your "I Buy Houses" classified ad.** Getting sellers to call you who are more strongly motivated is one of the keys to a sustainable, successful real estate investing business. Classified advertising in papers that sellers are likely to look at works wonders. This is a way to leverage the money for the ad to save you time finding deals. With one phone call you can have your ad out there 24/7, finding you deals.

3. **Put out your "I Buy Houses" signs.** Dollar for dollar, your tacky, ugly "I Buy Houses" signs are one of the best lead sources you can get working for you. Make sure you check with local ordinances in your area regulating their use, but seriously consider adding them to your marketing mix. I suggest a minimum of 50 signs per week on a regular and consistent basis.

4. **Test direct mail.** Once you've had some practice talking with sellers on the phone and have met with at least 10 sellers, test two simple direct mail campaigns to generate leads of motivated sellers. The first is a postcard campaign to out-of-town owners. The second is a postcard campaign to landlords.

5. **Spread the word that you have started to invest in real estate and generate referral business.** The easiest form of leverage to find great deals is to get other people who you know or meet to help you find deals. Your referral network is a critical piece of your long-term investment success. I have found my best deals from referrals. The only question is whether you will have the courage and discipline to consistently build your referral network.

Key Concept 6: The Big Picture of Structuring Real Estate Deals—
The Winning Deal Decision Tree

There are two main ways to buy a property and make a conservative profit. Either you buy the property for cash at a deeply discounted price, or you buy the property with attractive terms of financing that allow you to make your profit due to the great financing with which you acquired the property.

Key Concept 7: The Cash Price Formula

When you are buying for cash, the reason for the big discount is that as an investor your cash is a valuable commodity—one that most sellers want. It is also a limited commodity. Once it's committed by being invested in real estate, you lose out on the ability to quickly access it to purchase your next screaming good deal. Because of this, you need to always value your cash highly and use it to maximum effect. This means if a seller requires an all-cash purchase, you require a deep cash discount to move ahead with the deal.

When you are buying for cash, never pay more than 70 percent of the as-is value, and you'll be taking one of the most important steps to guarantee yourself a profit in your real estate deals. This is known as the Cash Price Formula.

So if you have a house that, if it were in great showing condition, would sell for $450,000 but conservatively needs about $50,000 of repairs to get it in that condition, then the as-is value of that house is $400,000. As long as the maximum you pay for that property is $280,000, with less being your goal, you'll conservatively come out of the deal with a fair profit.

Key Concept 8: The Three Most Important Terms Acquisition Strategies

In *Buying Real Estate without Cash or Credit*, you learned about all three of the most important Terms Acquisition Strategies: lease options, buying subject to the existing financing, and using owner-carry financing.

A **lease option** is when you lease out a motivated seller's property with a set purchase price at which you have the option of buying during the term of your lease agreement. Typically, the longer the period you lock in your option to purchase the property, the more money you'll end up making when you eventually re-sell or refinance the property.

Buying a property subject to the existing financing means you buy the property and leave the old seller's loan in place, secured as a mortgage against the property. You own the property, but your ownership claim is "subject to" the existing loan(s) in place. Since you are not formally assuming the underlying financing you technically have no liability on the loan, but as an ethical investor you are responsible to make sure that the mortgage payment gets paid each month. You usually accomplish this by renting the property (as a simple rental or a rent-to-own) for an amount greater than your monthly costs to maintain the property.

Owner-carry financing means that the seller you are buying from takes a significant portion of the money you owe in back in the form of a seller loan. You can structure this seller carryback with monthly interest payments, or with all the interest accruing for you to pay as a lump-sum payment due down the road.

Key Concept 9: The Six Best Sources to Fund Your Deals

1. **The Seller.** Any terms deal that you negotiate with the seller, whether it be a lease option, a subject-to deal, or an owner-carry deal, is in essence the seller funding part or all of the deal. The seller can lend you some or all of his equity, or the seller can let you tap into the existing financing against the property by accepting monthly payments from you. Either way, it is still really the seller funding your deal.

2. **The Buyer.** There are two main types of buyers who can help fund your deal. The first is a retail buyer—someone who wants to buy the property so that he or she can move in and live there. A retail buyer can fund the deal using their cash in the form of a down payment or option payment, their credit in the form of a new bank loan, or a combination of the two. The second type of buyer who can help fund your deal is another investor—also known as a wholesale buyer. You can quickly "flip"—that is, sell—your deal to another investor for a fast cash profit, and let this other investor use his or her money to fund the deal.

3. **Private Money.** After you have gotten a bit more experienced with your deals, you'll start to meet people who are willing to lend you money for your deals as long as they can have the loan secured by a first mortgage on the property. Often these private lenders are average people who prefer to earn market interest rates for a first mortgage versus the poor earnings of a CD at their local bank. The key for a private lender is that the loan be safe.

4. **Your Cash or Credit.** While I don't recommend you use your money to buy a property unless the first three sources of funds don't work for you, if the deal is a good one, and if you have the money, or if you have the credit to get easy access to conventional financing, then funding a deal yourself makes good sense.

5. **Hard Money.** Hard money comes from a third party lender, but whereas a private money lender only wants market rates, a hard money lender is an experienced investor who is willing to lend to you not based on your creditworthiness or character, but based on the security of the loan. The main difference between a hard money lender and a private money lender is in the rate of interest and fees charged.

6. **Equity Money Partner.** Sometimes you turn to a private party to provide the funding to make a deal work. When this person requires a share of the deal rather than a rate of return, you have an equity partner. An equity partner can put her own money into the deal, or she can agree to get a conventional loan in her name to fund the deal.

Key Concept 10: The Five Most Important Exit Strategies

Once you've bought the property, what is it you plan to do with it to make a profit? There are five main Exit Strategies you can tap into.

1. **"Retail" the property.** This means that you will sell the property for the highest price you can on the retail market. This is how most homes are sold, whether they are listed with a real estate agent or sold for sale by owner. When you retail a property, your buyer borrows from a conventional lender and almost always moves into the property to live there.

2. **"Flip" the deal.*** This is a fast-cash exit strategy where you lock up a property under contract and then sell your contract to another buyer, typically another investor, who will pay you a cash fee to assign your contract to them. The biggest benefit of flipping a deal is that it generates instant cash.

3. **Lease the property to a traditional renter.** This is perhaps one of the most common exit strategies of average investors. They buy a house and put a traditional renter in it. This renter leases the property either on a month-by-month rental agreement or a longer-term lease (typically for one year).

---

*To download the FREE ebook, *Three Simple Steps to Flip a Deal for Fast Cash Profits,* go to **www.InvestorFasttrack.com.**

4. **Offer the property on a "rent-to-own" basis.** The rent-to-own strategy comes extremely close to doing the impossible—it gives you all the benefits of a traditional rental property, while minimizing the three major downsides. The way this strategy works is that you find a tenant buyer who wants to rent-to-own your property. This tenant buyer will lease your property on a two- or three-year lease with a separate option agreement that gives them a locked-in price at which they can buy the home at any point over that two- or three-year term. As part of agreeing to give them this fixed "option to purchase" price, your tenant buyer will pay you a non-refundable option payment of 3 to 5 percent of the price of the property. In many cases your tenant buyer will also be paying slightly higher than the market rent because they aren't just renting the property, they are renting to own. This increased rent, when added to the option payment you collect up front, really boosts your cash flow on the property. The best thing about a tenant buyer isn't this increased cash flow, in my opinion. To me, the best part is that since you have an occupant with an owner mentality, not a renter mentality, your tenant buyer will treat the property with much more care and attention. I even get my tenant buyers to take care of all the day-to-day maintenance and upkeep of the property!*

5. **Sell with owner financing.** This means that as a seller you take back some or all of the purchase price as a loan that your buyer will pay you over time.

Key Concept 11: A Simple Five-Step System to Negotiate Any Real Estate Deal

This is where you learned the negotiating system called the Instant Offer System, which gave you the structure and scripting to effectively negotiate any real estate deal.

Key Concept 12: The Three Investor Levels

This breakthrough model outlined the road all investors must travel to be successful. In *Buying Real Estate without Cash or Credit*, I focused on how this unique investor map impacts Level One—beginning—investors.

---

*To download the FREE ebook, *Seven Simple Steps to Sell Your Property on a Rent to Own Basis*, go to **www.InvestorFasttrack.com.**

Key Concept 13: How to Mastermind with Other Investors to Guarantee Success

Over time, investors who have the whole-hearted support and encouragement of a core group of other investors will succeed at levels that far outpace the average investor. In the book you got to watch six beginning investors run two of their mastermind meetings, and you also got a step-by-step action plan for how you can use the same idea in your investor circle to tap into the skills, contacts, and resources of other investors.

Key Concept 14: The Real Difference between Speculators and Investors

Speculators are people who buy real estate at close to or even at full price as part of a cash deal, and then they hope-pray-gamble that the market will rapidly appreciate so they can resell the property at a profit. They are totally dependent on outside market conditions to produce a profit.

For example, a speculator might buy a $500,000 house as a cash deal for $475,000 in a hot market, hoping that if the market stays hot the house will rapidly appreciate and in one year he'll be able to resell the house for $600,000 or more. But what if the market cools off? The speculator always runs the risk of getting stuck with a property that is a dog.

Investors are smarter than that. When they buy a property they do so knowing that they are guaranteed to make a profit because of the way they purchased it. Either they have gotten great terms that make the property cash flow well, or they have negotiated a discounted cash price that ensures a profit when they resell. **The key distinction is that speculators gamble on outside forces to create a profit for themselves, while investors negotiate the price or terms they need to build their profit in from day one—no matter what the market does in the short run.**

Key Concept 15: How to Successfully Launch Your Investing Business in the Real World

It's one thing to learn all the fancy ideas in books and at workshops, but it's quite another to actually take the ideas and put them into practice in the real world. Many times the situations in the seminar seem to be unrecognizable when you work to implement the ideas in the real world. That's why the entire second half of the book was focused on the efforts of six beginning investors who were struggling to apply exactly what you learned in the first half of the book in the real world of their day-to-day investing. Sometimes the most important thing is not so much the raw technique or information, but rather the exact way you are supposed to translate that information into the world of your investing. Which leads us to the final key lesson from *Buying Real Estate without Cash or Credit*.

Key Concept 16: Your 90-Day Action Plan

It's not enough to just sit back and read. You need a game plan to turn that information into tangible profit in your bank account! That's why I shared with you the detailed eight-step action plan to launch your investing business in 90 days.

1. **Log onto the powerful online business planning tool.** We offered this valuable bonus to all readers of *Buying Real Estate without Cash or Credit* to help them translate the ideas in the book into cash in their pockets.

2. **Connect with your "burning why."** What are your driving motives to make your investing work no matter what?

3. **Clarify your dreams and goals.** This was the simple three-step process to gain total clarity about your investing goals.

4. **Take stock of your starting point.** This was the 19-question survey that was strategically designed to help you identify your real estate strengths to build from, and to uncover your real estate weaknesses so that you can overcome them. This way you know exactly where to focus your energy for maximum success.

5. **Identify the specific obstacles standing in your way.** You learned which of the six investor obstacles were most impacting your investing success.

6. **Create and commit to your action plan.** This is the key step to translate intangible goals into a concrete game plan to help you achieve your dreams. We ended this step with the three key action commitments all successful real estate investors must make when they are first getting started.

7. **Take consistent action with regular feedback.** Daily action, with consistent feedback on what went well and what you would do differently the

next time you are faced with the same situation, is crucial for you to develop and succeed as an investor.

8. **Perform your 90-day review.** There is something crucial about stopping to reflect and evaluate your investing business launch at the 90-day mark. That's why we gave you the outline of how to complete this powerful check-in.

An Overview of What You'll Learn from Reading *The Real Estate Fast Track*

By now you realize just how much useful investor information was packed into book one, *Buying Real Estate without Cash or Credit.*

This book is all about what happens next. What happens *after* you get your first few deals? How do you make sure that you aren't just doing a random deal or two, but rather building a real estate investing business that will consistently generate a $5,000 to $50,000 per month real estate cash flow for you—month after month, year after year?

You'll learn the key strategies you need to succeed and how to actually apply that knowledge in the real world to make you successful, including the often-overlooked link of how to adjust to individual circumstances as the best-laid plans get knocked off kilter by a variety of real-world realities.

Part One: The Advanced Investor Workshop

Part One takes place at the Advanced Investor Workshop held only once each year. This workshop has been carefully crafted to help investors just like you succeed as quickly as possible with their investing.

In Chapters 1 and 2 you'll get a clear overview of the big picture of how to earn $5,000 to $50,000 per month real estate cash flow. You'll also learn how to follow the Fast Track Map™ to become a Level Three Investor, financially free for the rest of your life.

In Chapters 3 through 7 you'll learn to master the five core investor skills that you need to succeed as a fully competent and self-reliant real estate investor.

In Chapters 8 and 9 you'll learn how to leverage your time as an investor for maximum profit. You'll also discover how to begin the process of building a successful investing business so that you can begin to make even more money.

In Chapters 10 and 11 you'll get a clear action plan to build a strong, independent real estate business that works even better when you're not working for the business. These key chapters lay out the three biggest barriers to going passive with your investing, and how you can break through to Level Three success. You also learn the "Master System"—the system to *build* investor business systems.

Part Two: The Real World—12 Months Building Your Investing Business

In Part Two of this book you'll learn exactly what it takes to transform the ideas and strategies from Part One into cash in your bank account. It takes place over the 12 months following the Advanced Investor Workshop, as these six Mentorship students apply the lessons they learned from the workshop to the real world.

Part Three: Your Turn—Turning This Book into Cash Flow

Now I'll turn the spotlight on you and your investing business as you create an individualized action plan to get immediate results growing your investing business.

The most important component to Part Three is the FREE online mentorship tool I've created for readers like you to tap into. It's called the Investor Fast Track Program™ and for a limited time it's free for readers like yourself.

The way the program works is you'll go online to **www.InvestorFasttrack .com** to register using the password listed in this book (See Appendix A for details). Next you'll take the Fast Track Intro Class that will share with you exactly how you can use the Investor Fast Track Program™ to grow your real estate investing business. It will give you the specific steps to take to use the program to leverage your investing efforts so that you immediately begin to grow your real estate cash flow. Then you'll just follow the 90-day action plan the program lays out, including taking the 10 FREE online investor workshops.

You'll literally get access to the same insider secrets and advanced investor strategies that I used to charge tens of thousands of dollars to share! This program is my gift to you for stepping up and reading this life-changing book.

The Investor Fast Track Program™ is literally jammed with powerful investor tools and resources to help you successfully launch your investing business. And best of all, for a limited time, it's FREE for readers like you. For complete details go to Appendix A. And for immediate access go to **www.InvestorFasttrack.com.**

Now let's get to work! Just turn the page and join me at the Advanced Investor Workshop.

PART ONE

THE ADVANCED
INVESTOR WORKSHOP

EARLY STAGE LEVEL TWO INVESTING—DEVELOPING THE FIVE CORE INVESTMENT SKILLS

CHAPTER ONE

The Big Picture of Taking Your Investing Business to the Next Level

As Vicki walked into the workshop on Saturday morning, she recognized several people who had attended the Intensive Training Workshop with her three months earlier. And while Vicki wasn't as scared now as she was three months ago when she did that first Level One workshop, she felt more than a little anxious this morning. The night before, when she met with her mastermind team of fellow investors, she shared a big decision she had reached about her investing, and the implications of that decision were starting to scare her.

"Vicki!" A bright, warm voice to her left called out.

Vicki turned and saw the wonderfully reassuring smile of Mary. "It's great to see you this morning Mary."

Mary cocked her head and asked, "You're not nervous at this one, are you? Why, after all you told us last night at our mastermind meeting, you should be strutting in here like you own the place." Mary laughed easily as she said this.

"That's what's got me so nervous. I'm having second thoughts about the decision I shared with you all last night," Vicki confided.

Mary touched her arm affectionately. "Don't worry Vicki. Didn't I say you'd be great at this investing when we first met at the Intensive Training?" Mary's laughter was infectious, and Vicki felt her anxiety ease a bit.

"Let's get a good seat," Vicki suggested.

They found a seat right up front, making sure to save a seat for Mary's husband and business partner, Leon. Looking around the room, Vicki waved to Mark, Nancy, and Tim, who along with Mary and Leon were members of her mastermind group. As Vicki was getting settled in, music started playing over the speakers. Vicki and the others instantly recognized the song as the words floated out over the room.

"We are the champions, my friend . . ."

Just then, the room burst into applause as a tall, athletic man in his mid 30s stepped out onto the stage.

"Welcome everybody!" David said with a warm smile as the applause and music faded into an expectant silence. "Are you ready for three days to revolutionize how you look at your real estate investing? Are you ready to take home with you a whole new game plan for taking your investing business to the next level?"

"Good," David continued. "But as we start here today, I want you all to realize that you are already champions. You are already among the elite of real estate investors. I know this to be true. After working with literally hundreds of thousands of wannabe investors I can tell you, the gap between them and you is huge. You want to know what the biggest difference between the wannabes and you is?" David waited a moment as everyone sat forward expectantly.

"The difference is that you showed up! I don't just mean that you showed up to this Level Two workshop. I mean that you show up each day in your investing too. The thing that stops the wannabes is their long list of excuses and rationalizations that they hide behind.

"They say things like," David switched to a whiney voice now, "*'I can't come to the workshop because I can't afford it.'* Or, *'I don't have time to do my investing.'* Or, *'That real estate stuff won't work for me, in my area, for people who have negative friends and relatives like I have . . .'* I think you get the idea here. The reason you are so special is that you showed up. You made no excuses. You took full responsibility for your life. Somehow you found the money to travel here. Somehow you arranged your life to make the time to be here. Somehow you sold your family on the idea of supporting you to be here. And because you did all that—because you showed up—I know that you also show up every day in your investing.

"Here's the key point to this." David turned and wrote on the board:

The way you do anything
Is the way you do everything!

"I know that you are able to consistently move forward with your investing because you are someone who doesn't give in to the little voice inside your head that whispers from the shadows. You have dealt with those excuses and rationalizations and blown right past them. In fact, from our work together in the Mentorship Program and reading your pre-attendance surveys, I know that each one of you has an inspirational story of how you earned the success that you are enjoying and that will be coming to you in the future.

"For example, I know that a third of you who are here are just on the front edges of your investing. You've either done a few deals or maybe you're still looking for your first one. The reason you're here is because you want to boost your confidence so that when you're out there in the real world doing your investing you move with assurance and certainty. Plus, you recognize that the best way to succeed is to start with the end in mind, and you want to get all the insight you can as to exactly what a successful real estate business looks like, smells like, and breathes like.

"Another third of you are solid Level Two investors. You've done five or ten or fifteen deals in the last year or two and are making good money with your investing. You're here because you recognize that up until now you've been winging it, flying by the seat of your pants. You don't want to *just* be an investor anymore. You're here to learn exactly how to build a successful investing *business* so that you can secure your income streams and earn more money with less of your time and effort.

"And the final third of you are seasoned pros who are on the verge of going passive with your investing and transitioning into Level Three. You're here because you want to learn strategies to solidify your investing business so that you can put it on autopilot."

David paused for a moment. "How many of you in this room realized that there are several investors here who already earn over a million dollars a year with their investing? Some of you might ask why in the world someone earning a seven-figure income would take a full three days out of their lives to be here this weekend. However, here's an even better question for you to ask. How do you think these investors built their investing businesses up to the point where they generate over a million dollars a year in profit? By *making* time to attend workshops and learn from their peers. I learned this lesson a long time ago when I attended a workshop like this—and yes, I want to make it very clear, I still attend at least two workshops a year to upgrade my knowledge base and sharpen my skills. I believe that to be truly wealthy you have got to be green and growing, and this means being open to learning new ideas and gaining new insights.

"So now we know why we're all here. In just a moment I'll give you an overview of what you're going to learn over the next three days. But before we do that, let's get three or four of you up on stage to briefly share your story. You're going to learn and benefit so much from the people you network with here so let's start getting to know each other." David quickly rounded up four volunteers to come share their stories.

"Okay," David said, when all four volunteers were up on the stage. "Who is willing to share your story first? I want you to tell us who you are and the two-minute version of your investing story."

A handsome man in his early 40s stepped forward and volunteered to go first: "My name is Mark and I'm a pilot with United Airlines. I joined the Mentorship Program about five months ago after reading David and Peter's first book. For me, things in my investing have just happened so quickly, it's almost overwhelming. Since the Intensive Training three months ago I have done five deals. Three houses that I purchased subject to the existing financing and one house that I picked up on a four-year lease option all have tenant buyers in them. These four properties generate about $800 per month of positive cash flow at this point, they netted me $12,000 in option payments from my tenant buyers, and I have over $90,000 of back-end profits waiting for me. The fifth deal was a duplex that I put under contract and flipped to another investor for an $18,000 profit.

"My biggest challenge has been time. Originally I had planned to transition into investing full-time over twenty-four months, but with all that's happened and the growth I've experienced as part of the Mentorship Program I've decided to make that transition over the next three months. I think this has been my biggest lesson, that in order for me to really grow as an investor I am going to have to make the leap of faith into doing my investing full-time. That's one of the reasons I am so excited about the Advanced Investor Workshop this weekend, because it will help me make the transition into being a Level Two investor much easier and faster."

"Thank you, Mark," David said. "Who wants to go next?" A tall, well-dressed man raised his hand.

"Hi, my name is Tim. My wife Nancy and I have worked in corporate America for the past twenty years. Nancy works as an IT manager for a Fortune 500 company, and I worked for the last fifteen years in technology sales. At least I did up until about six months ago when my company was bought by a larger company. I was laid off with about a hundred other people in my division. It was really a blow to my ego and self-esteem at first. But after joining the Mentorship Program a few months ago I realized that this was the push I needed to get out there and pursue my investing dreams. I was just way too comfortable with my old life and I needed that kick in the pants to get moving. It's been hard going for Nancy and me. We really struggled for the first month or two, with our biggest obstacle being ourselves. For me, it was all my old sales habits working against me when I was negotiating with sellers.

"For the first two months Nancy and I would argue over whether this would really work in our area. But even while we argued we kept at it. Every week I kept up my marketing efforts and made sure I met with at least two new sellers about buying their properties, no matter what. Even when we finally signed our first deal but had to give it back to the seller after we couldn't find a tenant buyer for the property, we still kept at it. We were scared about whether we could do this, but we knew this was the best chance we were ever going to get, and I did *not* want to have to go back to work for someone else again! Nancy and I had lots of long talks about what we wanted to do, and we came to the decision that no matter what, we are going to make this work—if it takes us another three months or three years, it doesn't matter. We are totally committed and know that this will happen for us. I feel like even though we haven't done a deal yet, we are already into the beginning stages of Level Two investing because we *know* this will work for us. It's just going to take a little more time."

David looked out at the room and asked, "Is there any question in your minds that Tim and Nancy are going to succeed with a commitment like that? Tim," David said, turning back to face him, "I admire your willingness to get yourself to show up week in and week out. All I can say is that when the door opens, success is going to come pouring out for you and Nancy because you're planting the seeds that can't help but yield fruit."

Tim handed the mic back to David, and Vicki stepped forward to share her story.

"My name is Vicki. For the past ten years I've been a full-time nurse. I'm also a single mom who is raising my two kids the best I can. It was really hard for me finding time to do my investing. I work three or four twelve-hour shifts at the hospital each week and my kids, who are seven and nine, take a lot of energy and attention to raise. The reason I got started with the Mentorship Program is because I want to be able to provide for my kids and to be there when they get home from school. When I look back, I realize that the biggest thing holding me back was my fear. But with the support of the coaches and my mastermind team who I met at the Intensive Training, I just kept taking action in spite of my fears. They encouraged me even when I felt overwhelmed taking care of my kids, working at the hospital, and then fitting in my investing around both those things.

"About six weeks ago I met with a motivated seller who was going through a divorce. I guess she and I had a lot in common because I'm divorced too. She agreed to sell me two houses at about 65 to 70 percent of their as-is value. The first week I had those houses under contract I felt paralyzed trying to find another investor to flip the deals to. I was scared that I wouldn't be able to do it, and I was even more scared of what it would mean if I *was* able to do it. It would mean that all the excuses I've made throughout my life were just that—excuses. And that the only one responsible was me." Vicki looked around the room and saw the caring looks she was getting.

"Well, four weeks ago I actually flipped one of the two contracts to another investor who paid me a $12,000 assignment fee!" Everyone was stunned. They could only imagine what this money meant to Vicki, who was struggling to raise her family on her nurse's salary. "I guess getting that $12,000 cashier's check in my hand gave me the boost of courage I needed to know I could do this. I approached my sister, who is an attorney in Chicago. I explained to her about my two deals and how I had just sold one contract to another investor and that I had one more house left but that I needed to cash the seller out in four more weeks. To make a long story short, she agreed to be my money partner on that deal. We actually closed on the house three weeks ago and immediately did all the cosmetic fix-up work and put the house back up on the market. We decided to sell it ourselves at a discount, and nine days ago we found our buyer! The escrow is set to close in three more weeks and when all is said and done, my sister and I will split a check for $58,000!" Everyone cheered Vicki.

"I've also just made a decision that I told my mastermind team about last night when we met here at the hotel. It's really scary, but it's also exciting too. I've decided that when I get my half of that $58,000 I will take a leave of absence from the hospital and do my investing full-time. That means I'll have more time to do deals and, because I can arrange most of my investing around my schedule, I'll have more time with my kids."

Again the room applauded as Vicki handed the mic to the last volunteer on stage.

"Hi, my name is Carl. I'm an ex–truck driver who got my start investing about six years ago. I bought my first few houses the old-fashioned way, with 20 percent down payments and bank financing. They were dinky little three-bedroom rental houses that I fixed up and rented. About three years ago I met David at an investor conference he was speaking at. After listening to how organized and simple he made his investing ideas, I joined the Mentorship Program. At that point I had already done fourteen deals, but I knew that I needed to learn how to make my business more organized because I was running around like crazy, driving a local route and doing my investing at night and on weekends.

"That was three years ago. Since that time I've quite driving my truck, and built my foreclosure business. I now have two rehab crews working for me with a full-time rehab manager. I buy about fifteen to twenty houses a year, mostly from sellers in foreclosure or pre-foreclosure, and I rehab and sell them. Some I sell to cash buyers, others I sell with owner financing or on a rent-to-own basis. Last year I made over $250,000 from my investing business, and this year I'm on pace to make over $300,000. I still pinch myself to see when I'm going to have to wake up and find this is all just a dream. I can't wait to learn this weekend how to get myself out of the day-to-day operation of my investing business. I'm not complaining, but right now it feels like it all revolves around me. I want it to work without me needing to drive it every day."

The room applauded all four of the students as the volunteers took their seats again.

David now put them to work networking. "Turn to someone you haven't met before and introduce yourself. Listen to their story and share yours with them. You've got four minutes—go!"

The room went into a frenzy as people scrambled to find a stranger to partner up with. After letting it go for a few minutes, David got everyone's attention back to the front as he continued, "So let's talk about this weekend. Once you've reached the place that you know real estate works for you, either by doing a deal or by collecting all the powerful experiences and references of other investors who've done it, it's time for you to begin the process of building a successful investing business. Remember, just being an investor isn't enough to make you financially free. To be a Level Three investor you need to build an investing *business* that works so you don't have to.

"You'll accomplish this in three stages. Stage one is called Early Stage Level Two. This is where you develop your investor skills and become a fluent and competent investor in your own right. Middle Stage Level Two is where you refine these skills and competencies and begin your first tentative steps to leverage yourself and your business. The final stage—Advanced Stage Level Two—is where you aggressively work to build your investing business to perform better when you're not involved in the day-to-day operation of the business.

"Most investors never reach this place where they can walk away from the daily operation of their real estate business, and as a consequence they are always tied to the business. Sure, they may be making a lot of money with their investing, but they are still limited. The real goal of your investing should be to create time and freedom so that your passive real estate cash flow pays for your desired lifestyle and at the same time your business, cash flow, and net worth grow—year in and year out.

"I urge you to raise your sights from just making money with your investing to building a profitable business that makes you money so you can have the freedom you've always dreamed about having. It's not easy, but what's worthwhile that is easy?

"I want to be clear here. This is *not* about getting rich overnight and never working again. This is about getting the specialized knowledge you need to secure your future over the next few years so that you have the freedom to enjoy the lifestyle you and your family deserve. You'll know that you can make this happen because you'll have the know-how to *make* it happen.

David asked the class, "So what are the qualities of those investors who make it *big* compared to those investors who only make it small-time? What are the top five things investors who earn $500,000 to $1 million per year have in common that enable them to earn big money investing in real estate? What skills, expertise, understanding, and qualities?"

Vicki raised her hand and answered, "I think that the really successful investors have the ability to make great decisions. They don't get stuck in analysis paralysis because of their fear. They trust their gut and also train their brain to accurately analyze deals."

Mark raised his hand and added, "The best investors also know how to ask the right questions so that while they can't know everything, they can get the key information they need laid out in a systematic way that supports them in making a decision."

Nancy nodded her head and said, "Yes, and the best investors know how to leverage themselves through other people, whether employees of their investing business or through their referral network of contacts."

David listened intently to their ideas, then said, "This is a great start. So what I'm really hearing you say is that the best investors are willing to make decisions, and the best investors are skilled at making decisions. By the way," David looked around at the whole class, "how do you think you develop the skill of making decisions?"

"By making them," two students shouted at the same time.

"Exactly! You become a savvy decision maker by making a ton of decisions and reflecting on them afterwards. This allows you to match up the decision, the process you used to reach that decision, and your intuition's message as you made that decision, with the actual outcomes of your decisions. This is how you train your intuition. Remember, your intuition is really just the accumulated total of your life experiences that you tap into in an instantaneous, holistic way instead of the linear, verbal process most people use to make decisions. It's the gut feel or flash insight or inner voice that you have learned to trust.

"Interestingly enough, a key part of this idea—the willingness to act, to decide, even when you're scared—is encompassed by the first of the five key qualities of successful investors that I have on *my* list."

David smiled as he said this, letting the anticipation build. "So just what is my list of the five most important investor qualities? In a moment I'll share my list with you, but before I do, it's important that you understand that great investors are made, not born. All five of the qualities I am about to share with you are learnable skills. This means that with the proper plan and coaching you can cultivate all five of these critical qualities so that you too can be a world-class investor.

"The first quality is in many ways the most important because without it, you won't be able to develop the other four. But if you are willing to work to foster this quality, the world of investing is yours. I call this quality **personal power.** The very best investors have learned to discipline themselves to consistently take action and do the things that they know will make the difference, even when they don't feel like doing them or are afraid of doing them. Basically, this is the quality that gets you to show up each day for your investing, no matter what.

"One of the best examples of this quality is Patty, a Mentorship graduate. When she first got started investing she was terrified. She was quiet and shy and scared to death to go out and meet with sellers. She had no background in investing and was intimidated by the contracts and negotiating. But she had personal power, and even when she was scared and her mind made up all kinds of excuses about how she could avoid doing those things that scared her, she got herself into constructive action anyway.

"As a direct result of her willingness to act in the presence of her fears, Patty made over $200,000 cash plus $300,000 of equity with her investing in just twenty-four months. You can too, if you are willing to do the things you are scared to do.

"Make no mistake about it, the biggest differentiator between wealthy investors and poor ones is that wealthy investors have a much higher tolerance for coping with their fears and taking constructive action in their presence.

"If personal power is the fuel that propels an investor forward even in the face of their own doubts or fears, then this second quality is the foundation that all great investing success is built upon. All great investors have developed **a strong affinity for and with other people.** Affinity simply means having a connection or attraction to and with other people. The most successful investors have both a deep understanding of how people work and a sincere enjoyment of connecting with other people.

"With the sincere enjoyment of people, you'll find that most of your interactions with people will flow smoother and produce better results. For example, many of you have worked with Emily, one of the coaches for the Mentorship Program. One of the reasons that Emily is so good with sellers and buyers is that she genuinely cares about other people. All the negotiating techniques in the world won't cover up for the person who is only out for themselves and has no ability to relate and connect with other people. All successful investors can quickly connect with other people, and the very best investors can connect at a very deep level. People intuitively trust them because these investors truly do care about and listen to the people they are working with.

The third quality of the world's best investors is that they have all developed **outstanding negotiation skills.** Notice, however, I didn't say they were outstanding negotiators, but rather that they had developed outstanding negotiation skills. Many people mistakenly think you are either born a top negotiator or not. This is total bunk. If I've learned one thing over the past decade mentoring so many thousands of new investors it's that negotiation is a skill and, like any skill, it can be learned. In fact, it's a skill that *anyone* can learn, provided it's taught the right way and provided it's practiced frequently enough so that you can develop fluency.

"In real estate, just like anything else in life, you don't get what you want, you get what you *negotiate*. Negotiation skills are what allow the highest earners to translate their people skills into tangible profits.

"I remember one Mentorship student I worked with who came from a sales background. He was engaging as a person, but he was incredibly pushy when it came time to negotiate with sellers. And to make matters worse, when he negotitated, he got nervous and began talking a thousand miles per hour and rarely listened to the other party's side of things. But over twelve months of working together, we got him to learn the mechanics of negotiating, which for him including coping mechanisms like forcing himself to breathe slowly at certain key points in the negotiation, slowing down, and repeating certain key language patterns that literally forced him to listen to the other party. By the end of that first year he had fifteen deals completed, and over the next twelve months he went on to buy over forty-five more houses!

"So no matter where you are starting off on the negotiating skill spectrum, don't worry, we can help you develop into a great negotiator if you just listen to our coaching and go out and practice what we teach you.

"The fourth quality of the top investors is that they have a **wide spectrum of deal structuring tools** to match to different seller and buyer needs. Remember, the more options you have, the easier it is for you to mix and match and find creative ways to structure a deal in which everyone wins. The highest earners in real estate consistently invest more time, energy, and money into increasing their knowledge base of investing tools than average investors do.

"The final quality of the most successful investors is their unwavering **commitment to leveraging their every action** in their investing business. Leverage simply means a way of magnifying the power of a specific action to create a bigger result with less effort. We all have limited time, money, and skills. The best investors leverage all three through systems, outsourcing, and modeling proven winners. They have a drive to consistently hone themselves and their investing business to produce bigger and bigger results with less and less energy.

The Seven Keys to Working *Smarter*, Not Harder

1. Systems

The first key to working smarter is to use powerful *systems* to help you get the results you want with less work and effort. A system is an organized process or tool that helps you and your team consistently produce an excellent result in an area of your business.

A system can be a script of what to say, a checklist to follow laying out a procedure, a sample document, a spreadsheet of key information, or a worksheet to fill out. **A system is a shortcut to help any person you have on your team, with very little training, succeed in getting a desired result in a specific area.**

Ultimately, to take your investing business as far as you want it to go, your investing business will need to be *systems* driven, not people dependent. You never know when a key person will leave your business. The key is to capture all the most important knowledge about how to successfully run your business into clear, simple systems that guarantee your business healthy profits, year after year after year.

One very important final point about systems is that the best systems empower your team to produce exceptional results. Systems are not about control, but rather freedom. The right systems free up your team from worrying about the details so that they can keep the bigger perspective in focus and spot unique opportunities to generate greater profits for your business.

2. Specialized Knowledge

The second way you can work smarter is to gain the specialized knowledge you need to more ably get results with your investing. What do you think makes the most skilled investors able to structure a hugely profitable deal while a beginning investor struggles with what he could even do with that seller? It is one thing and one thing only. The highly skilled investor has a stockpile of powerful experiences from which to draw on.

In today's complicated world, it's the investor with the access to the most varied and powerful storehouse of specialized investor knowledge that has the greatest ability to make big money investing in real estate. The key word here is *access*. You don't need to learn it all by trial and error. The biggest shortcut is to gather the best information on investing from the experience of other successful investors.

(continued)

The Seven Keys to Working *Smarter*, Not Harder (continued)

While we learn from our successes, it's when we fail that we tend to really search for the core lessons from our painful experiences. In fact, it's been said that pain is the greatest teacher of all. If this is true, the key question is, whose pain would you prefer to learn from—your own or someone else's?

That's the power of specialized knowledge. It can easily be borrowed from other successful investors without having to directly experience the pain yourself.*

3. Cohesive Action Plan

One of the most costly myths in the world of investing is that the best investors fly by the seat of their pants and go purely on intuition. The opposite is true. The best investors all have clear action plans that tie together all their investing activities. One of the best benefits of having this cohesive action plan is that it allows you to intelligently decide whether to step off of the plan to take advantage of an unexpected opportunity when you see it. The best investors all understand the power of quickly seizing an unplanned opportunity, and they have the ability to improvise to leverage this opportunity for maximum gain with minimum work and risk. But they will quickly modify their action plan to accommodate this new opportunity and tie it into the larger goals of their investing business.

4. Open Mind to New Ideas

The world of investing is constantly changing. New lending programs and legislative changes come at an ever accelerating pace. Breakthrough investor technologies are invented for you to harness to make your investing business grow faster. In order to work smarter you need to constantly be on the lookout and open to new ideas that you can tap into, whether they be directly from the field of real estate or from some totally unconnected field.

I can remember how when I redesigned my investing business to make it a passive enterprise, I took the technology infrastructure from another business I had and used that as the technology backbone. The result was a 1,000 percent savings in time! Great ideas to use in your investing business can come from anyone, at any time. Always be open to evaluating these ideas and ask the key question, "How can I use this?"

*As a reader of this book, you get FREE access to a special online program called the Investor Fast Track Program™ (Value: $2,497). For details on how to register see Appendix A, or go to **www.InvestorFasttrack.com.**

(continued)

The Seven Keys to Working *Smarter*, Not Harder *(continued)*

So if openness to new ideas is so important, why do so many investors struggle with it? The sad truth is that far too many investors are locked into archaic and habitual patterns of running their investing business, even if these practices are inefficient and far too costly.

In any time of great change, one of the most important tools for you to cultivate is that of a powerful eraser. It's not always what we know that gets us into trouble, but sometimes it's all the things we know that just *aren't* so that causes us so much aggravation. To work smarter, constantly look for places to prune and delete old practices and outmoded ideas to leave room for fresh ideas and strategies to thrive.

5. Integration of New Information

With all the change and explosion of information you have at your fingertips, as an investor, one of the keys to working smarter is to systematically develop your skill of integrating and putting new information to productive use. Remember, it's only the ideas that you profitably harness that actually matter. If you can't use the information and integrate it into your existing knowledge base, then all the new ideas are just fancy diversions. Information becomes power only at the point of application.

Here are five techniques to help you quickly integrate and apply new information:

- **Technique One: Fail Fast.** To make sense of new information usually involves trying it out. Average investors let fear of failure slow them down, but remember, the very best learning comes out of learning from what doesn't work. Look for ways that you can quickly do minitrials with the new information to get some real-world experience with which to make sense of the information (e.g., try out a negotiating language pattern the next time you are shopping at the mall; brainstorm three creative deal structuring techniques the next time you are structuring an offer before meeting with a seller).

- **Technique Two: Chunk It Down.** Don't try to learn it all in one large chunk; instead, break the new information into smaller, more manageable chunks. There is a reason why Mentorship students take weekly classes on investor skills in addition to the real-world help the coaches provide them on the deals they are putting together. We've learned that there is a practical limit on how much new information a Mentorship student can take in at one time. That's why we created the structured curriculum that layers in the investor knowledge chunk by chunk.

(continued)

The Seven Keys to Working *Smarter*, Not Harder *(continued)*

- **Technique Three: Layer It.** Just like a coat of paint covers best when applied in layers, so too does information work best when it's applied one layer at a time.

- **Technique Four: Daydream.** It's a powerful tool to visualize and use your imagination to see yourself using the new information that you are learning. It allows you to integrate the new knowledge at deep levels in an accelerated fashion.

- **Technique Five: Consistent Feedback.** The faster and more regularly you can get feedback in the real world by trying out a new technique or strategy, the faster you will begin to own the new ideas. After each trial of the new idea, ask yourself what you did that went really well, and what one or two things you will do differently next time as a result of what you learned this time.

6. Leverage

Leverage is when an effort produces a magnified result. In real estate, leverage is the greatest key to working smarter. It's what has allowed top Mentorship students to generate large and growing monthly cash flows while working fewer and fewer hours.

The Six Leverage Points:

- **Network Leverage.** Who do you know, or who do you know who knows someone, that can help you create a breakthrough in your investing? Do you know someone who can refer you deal after deal? Do you know someone who can connect you with a source of private funding? Leveraging your contacts is one of the critical steps to super-sizing your investing success.

- **Time Leverage.** How can you get more from your time? What activities give you the greatest return for the time and energy you spend on them? How can you leverage other people's time—either team members you hire or business contacts you tap into?

- **Information Leverage.** The right information can save you from going down the wrong path. The right information can give you a huge edge in your investing. Consistently ask yourself how you can leverage any new piece of information to create a magnified return in your investing business.

(continued)

The Seven Keys to Working *Smarter*, Not Harder (continued)

- **Skills Leverage.** Certain key investor skills you'll be learning about can be leveraged to produce amazing results. For example, take the skill of negotiation. Since you'll be involved in thousands of negotiations over your investing lifetime, one unit of effort invested to improve your negotiating skill will literally produce a thousandfold return.

- **Money Leverage.** One of the best features of real estate is the ease with which you can leverage your own money and other people's money. Whether it be by financing 90 percent of a new purchase with outside funding, or investing some of your money in a proven marketing campaign to find motivated sellers, intelligently leveraging money will make you a fortune.

- **Creativity Leverage.** This is perhaps the most overlooked form of leverage. Creative ideas are more valuable than just about any other resource you have as an investor, yet far too often new investors and rigid old pros forget this. One of the reasons I think all investors should learn to buy without cash or credit is because it forces these investors to get creative. We tend to grow in direct proportion to the demands we put on ourselves.

7. The Discipline to Let Go of the "Good" Things
"The biggest enemy of the *best* is the good."

As you blaze your way into Level Two success with your investing, you'll find that your biggest challenge won't be finding enough opportunity, but rather having too much opportunity to choose from. At any moment in time you are faced with choices of how to use your time. To work smarter you need to cultivate the "best and highest use" mind-set. Constantly ask yourself the question, "What's the best and highest use of my time here?" Then develop the capacity and discipline to do the best things and let go of the lower-order possibilities. This takes courage and a clear understanding of the end toward which you are working.

For example, as I've enjoyed success with my real estate investments, many investors now bring deals to me to either joint venture on with them or to lend them money to complete. I've learned certain rules that are now disciplines that I will not violate, because the cost in terms of wasted time is too great. For example, I won't even discuss partnering on a deal for more than two minutes if the person who brings the deal to my attention hasn't faxed me a copy of his or her signed contract. And I have learned that I simply won't lend money for a deal unless it's on an apartment building or single family house. Why? Because I've streamlined and systematized my business enough that I can safely and accurately lend on houses and apartment buildings quickly and easily. This means a higher return for the time and energy I invest. This is a form of leverage.

(continued)

> **The Seven Keys to Working *Smarter*, Not Harder** *(continued)*
>
> Time is your most precious resource. You need to start valuing it by investing it like your cash—with care and respect. Value your time like your cash, and value your cash like you would if you didn't have any. Then you'll learn to maximize your opportunities.
>
> There is a key concept called "opportunity cost," which is the cost of the time and money you have to put into a specific opportunity. Every opportunity has a potential reward, and it also has with it a specific expense—time cost, financial cost, emotional cost. The final key to working smarter is to remember to choose carefully to maximize your finite resources. The real risk of an average deal is not the money you have in the deal. The real risk is the potentially lost profit because you put your focus on this deal rather than on a great deal.

David continued, "This weekend is about taking your investing to the next level. You've already learned how to take the first step and get started investing in real estate. You learned what stops most people and how you can find and close your first deal in 90 days or less. Now you'll learn how to take your investing to the next level and build an investing business that leverages your efforts to give you maximum results. You'll learn how to build an investing business that magnifies your returns so that you earn more and work less. Make no mistake about it, ultimately your wealth building is not about working harder, it's about working smarter. It's about only doing those things that bring you closer to your end goal of being a Level Three investor.

"So it's time to get started learning to build a Level Two investing business. The first step is for you to develop your investing skills so that you have gained fluency in the five core investor skills. Then in the Middle Stage Level Two investing, you'll work to fine-tune these key skills while you also begin your first tentative branching out to build your investing business. Finally, in Advanced Stage Level Two investing, you'll build in earnest your profitable investing business.

"Ultimately, the only way to use real estate to become financially free is for your business to prosper without you there to run it day-to-day. This is the road to real freedom—cash flow that flows to you while you are not there working, in such a way that both the business and your net worth are growing day by day, month by month, and year by year.

"Tall order? Yes, but infinitely worthwhile. So let's roll up our sleeves and get to work."

CHAPTER TWO

Your Fast Track Map™ to Real Estate Riches

"Y" ou are all familiar with the Three Investor Levels," David continued. "This model of how to look at your investing is an important key to clearly identifying what you want to achieve and build with your investing business. But it's not enough to just know the Three Investor Levels—you need to have a clearly charted pathway to follow as you progress from where you are to Level Three. This pathway puts you on the real estate fast track.

"What I'd like to do now is clearly lay out your Fast Track Map™ so that you have a precise picture of the steps you'll take and the key focus you'll have as you accelerate your progression to becoming a Level Three investor."

David turned and drew a diagram on the board.

"Level One investors focus on the need to get into action. The key for them is belief. They are working to prove to themselves that real estate works, and that it works for them. We won't be spending much time on this level since you're all already past it.*

---

*For any readers who are just getting started, I urge you to get a copy of *Buying Real Estate without Cash or Credit* right away and read it cover to cover. It covers exactly how a Level One investor can get started today so that you can do your first deal in 90 days or less! To download two free chapters of this book just go to **www.InvestorFasttrack.com.**

The Fast Track™ Map

Level Three:
Passive Streams of Income!

Advanced Stage Level Two:
Building a Successful Investing Business
• Team
• Systems
• Outsourced Solutions

Middle Stage Level Two:
Refining Your Skills and
Leveraging Yourself

Early Stage Level Two:
Mastering the Five Core Investor Skills

Level One:
Proving to Yourself That Real Estate Works

"Our focus here this weekend is going to be on this middle area, on Level Two investing. As you can see, Level Two investing is broken down on the Fast Track Map™ into three distinct stages. Each of these stages has a different developmental focus for you, the investor. Here's a quick snapshot of each of these stages. We'll go into great detail on each one throughout this weekend.

"First there is Early Stage Level Two. The focus of this stage is on skill development. **Early Stage Level Two investors are learning to master the five core skills of successful investors: finding deals, structuring deals, negotiating deals, analyzing deals, and contracting on deals.**

"It usually takes an Early Stage Level Two investor 12 months to learn the core skills and gain the confidence and composure to use those skills in the real world. This leads them to the next stage—Middle Stage Level Two investing.

"**Middle Stage Level Two investing is about refining your investor skills and learning to leverage yourself so that you produce more for your investing business.** At this point in your investing, you are the central hub around which your investing business revolves. You're like a doctor whose whole office is organized to keep her as efficient as possible. As a Middle Stage Level Two investor you leverage your time every way you can by building the team and systems around you to keep you producing for your business.

"But ultimately there is a limit to what you are able to produce through your own efforts. This is why it's so important to progress to Advanced Stage Level Two investing.

"**Advanced Stage Level Two is about building the systems, teams, and outsourced solutions your business needs to consistently generate profits independent of you and your efforts.** When you've accomplished this you are able to transition into Level Three investing, where you are financially free and able to focus your time wherever you want. Many Level Three investors start to do big deals on commercial real estate because they have the experience, skills, and business infrastructure to do this in a Level Three way. This means they can buy an apartment complex and not get swallowed up by the project. In fact, they are able to take on a big project with less work and effort than they used to spend on deals as a Level Two investor.

"That is the overview of the Fast Track Map™. Right now we are going to start off with Early Stage Level Two investing."

Early Stage Level Two Investing

"Most people hit Early Stage Level Two investing fresh from the excitement of their first or second deal," David continued. "For some, it's the moment when they get that first cashier's check in hand from the option payment from a tenant buyer. Or maybe it's the moment when they sign up their first cash deal. Or when they walk out of a closing having sold their first property for a $35,000 net profit. Whenever it happens, they have come to the key moment where they know that real estate works, and more importantly they know it will work for them. This is their master key giving them entry to Level Two investing.

"When I meet a new Early Stage Level Two investor I can see the hope in their eyes. They start to dream again and believe that maybe, just maybe, their future can be what they used to dream it could be. How many of you can remember the moment when you reached Early Stage Level Two investing and hope blossomed in your heart?

"There is something else that I observe in Early Stage Level Two investors—relief! They tell themselves that no matter what happens next, at least I can tell all those naysayers in my life that I did it, I made some money at it!" Throughout the room students laughed and several nudged their partners with an "I told you so" look.

"Of course, for most Early Stage Level Two investors, there is still quite a bit of fear present. With your success you raise your expectations, and now you wonder if you can really meet these new expectations. *What if*, you ask yourself. What if you don't find more deals? What if these first ones were flukes? What if you wake up tomorrow and it was all really just a dream and never happened? And, gulp . . . what if you really do succeed in a massive way? Sometimes the only thing scarier than failure is success.

"But even with these fears, which are perfectly normal feelings, the biggest thing you feel is excitement. With the flush of your success comes the excitement for a future that is dramatically better than your old gray vision of just getting by. You awaken dreams long dormant, and these dreams begin to take on color and depth and become real. And they are a compelling pull for you to keep working on your investing.

"Early Stage Level Two investors often have a quiet determination about them to keep going after their investing—day by day and deal by deal.

"While most Early Stage Level Two investors are still only part-time, working around 15 to 20 hours a week on their investing, roughly 10 percent of them voluntarily take the leap to go into their investing full-time, with another 10 percent pushed into investing full-time because their jobs up and quit on them!

"Almost all of them work out of their homes, keeping their business overhead to an absolute minimum. They get on with the business of generating leads, negotiating with sellers, arranging necessary financing for deals, and looking after the properties they have added to their portfolios. Early Stage Level Two investors are at the steepest part of their learning curve, soaking up new information and focusing on mastering the five core investor skills.

"In fact, that's exactly what we are going to spend the rest of today and a good chunk of tomorrow covering—the five core investor skills. But you've all earned a quick break first."

The Three Biggest Pitfalls for Early Stage Level Two Investors

BRIGHT IDEA

One: Letting Your Comfort Zone Drag You Down

When you start succeeding with your investing, there is a temptation to relax and to stop doing the behaviors that brought you that success. There is a part of you that says, "Hey, you've done it. Now take it easy and enjoy yourself. You deserve it." Of course you can listen to this voice, but if you do you'll soon find yourself back where you started. This voice isn't the best part of you, it's the scared place trying an end-run to get you to go back to what feels comfortable.

There is a part of you that is focused on mere survival, and success can make this part of you feel uncomfortable. When this happens, this part of you pushes you to turn back to the life you used to live. You must fight this urge no matter what it takes.

When you have your early real estate success, that is not the time to relax. Rather, it is the time for you to step it up, build on the momentum, and push your investing business two more steps ahead as quickly as possible. It's like a sports team that is on a roll. This is the time to push your lead to make sure you win.

(continued)

The Three Biggest Pitfalls for Early Stage Level Two Investors
(continued)

Two: Thinking You've Arrived

The ancient Greeks called it "hubris"; in today's world we call it getting cocky and letting your head swell. Remember that your early success is just that—early success. It is not a guarantee that you've arrived, nor is it a sign that you've won the game. You still need to keep your focus and quietly get on with the business of investing.

Until you've had at least one major failure in your investing it's hard to recognize that we all make mistakes when buying real estate from time to time. Smart investors build in allowances for the fact that they may be wrong in their assessment of a deal. This can mean getting an outside pair of eyes to unemotionally give you their opinion on a deal, or it can mean creating a safety cushion in your deals in case your prediction of local market conditions is wrong.

The best investors are the ones who have learned that they are fallible and, because of this, learned to entertain the possibility that they may be wrong. Far from slowing you down, this humbling realization will help you accelerate your investing success because you aren't bogged down by the need to be right all the time. When you make a mistake the world doesn't come crashing down. You simply brush it off, learn your lessons, and get on with your investing. This was one of the toughest lessons for me to learn, and one of the most important.

Three: Delaying Investing in Your Real Estate Education Until You've "Made More Money"

It never ceases to amaze us the number of new investors who say they will wait to invest in their real estate education until after they have made a lot of money with their investing. That makes about as much sense as standing in front of an empty fireplace and saying that as soon as the fireplace gives them heat then they'll be willing to put in wood!

Let's get one thing absolutely clear—one way or another, *everyone* pays for their education. You either pay by learning the slow, painful route of "self-education," also known as trial and error, or you get on the fast track and learn from experienced mentors who have done what you want to do and who can save you years of wasted effort and help you reclaim thousands of dollars in profits that you would have otherwise missed out on.

(continued)

The Three Biggest Pitfalls for Early Stage Level Two Investors
(continued)

It is not a sign of weakness to get someone to help you learn and succeed faster in your investing, it is a sign of strength. Intelligent investors know that learning from other people's experiences is one of the best short cuts to success available to them. Look for people who you can model to accelerate your success in investing. While it's important to look for people from whom you can learn techniques and specific strategies, as an Early Stage Level Two investor it is even more important that you look for a successful investing *model* upon which to build your fledgling investing business.

In order for you to reach the levels of success you really want, make sure that whatever investor model you base your investing business on is one that is laid out all the way *through* the finish line you've set for yourself, and not just *to* the finish line. I've seen too many investors who only had a model that took them to the finish line and, as a result, they are stuck, still actively working their real estate business. Granted, they make a great living, but they're still not passive Level Three investors enjoying real financial freedom. If they stop working, in fairly short order their investing machine will come to a grinding halt. Make sure your model takes you to Level Three success, where your real estate business runs better without you there in it day to day. Remember, *passive* cash flow is the ultimate goal of your investing business.

CHAPTER THREE

Core Investor Skill One:
Creating a Deal Finding Machine

David then posed the following scenario: "Imagine walking into your office each day and having two highly motivated sellers waiting to talk with you about your buying their properties. Do you think if you talked with two motivated sellers a day, five days a week you'd be able to close on some highly profitable real estate deals? Let's think through the numbers: two motivated sellers a day, multiplied by five days a week, multiplied by 40 weeks each year—I think you should take 12 weeks of vacation a year, I hope that's okay with you," David smiled. "That equals a total of 400 potential deals each year for you to choose from. How many of those deals do you think you could handle? When you let the math add up, the potential for your investing business is huge. But there are two looming challenges to all this.

"First, the average investor is not able to handle even a fraction of this volume of lead flow because he has no business infrastructure to lean on and leverage. This is why I've stressed so heavily so far, and will continue to press, the urgency and rewards of building an investing *business* rather than just being an investor.

"Second, as you can probably imagine, the single greatest bottleneck to your business initially is your ability to create deal finding systems that consistently churn out quality leads—one after another after another. When you are building a profitable investing business it's not enough to just be able to find one deal. To really take it to the next level you've got to create marketing systems that consistently produce deal after deal.

"This is a tall order. In fact, in the beginning a great deal of your energy is going to be tied up in creating this deal pipeline. But once you've built it, it only takes a fraction of the time to *maintain* it. Is it worth the weeks and months of effort to build this kind of real estate deal factory? You better believe it!

"Just look at someone like Stephen. I know that many of you have worked with him on the Mentorship Program coaching sessions. It took him and his wife Susan over 18 months to really establish their deal finding systems. That's a lot of time and energy they had to put in to build this infrastructure. But they now enjoy a foreclosure business that generates over a dozen profitable deals each year. Plus their commercial investing part of the business generates several highly lucrative big projects each year. If you invest the energy over the next 12 months, you can enjoy the same success as Stephen and Susan.

"So let's start with the foundation and work from there. The foundation of all winning real estate deals is the Winning Deal Formula. I am hoping that you all remember this formula from the Intensive Training you attended at the start of the Mentorship Program."*

David clicked an image up onto the screen.

Winning Deal Formula

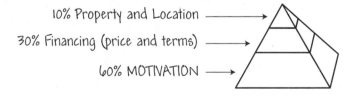

---

*Would you like to get an insider's seat at the Intensive Training? Then grab a copy of *Buying Real Estate without Cash or Credit*. The first half of the book is just that, a step-by-step workshop on exactly how to start your investing business in 90 days or less. To download two free chapters, go to **www.InvestorFasttrack.com.**

"As you can see, the foundation that great real estate deals are built on is *not* location, but motivation. The first concern when you are looking at a deal is why the seller is selling the property. **This is the first key ingredient of a great deal—finding a seller who has a strong motivation to sell.** It's the seller's compelling reason to sell, with a perceived time crunch within which to do it, more than any other factor, that helps you get a great real estate deal. Remember this and say it to yourself over and over again—the foundation of all winning real estate deals is the seller's motivation to sell. It's almost as if what the seller initially tells you is his reason for selling is the tip of an iceberg. The real reason is the hidden 90 percent that is below the surface. And it's this hidden 90 percent which is the key ingredient for a winning deal.

"**The second level of a winning deal is the financing—the price and terms.** To make money on a deal you need to either purchase the property for cash at a steep cash discount, or you need to get great terms of financing. If you buy for cash at a discount, your low cash price guarantees you a profit. If you buy on flexible terms where you are making the seller payments over time, then the financing lets you hold on to the property over time with positive cash flow and make even more money on the back end when you eventually resell or refinance the property to tap into your accumulated equity. For any deal to be a winner the numbers must make sense.

"**Now third in line in importance are the location and physical structure and condition of the property.** Over the long haul the location does matter. The right location will appreciate in value significantly more than the wrong location. But, and this is a *big* but, the only way you can safely know you'll be able to hold on to the property over the long haul is for the first two ingredients—motivation and financing—to be in plentiful supply.

"Any property at the right price and terms is a great deal. But the only way you'll ever find a seller who is willing to give you the best price and terms is if that seller is a motivated seller. That's why a strongly motivated seller is so important. As I've just mentioned, the right price and terms—the financing—guarantees you a profit.

"The location and the physical condition of the property are important for two reasons. First, they matter because they significantly impact what the right price and terms for a property are. After all, if the property needs a huge amount of fixing up, then that needs to be factored into the price. Or if the property is in an area with zero appreciation, then the numbers you agree on for the price and terms need to be such that you build a profit into the deal from day one. Second, the location and physical structure impact your exit strategy on the property. If the house you are buying is in a great area, you may be much more likely to hold on to the property over the long term. This may mean that you structure the deal in such a way that you trade the seller a higher price in exchange for you getting great long-term financing to enable you to profitably hold on to the property over time. Or if the building is in a war zone, perhaps you want to negotiate a very low cash price with the plan to immediately resell the property to another investor who specializes in lower income housing in that neighborhood.

"So I hope you see that location matters, but only after the first two levels of the Winning Deal Formula are factored in. This is a major shift from how most people think about investing in real estate. **This shift—from real estate being about location, location, location, to real estate being about motivation first, price and terms second, and then as a distant third about location—greatly impacts how you structure your real estate business.**

The Seven Clues to a Seller's *Real* Motivation

So what are the key clues that let you know you are on the trail of a motivated seller? What things should you be looking for when you are talking with property owners or people in your referral network that will let you know you have found a motivated seller?

Here are the seven key clues to determining if you have found a motivated seller, along with the scripted questions you'll need to ask the seller, either over the phone or when you meet with them in person, to uncover the seller's real motivation.

Clue One: They have a compelling reason to sell!
Key Question to Ask: *"This sounds like a wonderful property, why in the world would you ever consider selling it?"*

Clue Two: They are under a perceived time crunch to sell.
Key Question to Ask: *"When did you want the property handled? Six months, or twelve months? You tell me, when did you ideally want the property handled?*

Clue Three: The property is vacant.
Key Question to Ask: *"Who's living in the property now? Is there a renter that we're going to have to deal with (using a negative tone), or is the property hopefully empty right now (using a brighter tone)?"*

(continued)

The Seven Clues to a Seller's *Real* Motivation *(continued)*

Clue Four: If it's a rental property, they've had a bad renter experience.
Key Question to Ask: *"You've probably never had a bad renter here, huh?"*

Clue Five: The property hasn't been properly advertised so buyers are scarce.
Key Question to Ask: *"You've probably been flooded with people coming through the house, huh? May I ask why you haven't accepted any of the written offers you've gotten so far?"*

Clue Six: The seller perceives the local real estate market is slow.
Key Question to Ask: *"I'm sure you're really up to speed on the local real estate market. What's your take on the stage in the real estate cycle we're in right now?"*

Clue Seven: The property is an emotional anchor to strong negative feelings for the seller.
Key Question to Ask: *"I'm sorry, I'm still just a little confused. Can you tell me again why it is you'd even want to sell such a lovely home?"*

The Two Clues to Great Financing

"Once you've determined a seller is truly motivated to sell, next you'll need to explore the financing potential of the deal. Remember, to be a winning deal, the seller either has to have enough equity to discount the price of the property so that a cash sale makes sense, or the seller has to be willing to significantly participate in the financing to allow a terms deal to work.

"**There are two key questions to ask when looking for clues to great financing. The first is, how much equity does the seller have in the property?** Having more equity means the seller could either discount the price of the property for a fast cash sale, or carry back more of the financing in some form of seller financing.

"**The second key question is, what is the market rent in comparison to the total payments on the underlying financing?** This question tells you if the property will cash flow as a terms deal. To make a terms deal work, your total monthly payment for the property must be no higher than the market rent. In fact, I recommend that you always build a cash flow cushion into all your terms deals.

This means that ideally the total property monthly payment needs to be no more than 85 to 90 percent of the market rent."

"But David," Nancy asked, " I live in an expensive area with home values that just seem so out of line with the market rents. How am I supposed to make a deal cash flow in my market?"

"That's a great question. In fact, probably about a third of you here are in very strong real estate markets right now where home prices are quite high in relation to the market rents, making it harder to buy an investment property conventionally and have it cash flow for the first several years. The key word though is *conventionally*. If you are going to buy using conventional financing to fund the deal, then you're right, it will be almost impossible to get the property to cash flow. But you're not limited to buying conventionally. You're also able to buy creatively. Now if you buy for a deep cash discount the property will often cash flow based on the fact that you are buying it for 60 to 70 percent of value. But one of my favorite ways to buy is on terms.

"For example, I picked up one upper-end home in California during the height of the market rush in San Diego where the only reason it cash flowed from the start was that the owner was motivated enough to carry back the financing at a very low interest rate. Remember, when you are buying from a motivated seller, you can often structure a deal that takes care of the seller's most pressing need and at the same time allows you to get a monthly payment that is lower than the market rents. Later today we'll discuss techniques like graduated payments, equity splits, and owner-carry notes and I'll give you the details you need to structure these deals. But the bottom line for now is to realize that, regardless of the market, you can always find profitable deals. You can buy cheaply for cash, or you can buy at a higher price but with attractive financing from the seller. Both will allow you to get at least a breakeven, if not a positive cash flow from your properties."

BRIGHT IDEA

The Eight Clues to a Great Property and Location

Once you know you have a motivated seller, and you know that the financing of the deal makes sense, next you need to factor in the physical condition and the location of the property. When you're looking for a great deal, here are the eight clues to look for that let you know you have a great property and location.

(continued)

The Eight Clues to a Great Property and Location *(continued)*

Clue One: The property has a cosmetic problem that makes it show poorly.
I love houses that have cosmetic defects that are cheap and easy to cure, but hurt the short-term value of the property. Why? Because once you fix them, the house is instantly more valuable.

For example, I bought a three-bedroom, two-bath house several years ago which was in dire need of new paint and carpet. The sellers had left the old, dated wallpaper and dingy carpet in the house while they were trying to sell it, and most buyers were turned off. I ended up getting a great deal on the house, and it only took me $4,000 to repaint and recarpet it. Once I did, it was easy to find a great tenant buyer who rented to own the property from me for $30,000 more than I paid for the property. This is a simple example of "forced" appreciation.

Clue Two: The property was well built.
This matters most if you plan on holding on to the property over time, either as a rental property or a rent-to-own property.

Clue Three: The area is well established and consistently in demand.

Clue Four: The area is close to the jobs and amenities that the potential buyers or renters for that level of home want.

Clue Five: The area has easy access to the main roads that will take residents to jobs, shopping, and schools.

Clue Six: The area has low *perceived* crime.

Clue Seven: The area has highly desirable schools.

Clue Eight: The property has four walls and a roof.
All kidding aside, I listed this one to remind you not to get too carried away with the house or area. *Any* house at the right price and on the right terms is a great buy. Don't lose yourself in the imagined possibilities of the house from the perspective of the occupant. Instead, keep focused on what the possibilities are from the perspective of an intelligent investor looking to make a conservative profit.

Seven *More* Techniques to Find Great Deals

I just couldn't resist sharing with you even more ways to find motivated sellers. Here we go!*

Technique One: Referrals from Real Estate Agents

As an investor, one of your most important relationships for you to establish is with the real estate agent community. I suggest that as a Level Two investor you network with at least two new agents each month. Invite them to lunch and get to know them. Find out how you can source and serve them. Share with them your buying criteria and how they can profit by helping you consistently find great deals. (See Chapter 13 for details.)

Technique Two: Establish a Farm Area

A *farm area* is simply a section of town where you focus a definite portion of your efforts. It's almost impossible to be an expert on the trends and hidden opportunities in an area that is too large. It's by creating one or two smaller farm areas that you are able to narrow your focus and find those hidden deals. You want to know before houses come up for sale, and you want to know when a landlord is dealing with a nasty eviction. To be privy to this type of insider information it's going to take effort to develop the network of contacts who will call you when they hear of new developments. Also, you will become *the* investor who people turn to in that area when they need a fast and *fair* solution.

Technique Three: Door Hangers and Flyers

One of the disadvantages of direct mail is that the postage is so expensive (not to mention that you are competing with all the other mail the homeowner receives for his or her attention). Did you know that you can hire someone to put out "I Buy Houses" door hangers or flyers in your farm area for about half the cost of a direct mail postcard and about a third of the cost of a direct mail letter? I had one student use this idea to find two houses from a seller who was literally a few weeks away from moving overseas. Our student bought both houses with attractive owner financing for less than $3,000 down!

*For a complete online workshop on finding great investment deals go to **www.InvestorFasttrack.com.** (See Appendix A for details.)

(continued)

Seven *More* Techniques to Find Great Deals *(continued)*

Technique Four: Call Expired Listings

A listing is simply the term for a house that a seller has agreed to allow a real estate agent to sell for them. If for some reason that house doesn't sell during the listing period, which is usually three to six months, then we call that house an *expired listing*. For every expired listing you generally have a much more motivated seller. Contact one of the real estate agents you have networked with and ask them to pull a list of expired listings for you to call through. It's easy for them to do on their computer and should take them less than 10 minutes tops to do this and e-mail the list over to you. They pull the list together and you agree that if you need an agent in the transaction, you'll use them as your buyer's agent. Plus, if any of the homeowners you talk with aren't motivated enough for you to make a deal work as an investor, then you'll refer these sellers over to your real estate agent friend so they have a good shot at getting a new listing. It's a total win-win for you and the agent.

Technique Five: Billboards and Bench Ads

If you can't afford it on your own, co-op with a group of fellow investors and rent some concentrated outdoor advertising in key, high-traffic areas. Make sure you diligently track your marketing to make sure the return is there for you, and just split the leads. I know of one group of five investors who collectively buy space on 30 bus benches and generate a sizable lead flow for themselves from this source.

Technique Six: Bird Dogs

Empower other people who are around houses every day to sniff out motivated sellers for you. Talk with landscapers, contractors, delivery people, postal workers, anyone who is regularly in contact with homes and homeowners in the course of their day and who can turn you on to potential leads. You just pay them a $250 to $1,000 finder's fee for every lead they share with you that you close on.

Technique Seven: Online FSBO Web Sites

There is a growing trend for homeowners to sell their own homes online through various "For Sale By Owner" (FSBO) web sites. For a list of links for powerful FSBO sites, just log onto **www.InvestorFasttrack.com** and click on the "Investor Resources" button.

Leveraged Strategies and Systems for Finding Motivated Sellers

"As Level Two investors who are looking to progress further in your investing, it is critical that you begin to make the shift away from 'looking for a deal' and instead focus more and more of your efforts on building leveraged deal finding systems that will yield your investing business deal after deal. It's the difference between being a hunter-gatherer scratching for a deal here or there, and being a sophisticated farmer who invests in the agricultural infrastructure so that each season you are able to harvest field after field of deals.

"This isn't an easy shift to make, and in the beginning you'll have to balance your need to keep deals coming into your business with taking the time to step out of the activity of your business and work *on* your business's deal finding systems. The best advice I can give you is to shift your thinking so that every time you implement a marketing strategy to find motivated sellers, you ask yourself **three key questions.**

"**First, ask yourself how you can leverage your efforts. How can you take the energy you are putting into a marketing channel and magnify your return?** I suggest you go back to the six forms of leverage we talked about earlier in the workshop and brainstorm ways you can take your efforts and get more from less. I call this 'super-sizing' an idea. You take it and make it bigger and better than ever."

Vicki raised her hand and asked, "David, can you give us an example of this?"

"Sure. Let's super-size the idea of networking with real estate agents by leveraging your time. How is it that most investors network with real estate agents?"

Vicki thought for a moment and then answered, "They randomly meet an agent here or there and then they follow up to establish a professional relationship. Sometimes they even get a referral to talk with a specific agent from another contact they have in common."

"Exactly! Now if it was me, I'd like to speed up this process and connect with more agents with less time and effort. To do this we need to leverage our efforts. One way would be to actually go to one real estate office each month and give a quick 10- to 15-minute talk at their regular office meetings about how these agents can generate a lot of repeat volume business by aligning themselves with local investors. This is your opportunity to share with 20 or 30 agents in one shot exactly what your buying criteria are and how you can help them generate more sales volume fast for any of their hard-to-sell listings, or anytime they come across a listing that the seller needs to sell fast. Can you see the leverage in talking with so many agents at one time versus one by one?"

David continued, "Now that's just one form of leverage—leveraging your time. Another way to leverage yourself is to leverage your money. For example, hire someone to put out your 'I Buy Houses' signs for you each week rather than spending the four or five hours yourself. For $10 to $12 an hour you can leverage this third party's labor to find you deals.

"Another example would be to leverage your network of contacts. Let's say you know a few local business owners. Ask them to let you put up your 'I Buy Houses' flyers at their businesses. I know one investor who found a deal that netted him over $85,000 from a lead that came from a contact who let him advertise in her place of business. Another example I heard about from reading the Mentorship student discussion board was how one of our students enlisted the help of a friend who worked at Target. Normally the store gets its employees to park at the back of the lot. Our student paid his friend five bucks a week to put a special 'I Buy Houses' magnetic car sign on his car and park right near the entrance to the store parking lot. Our student used a separate extension on the sign to track the calls and agreed to give his friend $500 for any deal he signed up as a result of the signs. He reported on the discussion board that he got four leads the first weekend his friend had the signs on his car! I hope you are getting the idea.

"The key is to start consistently asking yourself how you can leverage a specific deal finding strategy so that you find more deals with less of your energy and effort.

"The second question to ask yourself when you are implementing a marketing strategy is how you can systematize it so that this marketing stream goes on autopilot. How can you make this marketing strategy work without you needing to focus your mental energy on running it?

"Let's look at the example of creating a mailing campaign to find motivated sellers. The average mom or pop investor just 'does a mailing.' They give no thought to how to make this an automatic, repeatable process; they just do it on a one-shot basis. This is just too expensive a way to run your marketing, with all that wasted energy ramping up your mailing campaign each time you consciously choose to do another mailing. Instead, let's sketch out a sample system that you can build for your investing business so that your *business*, not you, regularly generates leads of motivated sellers.

"The first step is for you to find a secure source of homeowners for you to mail to. For our example we'll use a mailing campaign to out-of-town owners. These are people who own a property in your farm area, but who live at least one hour's drive away. The average investor just calls up a title company and asks for the list from them. You, however, will create a script for calling up the title company and asking for the mailing list. You'll systematize how your title company will get you updates of this mailing list via e-mail once a quarter. This way you don't have to be the one calling to get the updated list from the title company each quarter—you can have a staff member do it. You'll also checklist out your Master Mailing Calendar that includes a timeline of when you'll need to get the mailing pieces printed, when you'll be dropping your letters or postcards into the mail, and your schedule for follow-up mailings.* You'll create a step-by-step instruction sheet for your marketing assistant to follow to execute on this master mailing calendar.

"I think you get the idea. I know this is a lot more work than just 'doing the mailing,' but the payoff is that you'll get a much better, consistent result for your business. Plus you'll be able to hand off responsibility for this marketing channel to someone else in your business, thus freeing yourself up to invest your time on higher-value activities. **Ultimately, if you want to be a Level Three investor enjoying a Level Three lifestyle, you'll need to have your business *systems* driven, not people dependent.**

"**The third and final question you need to ask yourself with your marketing to massively grow your investing profits is how you can optimize your marketing results. How can you optimize all your marketing efforts to maximize your net profits in the simplest, stablest way?**

"The key component to this step-by-step optimization of your marketing efforts is the disciplined and effective tracking of your marketing activities."

David got a little playful with the group and said, "Everyone raise your right hand and repeat after me: 'I hereby affirm and declare . . . that I will never . . . ever . . . engage in a marketing activity . . . unless I have a reliable mechanism in place . . . to track the results of the marketing effort . . . so that I will know how

---

*Would you like to see a sample "Master Mailing Calendar" and get your hands on my script to get your out-of-town owner mailing list for free? Just log onto **www.Investor Fasttrack.com** and click on the "Free Offers" button.

much money and time I put in . . . and what tangible benefit I got out . . . and over time I will test . . . and test . . . and test . . . to find the optimum mixture and methods . . . to get the most for the least. So help me God.'" By this point the class was hamming it up as much as David, but the point went home—they were just having a blast while they were learning it.

"If you don't track all your marketing efforts then you are shooting in the dark. I used to fool myself into thinking that I could get a gut sense of which of my marketing efforts was most effective, but sadly I've come to realize that my gut was wrong much of the time. It was only when I had hard numbers to look at that I started to make the right marketing decisions and was really able to optimize my marketing efforts and dollars."

The Mechanics of Tracking Your Marketing

One of the key lessons of successful investing businesses is that a successful investing business always gets paid for every dollar or hour it spends on a marketing campaign. And so should you.

Every campaign you run should either make you money by finding you great real estate deals, or it should profit you by expanding your learning of what works or doesn't work with your marketing efforts. Ideally you will get "paid" both ways—in profitable deals and in valuable marketing insights.

You need to track what goes into the campaign in terms of time and money, and what you get out of the campaign in terms of leads, lead quality, and the ultimate results. This way you will be able to refine and optimize all your marketing activities.

How do you track your marketing? Simply have every ad, every mailing piece, every campaign send responses to a voice mail system that uses a specific extension or voice mail box for each marketing channel. So, for example, responses to your classified "I Buy Houses" ad go to extension 31; to your signs, extension 32; to your first postcard to landlords, extension 33; and so forth. Then you just tally up your responses weekly in a simple spreadsheet or worksheet to track your results.

(continued)

The Mechanics of Tracking Your Marketing *(continued)*

It's essential to be able to track the specific, demonstrable results of all your marketing campaigns. I recommend that you use a toll-free voice mail system to point all your marketing efforts toward, because of the ability these systems have to help you track your marketing results. The system that Mentorship students use lets them track up to 90 marketing campaigns concurrently by the use of specific extensions placed in the advertising. The system has all the outgoing messages pre-scripted and installed with professional voice recordings. In fact, the system is set up and ready to use right from day one to save students time and effort.*

Also, since it's a toll-free system, you'll capture the phone number of every caller, regardless of whether they leave you a message or not. What this means is that you can actually increase your marketing results by 50 to 200 percent! How? I've found that for every 10 messages from sellers your marketing generates, on average another 5 to 20 sellers have called into your voice mail in response to your marketing, but they hung up without leaving you a message. Most investors think that particular marketing effort only produced 10 calls, but in reality it produced 15 to 30 calls. The power in a toll-free voice mail system like the one that Mentorship students use is that it lets you generate a "call detail report" that lists the phone numbers of *every* caller—including the ones who didn't leave a message! You can then call back *all* your leads to follow up.

*For a limited time, readers can sign up for the same investor voice mail system that Mentorship students use, for a small monthly fee. To find out more and to quickly get your toll-free voice mail system operational, log onto **www.InvestorFasttrack.com** and click on the "Investor Resources" button.

"Here's an example of a worksheet to track your marketing." David clicked an image up onto the screen.

Lead Tracking Worksheet

Week of June 15th, 2010

Lead Source	Voice Mail Extension	Cost/ Week	# of Leads	# of Appointments	# of Deals	Results $ of Deals
Classified Ad (*Tribune*)	33	$158	4	2	1	Estimate: $38,000
Calling System	N/A	$450	5	1	0	0
Out-of-Town Postcard	34	$345	3	1	0	0
"I Buy Houses" Signs	35	$125	5	3	1	Estimate: $55,000

"To use this worksheet, you just keep a running tally of each of your campaigns as they are running, and each week you fill out the form."

"David," Mary asked. "What's the difference between a 'lead' and an 'appointment'?"

"Great question. A lead is simply anyone who responded. Let's face it, plenty of the people who respond to your marketing won't be worth meeting with. The difference is that an appointment is a qualified lead that you determine is actually worth sitting down and meeting with, even if they are long distance and you hold that meeting over the phone.

"Also note that you won't know the actual profits in a deal until down the road, so make sure you make your best guesstimate, but come back later to enter in the actual number so that when you do your quarterly marketing overhaul you have *real* numbers to look at, not just estimates.

"Now let's go to the next worksheet, which is the Marketing Analysis Worksheet." David clicked a new image up onto the screen.

Marketing Analysis Worksheet

Month of June 2010

Lead Source	# of Leads	# of Appointments	# of Deals	Cost/ Month	Cost/ Lead	Cost/ Appointment	Cost/ Deal	Profit from Lead Source	Return on Marketing $(Profit/Cost)
Classified Ads	12	5	1	$ 632	$ 52.67	$126.40	$638	$38,000	6,012%
Calling System	N/A	18	2	$1,800	N/A	$ 100	$900	$72,000	4,000%
Out-of-Town Postcard	9	4	0	$1,380	$153.33	$ 345	N/A	N/A	N/A
"I Buy Houses" Signs	22	8	2	$ 500	$ 22.73	$ 62.50	$250	$65,000	13,000%

"I recommend you sit down monthly, quarterly, and annually, review your marketing systems, and see which systems are yielding the best results. Invest the bulk of your marketing resources in these proven winners, but invest 5 to 10 percent of your marketing energy and dollars and test new versions to see which pulls best. The key is to keep all the variables you can constant and test one element at a time. Change the headline on your postcard. Try out a new paper to run your classified ad in. Try a new color on your 'I Buy Houses' signs. As long as you track things, over time you'll come up with the hard numbers, which will make your marketing decisions easy and fast.

"Okay, you've all been so good you've earned a short break. When we come back we'll get into the second Core Investor Skill: structuring deals."

CHAPTER FOUR

Core Investor Skill Two: Structuring Highly Profitable Win-Win Deals

After the break, David jumped right in: "At the most basic level there are **three steps to any deal. Step one is to find a motivated seller who has the right motivation and situation.** Remember that you bring value to the deal by helping a seller solve a pressing real estate problem. If they're not motivated, then there is no way for you to bring enough value to the table to make it a win-win deal. This is why it's essential that the seller you work with have a compelling reason to sell.

"**Step two is to meet with this seller and find a way to structure a deal that meets the seller's most important needs while building a conservative profit in there for you.** Once you have created this win-win solution with the seller, you need to make sure that agreement is in writing and signed by both you and the seller. We call this 'putting the property under contract.'

"**Step three is to execute your exit strategy for the property.** This almost always means you must find your end user for the property. This end user might be a retail buyer who is purchasing the property from you if you've decided that your exit strategy is to immediately resell the property. Or your end user could be a renter if your exit strategy is to lease out the property for a period of time. Or your end user could be a tenant buyer if your exit strategy is to sell the property on a rent-to-own basis.

"As you can imagine, the seller's needs and situation are going to determine to a large degree how you structure the deal, as is your plan for dealing with the property once you've acquired it. The key to structuring a winning deal is to plan both your way into and out of any deal. Your way into a deal is called your '**acquisition strategy.**' This is how you structure your *purchase* of the property.

"Intelligent investors know that they make their money when they buy, not when they sell. This requires them to make sure that any deal they do has a built-in profit at the time of *acquisition*.

"Your way out of the deal is called your '**exit strategy.**' This is when you harvest the profit you have created from the deal. *Notice you don't make the profit when you sell—you make your profit when you buy.* You merely harvest your profit when you sell. The key lesson here is that you will never enter into any deal that you do not have a clearly laid out strategy for gracefully exiting.

"There are two main ways to buy a property and make a conservative profit. Either you buy the property for cash at a deeply discounted price, or you buy the property with attractive terms of financing that allow you to make your profit due to the great financing with which you acquired the property. Picture this as a decision tree. At the first juncture you have your first real decision to make as you structure the deal—will it be a cash deal or a terms deal?"

David drew a diagram on the board:

Winning Deal Decision Tree

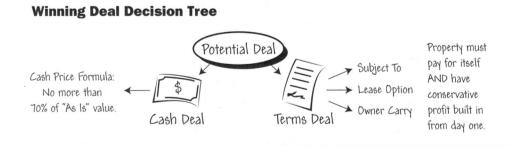

Cash Price Formula: No more than 70% of "As Is" value.

Cash Deal

Potential Deal

Terms Deal

Subject To
Lease Option
Owner Carry

Property must pay for itself AND have conservative profit built in from day one.

"Depending on which way you go, there are specific formulas and techniques for how you'll structure the deal. When you are buying for cash you'll need a price that is at least 70 percent or less than the 'as is' value of the property. We call this formula the 'Cash Price Formula.' Here's what it looks like." David clicked a new image onto the screen.

Cash Price Formula

<u>Highest</u> "All Cash" Price You Can Pay = 70% of the "As Is" value of the property

↳ (Go for less!)

"As Is" Value = The after-repair value of the property less the CONSERVATIVE cost of getting the house in the condition so that it will SELL in 90 days or less.

"One very important distinction when you are doing a cash deal is that the cash you are using doesn't have to be your money. It *could* be yours, or it could be money you borrowed from some third party like a bank or private lender. The critical distinction in a cash sale is that the *seller* is getting all of her money up front from you and not waiting for payments over time. Once you've purchased a property for cash, you can either hold on to the property over time or move to sell it right away for more than you paid.

"When you are buying for cash, the reason for the big discount is that as an investor your cash is a valuable commodity—one that most sellers want. It is also a limited commodity. Once it's committed by being invested into real estate, you lose the ability to quickly access it to purchase your next screaming good deal. Because of this, you need to always value your cash highly and use it to maximum effect. This means that if a seller requires an all-cash purchase, you require a 'deep cash discount' to move ahead with the deal. Remember, anytime you get cash to a seller, you need to get something of equal value in return—like a deep cash discount. When you buy for cash, you typically take on more risk than if you enter into a terms deal—having more money in the deal means you potentially have more to lose—and risk always needs to be rewarded. If your risk isn't being adequately rewarded in a deal, then why take it? In a cash deal the way you get rewarded is by getting a deep cash discount.

"Let's do a brief review of buying on terms. This means you structure the deal so that the seller is not getting all her money up front but instead is going to get paid at some future date. With a terms deal you use the excellent financing that the seller participates in to make your profit. Usually on a terms deal you make sure that the property can afford to pay for itself long enough for it to go up in value to resell at a profit. Or you make a deal in which the financing is so valuable that you are able to use it to make your money regardless of whether the property goes up in value.

"Now all of you remember the Intensive Training you went through as part of the Mentorship Program where you learned some of the creative financing strategies we teach, such as lease options, buying subject to the existing financing, and using owner-carry financing.* We'll be building on these main acquisition strategies in just a moment."

---

*For more information on these basic terms deal structuring strategies, check out Appendix A for the list of FREE Online Investor Workshops you get when you register for the Investor Fast Track Program™ at **www.InvestorFasttrack.com**.

The Three Most Important Terms Deal Acquisition Strategies*

Terms Deal Acquisition Strategy #1: Lease Option

Long-term lease + agreed upon option price.

The first and perhaps the most common way to structure a terms deal is to negotiate a long-term lease on the property along with an option to purchase the property. What this means is the seller agrees to let you take possession of the property (i.e., lease) and the seller has agreed to give you a fixed price at which you can buy the property at any point over your lease period (i.e., option). The lease portion of the deal lets you control possession of the property, including allowing you to sublease the property to a tenant. The option portion of the deal gives you control over the sale of the property and any future appreciation by locking in a price at which you have the exclusive right to buy for the specific period of the lease term.

Case Study: Two Mentorship students, Mark and Trish, found a seller who was making double payments on two properties after a recent move, who wanted to just get out from under the second payment. They agreed to step in and do a three-year lease option on the property for a price of $235,000. They sold the property on a two-year lease option for $295,000 and netted over a $65,000 profit for their efforts.

Terms Deal Acquisition Strategy #2: Buying Subject To the Existing Financing

Seller deeds you the house and you make payments every month on the existing loan(s).

On most properties you buy, the seller doesn't own the property free and clear. She has a loan against the property for some amount. Now how did the seller get that loan in place? She applied with a mortgage lender who required her to show three things to qualify for the loan: her credit score, the financial resources to pay for the loan, and often a cash down payment, Of course the lender didn't do the loan for free; it charged the borrower application fees, appraisal fees, origination fees, and points on the loan. And the lender required the borrower to personally guarantee the loan.

*For more details on all three terms deal acquisition strategies, go to **www.InvestorFasttrack.com** and download a FREE ebook titled *Five Fun, Easy Ways to Structure Terms Deals to Generate Over $100,000 in Profits This Year.*

(continued)

The Three Most Important Terms Deal Acquisition Strategies
(continued)

With subject-to financing, you get all the benefit of the loan that's already in place with none of the risk, with none of the cost, in fact with virtually none of the downsides of conventional financing. What you do is simply buy the property and *leave* the existing financing in place. *You* own the property, the seller owns the debt. Of course you agree to pay the payment each month on the existing loan, because if the loan isn't paid each month the lender's claim to the property comes before your claim to it. In fancy terms we'd say you own the property "subject to the existing financing that exists against the property."

Case Study: John, one of our Mentorship graduates, got a referral to meet with a couple who were four months behind on their mortgage payment and about to lose their home to foreclosure. After meeting with them he agreed that he would make up the back payments, buy the property, and simply take over making payments on the underlying loan. Here are what the numbers looked like on the front half of the deal:

Value	$180,000
Existing Mortgage	($155,000)
Back Payments (with late fees and attorney's fees)	($9,000)
Money Given to the Seller	($1,000)
Closing Costs (title insurance, escrow cost)	($1,000)
Effective Purchase Price	$166,000
Total Cash Needed for Deal	$11,000

To make this deal work for him, John immediately found a tenant buyer for the property who gave him $6,000 of option money plus the first month's rent of $1,600. In essence he recouped $7,600 of the $11,000 he needed to do this deal within three weeks of buying it. Over the next five years he had two different tenant buyers go through the property and choose not to exercise their option to purchase (remember, his tenant buyers had the *option* to purchase, not the obligation). During that time, these tenant buyers paid him rent every month, took care of maintaining the property, and both gave him sizable nonrefundable option payments. Five years later the property had increased in value to $300,000. He ended up selling the property to his third tenant buyer for $280,000. In the end he made $110,000 from this one deal!

(continued)

The Three Most Important Terms Deal Acquisition Strategies
(continued)

Terms Deal Acquisition Strategy #3: Owner-Carry Financing

Seller accepts a promissory note for some or all of the money owed to her.

When you are doing your investing you will at times run across sellers who have a very large chunk of equity in their properties, or perhaps even own the property free and clear. In situations like this it is often possible to structure the deal with the seller agreeing to finance your purchase of the property by "carrying back" some or all of the purchase price as a mortgage that you will pay back over time.

Case Study: Peter and I called about a FSBO ad in the newspaper. The seller owned a large five-bedroom house in an upscale section of San Diego. He not only owned this property free and clear, but he had already purchased another home near Palm Springs that he wanted to retire to.

After negotiating over three days we agreed on a purchase price of $595,000 with a down payment of 10 percent and the owner to carry back the balance as a first mortgage at an interest rate that was about 2 percent lower than the best rates conventional lenders would offer at that time. Why did the seller agree to give us such attractive financing? Because he wanted a fast and easy sale. We gave him a price that was fair and we told him not to worry about repainting the interior of the house. We held on to the house for four years, put a little money into sprucing it up cosmetically, and resold the property for $925,000.

Case Study: A Mentorship student in Virginia found an elderly couple who were selling their home. Since the couple owned the property free and clear, our student, an attorney in the area, talked with them to see if they would participate in the financing.

After going back and forth, they agreed on a purchase price of $380,000, with our student to bring in a new conventional first mortgage of $180,000 and the sellers to carry back a second mortgage for the other $200,000. The sellers got the $180,000 from the new conventional loan up front at the closing, and our student was able to 100 percent finance the deal (roughly half from a conventional first mortgage and half from the owner-carry second mortgage). Why wasn't this a "cash" deal since the owner got so much money up front? Because the seller carried back a second mortgage for $200,000 with an interest rate of just 2 percent! This allowed the property to have incredibly low mortgage payments. In the end our student decided to move into the property and live there for a few years before he resold it for a healthy profit.

The Deal Structuring Wizard™— Two Simple Steps to Determine the Right Way to Structure the Deal

"All of you understand the basic deal structuring techniques, but the real skill isn't just having enough tools in your investor toolbox. The real skill is being able to quickly determine which tools are appropriate for which seller situations. Let's face it, if you try to force a terms deal on a seller who really is ready for an all-cash offer, then you're in for a lot of frustration. Or if you try to push a seller to discount the price for a quick cash sale, but they don't have the equity to discount the price as much as you need, you can be the world's best negotiator but you're still not going to close the deal.

"What I would like to do right now is to cover a simple two-step process you can go through to quickly determine which of the deal structuring strategies is most appropriate for a given seller's situation. When we're done, you'll be able to meet with a seller and quickly diagnose, just like a doctor does, what solution best cures their real estate ailment.

"Let's start with Part One of the Deal Structuring Wizard™." David drew a diagram on the board.

Deal Structuring Wizard™ (Part One)

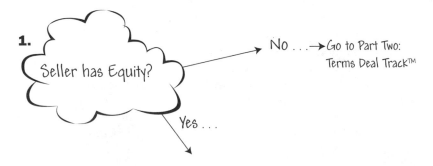

(continued)

Deal Structuring Wizard™ (Part One) *(continued)*

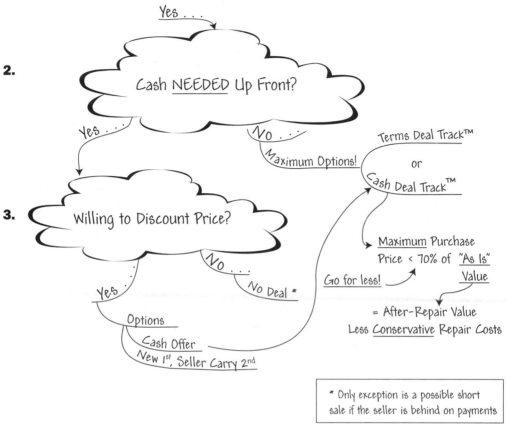

2. Cash <u>NEEDED</u> Up Front?

Yes . . .

Yes . . .

No . . .

Maximum Options!

Terms Deal Track™

or

Cash Deal Track™

3. Willing to Discount Price?

No . . .

No Deal *

Yes . . .

Options

Cash Offer

New 1st, Seller Carry 2nd

Go for less!

Maximum Purchase Price < 70% of "As Is" Value

= After-Repair Value Less <u>Conservative</u> Repair Costs

* Only exception is a possible short sale if the seller is behind on payments

"The first question you need to ask is, does the seller have a lot of equity? If the answer is no, then chances are you'll need to choose the Terms Deal Track™. If the answer is yes, then you have maximum flexibility because either a terms deal or a cash deal could work.

"Next you'll ask yourself, does the seller absolutely need their equity in cash up front? Now understand that almost every seller *wants* their cash up front, but not every seller *needs* it up front. The single biggest reason why a seller would need all of their equity out of a house up front is so that the seller can use it for a down payment on their next property.

"Indirectly explore whether the seller needs his equity, or if he just wants it up front. If he just wants it, and if he is truly a motivated seller, then many times a terms deal could work for him. If he needs all his equity up front then your only choice is the Cash Deal Track™. If he isn't motivated enough for this route, then you'll have to walk from the deal.

"The final question to ask in Part One of the Deal Structuring Wizard™ is, if the seller has a lot of equity, is she willing to give you a big discount in exchange for an all-cash offer? If the answer is no, then your only option is the Terms Deal Track™. If the seller isn't willing to go that route, then you are going to have to walk from the deal. If the seller *is* willing to take a big discount on the price, then your best route is to choose the Cash Deal Track™ and go for a discounted cash price for the property.

"And that take us to the end of Part One. At this point you know whether the seller has a lot of equity or not. If he does have a lot of equity, you know whether he needs it all up front or just wants it all up front. And finally, you know if he is willing to give you a big discount in the price in exchange for an all-cash closing. In essence, these three questions will help you determine which track to take. You'll either take the Cash Deal Track™ or the Terms Deal Track™." David paused as students let these ideas sink in.

"Let's move on to Part Two of the Deal Structuring Wizard™. This is the Terms Deal Track™ and it's your chance to determine if a terms deal will work. Here's what it looks like." David turned and drew on the board.

"The first question to ask is, what is the property's current monthly fixed expense of mortgage payment, property taxes, and insurance in relationship to the market rent for that property? This matters because if you are going to structure a

Deal Structuring Wizard™ (Part Two)

Terms Deal Track™

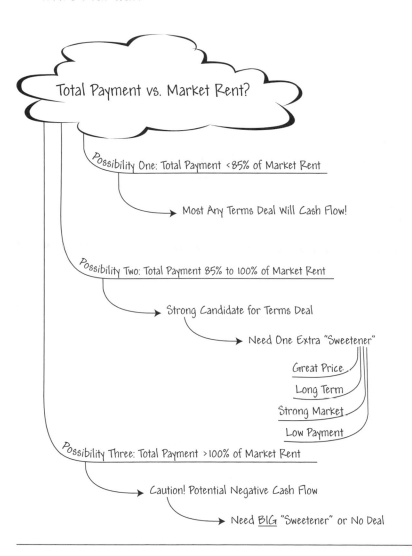

Total Payment vs. Market Rent?

Possibility One: Total Payment <85% of Market Rent

Most Any Terms Deal Will Cash Flow!

Possibility Two: Total Payment 85% to 100% of Market Rent

Strong Candidate for Terms Deal

Need One Extra "Sweetener"

Great Price

Long Term

Strong Market

Low Payment

Possibility Three: Total Payment >100% of Market Rent

Caution! Potential Negative Cash Flow

Need BIG "Sweetener" or No Deal

terms deal, then the property will need to be able to generate enough income from rent to cover the monthly expense.

"There are **three possibilities. First,** the payment could be very low in relationship to the market rent, which I define as **less than 85 percent of the market rent.** If this is the case then a terms deal would cash flow great. Now it's just up to you to negotiate it! Don't worry, I'll cover how to get the seller to agree to your creative terms deals later.

"Possibility two is that the monthly payment is 85 to 100 percent of the market rent. If this is the case then you can still structure the deal, but you need at least one other small sweetener to make the deal worthwhile. This could be that you're getting a great price in combination with the terms deal. Or it could be that you're getting a real long term on the financing of more than five years. Or it could be that the property is in a strongly appreciating area, in which case it is almost certainly worth doing the deal.

"The **final possibility** is for the monthly payment to be **greater than the market rent.** This means if you took the deal you'll probably have a negative cash flow. This is a big warning flag. The only way you'll take on a deal that has negative cash flow is if you have some other big sweetener in the deal. This could be a great price that guarantees you a conservative profit after you factor in the extra holding costs of the negative cash flow. This could be a red-hot market and a long term that will conservatively make you a lot of money on the back end. Or, in one deal I did with Peter, we got a free lot of land with the sale of a house that had a small negative cash flow. We immediately sold the lot and made a nice profit, some of which went to cover the negative cash flow for a few years until the property was sold.

"I think you get the idea. If you are going to buy on terms, then chances are you are going to hold on to that property over time. And this means the property needs to be able to pay its own way. If not, you need some other sweetener in the deal to offset the cost of carrying the property."

Advanced Secrets to Structuring Deals

"Once you master the basics—buying for cash and buying on terms—then you'll start to get more comfortable combining buying strategies to tailor a solution to the seller's situation, earning a healthy profit for yourself.

"For example, I remember a Mentorship student who found a motivated seller with a $300,000 house that he locked up to buy at $180,000 cash. The challenge was that this student didn't have the money to close. So what he did was get the seller to agree to let him buy the house subject to the existing $100,000 mortgage, as long as he finished the rehab and cashed the seller out within six months. The seller actually did ask for a down payment to make sure the deal was for real, so our student agreed to put $20,000 down. But rather than give that money to the seller, the investor got the seller to agree to allow him to put the money into the rehab of the house. It took two months and $23,000 to fix it up, at which point he put it on the market and sold it nine weeks later for $285,000. The seller got his money at that point and the investor ended up netting $55,000. The way the student was able to save the deal was simply by combining the all-cash acquisition strategy with a short-term subject-to acquisition strategy.

"Another way you can combine strategies is to negotiate a cash price but make the seller your partner by using an *equity split*, whereby you agree on the price that you'll pay the seller, and you also agree that the seller will get a percentage of the profit you make when you resell the house for more.

"Or you could even combine a subject to the existing financing purchase with an owner-carry second. I did that on a pre-foreclosure property I bought several years back. The owner was four mortgage payments behind and headed toward foreclosure. The house was in great need of new carpet and paint, but other than that it was structurally sound. I bought the place subject to an existing $65,000 first mortgage, and I gave the seller $15,000 in the form of a second mortgage on the property with an annual interest-only payment and the balance due in full in five years or less. The deal saved her from being foreclosed on and made her $15,000 plus interest. I got a house that five years later was worth over $200,000 more than I paid for it.

"The point I'm trying to make here is that when you master these basics and add a little creativity, the sky is the limit. You will need the nerve to ask the seller to go along with your creative ideas, and the skill to negotiate the deal. Plus you'll need the fluency to write up the deal initially, and the business systems to follow through and execute your exit strategy for the deal. But when you do, a whole new world of opportunity will open up for you.

"The average investor only knows one way to buy an investment property—

for a discounted cash price. To grow a thriving investing business you need to master more creative ways to buy so that you have more tools with which to structure win-win deals with motivated sellers."

21 Advanced Deal Structuring Strategies to Unstick Even the Toughest of Deals

Advanced Strategy 1: Delay Your Down Payment

Is the seller flexible as to when you give them your down payment? Sometimes it's to your advantage to give a small earnest money deposit, with any down payment coming later. Can you push the closing out 90 to 120 days? Often this gives you the chance to put together your financing or to use Advanced Strategies 2 or 3 (which you'll read about in a moment). If you just need more time, see if the seller will let you make a fair payment of principal to extend the closing date by 30 to 60 days.

I've also seen deals structured where the down payment was used by the investor buying the property to fix up the property. This let the seller know the investor had something at stake, plus all that money went into improving the property, which made the seller's protection greater. For the investor, this allowed them to significantly reduce the cash they needed to close on the deal. Once they had the house fixed up they either sold the house or, six months after they bought the house, they refinanced the property and cashed the seller out at that time.

Advanced Strategy 2: Wholesale the Deal

Some new investors are scared to lock up a contract to buy a house for cash because they mistakenly think they don't have the money. Remember, you don't need to have the money. If the deal is right you will *find* the money. One source of money is for you to sell your right to buy the property to another investor. This is called wholesaling or "flipping" the deal. Start to build your investor's list of rehab investors and other cash investors in your area who might want to buy one of your lucrative cash deals from you at a wholesale price.

(continued)

21 Advanced Deal Structuring Strategies to Unstick Even the Toughest of Deals *(continued)*

Example: A Mentorship student in Phoenix found the owner of a beat-up, ugly house and put the property under contract for a discounted cash price of $14,500. Then a short while later the student found another investor who gutted and rehabbed homes in that area, who paid the student $10,000 to buy the contract to purchase the house. The Mentorship student made $10,000 cash for assigning his contract to this new investor. The new investor used his money to rehab the house and later resold it for an even larger profit. The buyer, who in this case was the rehab investor, "funded" this deal by paying the student cash for the right to buy this house at a deep discount, and also "funded" the deal by using his own money to pay the original seller the $14,500 owed to him.*

Advanced Strategy 3: Presell the Property to a Retail Buyer
A retail buyer is someone who wants to buy the property so that he can move in and live there. A retail buyer can fund your deal using his cash in the form of a down payment or option payment, his credit in the form of a new bank loan, or a combination of the two.

Example: A past Mentorship student in Washington, D.C., found a motivated seller through the Internet. He negotiated over the phone and put the property under contract to purchase at a discounted cash price. He aggressively advertised and marketed the property and found a buyer who fell in love with the home. The student was able to sell the property for a $45,000 profit to this new buyer. He structured the sale to be what's called a *simultaneous closing*, which meant he did a double closing where he took his new buyer's money from the loan his new buyer secured, and gave most of it to the original seller to pay the original discounted cash price, and in the process the $45,000 spread in prices became the investor's profit. The buyer "funded" this deal by getting a conventional loan to pay for the property, with our student using a large chunk of this cash to pay to the original seller.

Advanced Strategy 4: Joint Venture with the Seller
Imagine you came across a seller who is motivated to do a deal with you, but not quite motivated enough to give up her existing equity or to give up all the future appreciation of the property. The seller wants to do the deal, but you need one last sweetener to spur the seller to do it. This is a perfect scenario to try using an *equity split*.

*To download a FREE copy of the ebook *3 Simple Steps to Flip a Deal for Quick Cash Profits*, go to **www.InvestorFasttrack.com**.

(continued)

21 Advanced Deal Structuring Strategies to Unstick Even the Toughest of Deals (continued)

An equity split is any deal where you, the investor, split part of your future profit with the seller of a property. Typically this is used to give the seller an extra bonus on top of the agreed-on purchase price for the property. For example, you and the seller agree on a cash price of $350,000 and you also agree that after you're done fixing up the property and reselling it, you'll split part of your profits from the resale of the property with the seller. How much should you give the seller when you resell? That is totally up to you to negotiate. You can give the seller a percentage of your future profit, say 10 to 15 percent. Or you can give them an extra bonus of $5,000 to $25,000 when you resell it for more than a specified amount.

Example: You find a seller who owns a rental house and is open to selling it to you on a two-year lease option. But he's just not motivated enough to give you any longer on the term. You ask him, "Mr. Seller, if there was a way where we could get you your asking price of $180,000 and even a small percentage of the appreciation too, in exchange for a bit longer period of time, is this something you'd even be open to, or probably not?"

The seller scratches his head and thinks for a moment. You negotiate back and forth for a while and this is what you agree on: a six-year lease option for a purchase price of $180,000 with a monthly rent to the seller of $1,200. Plus you also agree on one more thing. You agree to give the seller 30 percent of any amount over $180,000 that you get when you resell the property to your tenant buyer. This is an equity split.

The seller gets all of the first $180,000 (which is your option price) and 30 percent of the difference between $180,000 and the amount you resell it for to your tenant buyer. Imagine your tenant buyer buys it from you for $230,000. The seller gets $180,000 plus 30 percent of the $50,000 profit you made, for a total payment to the seller of $195,000. You make $35,000 from the resale plus any cash flow from the spread between your tenant buyer's rent and your rent to the seller, and you also make any forfeited option payments from earlier tenant buyers who didn't end up buying.

Remember, there is no set rule that says you have to do a 50-50 equity split. You can negotiate the deal any way you want. If you want to negotiate a 60-40 split or a 75-25 split, or even a 95-5 split, you can—whatever you and the seller agree to.

(continued)

21 Advanced Deal Structuring Strategies to Unstick Even the Toughest of Deals *(continued)*

Advanced Strategy 5: Use the "Hybrid Equity Split" to Make an Extra $25,000 or More on Every Equity Split Deal You Do

Peter and I developed a smarter way to do an equity split several years ago where you the investor will make an extra $25,000 or more on every equity split you do, with zero extra work or effort! It's call a *hybrid equity split*. I think you'll like this simple yet highly profitable technique and want to add it to your toolbox of investing ideas.

In essence, a hybrid equity split is taking a normal equity split and adding in a minimum "base profit" that you the investor need to earn before the equity split kicks in.

Example: Several years ago I met with the owners of a two-bedroom, two-bath condo. The sellers were motivated because the husband had been transferred. When I met with them we talked through doing a five-year lease option on the property. Right at the very end they started to balk, so I introduced the idea of adding an equity split. In fact, by adding in this extra incentive to the seller, it was almost like they were my partners. The more money I made, the more money they made. They even agreed to extend my term with them to eight years!

Watch this part very carefully. I told them that as a conservative investor, obviously I would need to build in a base profit for myself of $25,000. But if I sold it for any amount above that, they would get all the purchase price we had agreed to, plus they would get 10 percent of the amount I sold it for above the base profit. We went back and forth a little and I let them negotiate me all the way up to 12 percent. Here is what the final details of the lease option turned out to be: a term of eight years and a purchase price of $102,000. The up-front option consideration I paid was $1. I also agreed to an equity split on anything I resold the property for above $127,000. In other words, the first $25,000 in profit would be mine alone and I would only do the equity split on any amount above that.

(continued)

21 Advanced Deal Structuring Strategies to Unstick Even the Toughest of Deals *(continued)*

Advanced Strategy 6: Use Hard Money

A hard money lender is an experienced investor who is willing to lend you money to purchase a property, based not on your creditworthiness or character, but based on the security of the loan. The security in this case is the property itself and not the borrower's creditworthiness or other assets. Since most conventional lenders will only lend you money based on the appraised value or purchase price, whichever is *less*, it's often impossible to 100 percent finance a cash purchase through a conventional lender, even if you have the price at 50 cents on the dollar. A hard money lender, however, will lend you money based solely on the appraised value of the property. This means that you can easily finance a cash sale through a hard money lender as long as your price is right. In fact, you can often borrow all the money you need to fix up the property too.

What's the catch? The hard money lender is going to make you pay a whole lot more for the money. Hard money lenders typically require five to eight percentage points higher in the loan interest rate than conventional lenders charge. Plus, hard money lenders will usually charge you three to eight "points" on the loan. A point is prepaid interest, with each point equal to prepaid interest of 1 percent of the value of the loan. While this sounds like and is a lot to pay for your money, if the deal is a good one, and you only need the money short term, a hard money loan may very well be the way to go.

Two easy places to find a hard money lender are, first, the "Money to Lend" section of your local newspaper. Second, go to your local real estate investors association.* Usually there are several hard money lenders who are members solely for the purpose of finding new investors to lend money to.

Example: One Mentorship student put a four-bedroom house under contract for a discounted cash price of $130,000. The property was conservatively valued at $220,000. The student borrowed $150,000 from a local hard money lender. The money was used as follows:

Purchase Price	$130,000
5 "Points" the hard money lender charged	$ 6,500
Closing Costs	$ 2,000
Fix-Up Costs:	$ 11,500
Total Loan	$150,000

*For a complete state-by-state listing of 200 local real estate investor associations go to **www.InvestorFasttrack.com**.

(continued)

21 Advanced Deal Structuring Strategies to Unstick Even the Toughest of Deals *(continued)*

It took the student four months to fix up and resell the property. During that time she had to pay the hard money lender 12 percent interest payments on the loan. But because she only needed the money for a short time, when she resold the property for $220,000 she ended up netting $40,000.

Advanced Strategy 7: Use Private Money

Once you have a track record of proven results, you should start to establish sources of private money. Private money comes from people who are willing to lend you money secured by a mortgage on a property, but at a substantially lower cost than a sophisticated hard money lender would charge you.

Example: Two investor friends of mine recently bought a mobile home park. They borrowed roughly $300,000 from a person they knew who wanted to get a good rate of return on his money without much risk or effort. My friends got the money for 10 percent simple interest with no loan fees or credit checks, and the lender was able to have his loan secured with a first mortgage with over $500,000 of equity protecting the loan. A win-win.

Advanced Strategy 8: Use Graduated Payments to Protect Your Cash Flow in the Early Years

See if the seller will accept lower interest payments in the early years with built-in increases in the interest payments in the later years of the note. For example, "Mr. Seller, what if we were able to pay you $300 per month for the first 24 months, and then for the next 24 months we'd pay you $400 per month, and then for the final 24 months you'd get $600 per month?" There are no rules governing this, so be creative. The key is to protect your cash flow in the early years. Who knows, you just may sell or refinance the property before the interest or payment bumps up too high!

Advanced Strategy 9: Use Graduated Prices to Get a Longer Term

Imagine you are working to negotiate a terms deal with a motivated seller. The seller is only willing to give you a three-year term before you have to fully repay the $365,000 owner-carry note. Try this with the seller: "Mr. Seller, I know that this may seem crazy for me to even suggest it, and you'll probably hate the idea anyway, but what if we did it exactly like you

(continued)

21 Advanced Deal Structuring Strategies to Unstick Even the Toughest of Deals *(continued)*

wanted with a three-year term, and then if for some reason we needed more time, we'd have up to another 24 to 36 months, but the price we'd be paying you would jump all the way up to $375,000. Is that something we should even talk about, or probably not?" Is it worth it to pay an extra $10,000 for two or three years added onto the term of the note? Who knows? But remember, you don't have to use the extension, but you'll be awfully glad you have it *prenegotiated* if you end up needing it.

Advanced Strategy 10: Use a Reverse Credit to Incentivize the Seller to Carry the Negative Cash Flow
A reverse credit is when you *increase* your purchase price each month. It's similar to a reverse amortizing loan. It is useful when you want to keep your payment to a seller low enough to have a property cash flow, and you need the seller to be willing to cover the negative cash flow.

Example: You are negotiating a five-year lease option on a three-bedroom house. You agree on a price of $350,000, which is $30,000 below market value. The sticking point is that the seller wants you to cover his full monthly mortgage payment (which includes the property taxes and insurance) of $2,200 per month. You, on the other hand, know that the most the house will rent for is $2,000 per month, so the most you want to pay is $1,900 per month to the seller. But this leaves a negative cash flow of $300 per month for the seller. Being the well-trained investor you are, you pull the "reverse credit" advanced strategy out of your tool box and say to the seller, "Look, what if I could get my partner to go along with adding that $300 that you are covering onto the purchase price each month. What this would mean is that each month you cover that money, it will get added into the purchase price." In essence, your purchase price will increase by $3,600 per year with the seller taking on the risk and burden of the negative cash flow. And just in case you need one more kicker to make this work, you can always offer to pay the seller an interest rate of 5 to 12 percent on that money, to be added into the purchase price, so at least he feels like he's getting paid something extra for tying up the money covering the negative cash flow. (Remember, though, this interest rate is *only* on the $300 per month as it's paid and *not* on the full amount you owe him.)

(continued)

21 Advanced Deal Structuring Strategies to Unstick Even the Toughest of Deals *(continued)*

Advanced Strategy 11: Turn the Seller into Your Bank

My favorite source of funding a deal is the seller I am buying from. Whether the seller actually carries back a mortgage as part of your purchase, or whether you buy the property subject to the seller's loan (both strategies were discussed earlier in this chapter), the seller is making your purchase of the property possible.

The following is an example of how you can put together a deal with owner financing. In the next several advanced strategies I'll build on this strategy to give you even more insider options.

Example: A Mentorship student called on a "For Sale" ad in her local paper. She talked to a nice man on the phone and set up an appointment to see this midpriced home in a quiet suburb. When she met him at the property she found out that he wasn't actually the seller, he was the attorney for a seller who lived out of state. They sat down and talked the purchase over and agreed on our student buying the house with $2,500 down with the owner carrying back a 30-year first mortgage at 8 percent interest. (Originally the attorney told the investor she would have to put $10,000 down, but she used the negotiating techniques you'll be learning later in this book to talk him down to just a $2,500 down payment.) The best part about loans like these is that the investor didn't have to pay points or loan origination fees or appraisal fees or any of a number of loan costs you'll have if you finance a property with traditional sources. The investor later sold the house on a two-year rent to own for roughly $15,000 more than she bought it for. (And the funny thing was that she liked working with this attorney so much that she later hired him to be her family's attorney!)

Advanced Technique 12: Combine Subject-To and Owner-Carry Financing

Better by far is to combine the subject-to financing strategy you learned about earlier with owner financing. What I mean is that you buy the property subject to the existing financing and the owner carries back a note for her equity. This is much lower risk to you the investor, plus it will save you money not having to pay to assume the existing loan.

Example: Two Mentorship graduates got a call from a motivated seller in response to the "I Buy Houses" ad they were running in the paper.

(continued)

21 Advanced Deal Structuring Strategies to Unstick Even the Toughest of Deals *(continued)*

The seller had bought a new house but hadn't been able to sell his first house and was feeling the pressure of the double payments. While they didn't sign the deal on the spot, the investors followed up every few weeks and eventually, six months later, the seller sold them the house. By this point the seller had refinanced out much of his equity with a new first mortgage of $280,000. The investors gave the seller $100 down and bought the house for a price of $350,000. They agreed to take over the payments on the existing $280,000 mortgage of $2,300 with the seller to carry back a $70,000 second mortgage with no interest and no payments, due in full as a lump-sum payment within 60 months of closing.

Next the investors sold the house on a two-year rent to own for $400,000. They collected a $24,000 option payment and got $3,300 a month in rent! All totaled, this deal netted the investors $65,000!

Advanced Strategy 13: Write Up a Zero Interest, Zero Payments Loan
Can you really do this, you ask? Yes! The simplest way to do this is to negotiate to pay off the mortgage the seller carries back as a "lump-sum payment due in full" down the road. This is the prettier way of saying zero interest, zero payment loan.

Here's the fancy way to say this in your purchase contract:

"The Seller shall carry back a second purchase money mortgage in the amount of $150,000 to be paid as a lump-sum payment due in full within 60 months of closing of escrow."

Advanced Strategy 14: If You Have to Make Payments, Pay Pure Principal
Obviously as an investor you would prefer a loan without payments and without interest. That's why, whenever possible, you'll use the language of paying your seller a "lump-sum" payment due down the road. But if you have to pay them as you go, pay them *principal*, not interest. Principal is money that goes towards the purchase price or loan amount.

Here's the fancy way to say this in your purchase contract:

"Seller to carry back a second mortgage in the amount of $100,000 to be paid by Buyer in 100 monthly payments of $1,000 including principal and interest with the first payment of $1,000 due within 30 days of closing."

(continued)

21 Advanced Deal Structuring Strategies to Unstick Even the Toughest of Deals *(continued)*

Advanced Strategy 15: Agree to Pay "Thank You Payments"
Many times the only way to make a highly leveraged purchase of a nice house cash flow from the start is to get the seller to accept below-market interest rates on the money they are carrying. One languaging tip that makes this more palatable to a seller is to call these monthly or quarterly payments "thank you payments" versus interest payments. Just by labeling the payment this way, you deemphasize the seller's need to get an interest rate and lower the seller's expectation as to the amount. Tell the seller, "Mr. Seller, I'm even willing to give you a thank you payment of $300 every month as my way of saying I appreciate you being a bit patient waiting to get cashed out and getting that $100,000 check."

Advanced Strategy 16: Let the Interest Accrue
As an investor you need to protect your cash flow. If you are negotiating with a seller who insists on interest, see if you can get them to let the interest accrue to be paid off down the road, ideally when you resell the property. This works especially well for properties you are buying far enough below value that you are going to have the margin to pay for this accumulating interest cost when you resell it to your buyer. Use caution here to make sure there is enough profit to make this possible.

If you use this strategy, your first choice is to pay simple interest versus compound interest. To do this, simply label the interest rate with the words "simple interest."

Here's the fancy way to say this in your purchase contract:

"The Seller shall carry back a second mortgage in the amount of $100,000 with simple interest of 7 percent which shall accrue. The entire balance of principal and interest is due in full as a lump-sum payment within 72 months of closing."

Advanced Strategy 17: Ask for Interest-Only Payments
If you have to pay money each month, and it can't be principal, then make the owner-carry note "interest only." In effect, this means you won't be paying any principal each month when you send the seller her check. This lowers your monthly payment and protects your cash flow. Remember, you can always voluntarily prepay principal anytime you want. Don't obligate yourself to pay principal if you can avoid it. This gives you more flexibility.

(continued)

21 Advanced Deal Structuring Strategies to Unstick Even the Toughest of Deals *(continued)*

Advanced Strategy 18: Consider Adding Up Your Monthly Payments into Quarterly, Semiannual, or Annual Payments

If the amount of your monthly payment to the seller doesn't seem like much, consider adding it up and offering a "larger" payment to your seller every quarter, semiannually, or annually.

Example: If $300 per month doesn't sound like much, why not add up the payments and pay your seller annually. Say, "Mr. Seller, I'm even willing to pay you $3,000 to $3,500 every year as a thank you payment for your willingness to work with me to make this a win for both of us."

Advanced Strategy 19: Prenegotiate an Extension or Renewal of the Loan

The best time to arrange an extension or renewal of the seller carryback is *before* you buy the property. The seller will never be as motivated, and you'll never be as unmotivated, as at that moment. You can always agree to pay the seller a "renewal" payment to renew the loan term. (Just make sure that if you do make a renewal or extension payment, you label it as *principal* and not interest!)

Here's the fancy way to say this in your purchase contract:

"Buyer may extend the Seller second mortgage by paying to Seller $5,000 of principal to extend the Seller second mortgage by 24 months."

Advanced Strategy 20: Offer to Cross Collateralize

Cross collateralize is a fancy name for you giving the seller a lien on another asset you own, like another house, as extra security so that the seller is more willing to carry back financing. Be careful not to offer this except as a last resort, and even still, use it only when you are confident that you have negotiated a really strong deal. If I agree to cross collateralize by giving the seller a second mortgage on another property as security for the seller carry, I also make sure to prenegotiate that the seller will release that mortgage after I have a 12- to 24-month track record of making the seller on-time mortgage payments. This gives the seller time to get to know how upstanding I really am, but it also makes sure I don't tie up my other property recklessly.

(continued)

21 Advanced Deal Structuring Strategies to Unstick Even the Toughest of Deals *(continued)*

Advanced Strategy 21: Ask for Seller Subordination—Pay a Seller with Borrowed Money

Have you ever run across a seller who owns a property free and clear, and who has a strong motivation to sell, but who doesn't want to do a lease option or carry back all the financing? In other words, they are willing to carry back some of the financing as long as they get a good-sized chunk of their equity now.

In these situations, the Big Money Cash Close is a powerful buying strategy to use. This technique means getting a new first mortgage secured against the property to get the seller some cash at closing, and then the seller simply carries back a second mortgage for the balance of his equity for a period of time.

Example: Imagine a $100,000 house. Using this technique you would bring in a new first mortgage of between $30,000 and $50,000 and have the seller carry back the balance as a second mortgage. Because the bank you are seeking the first mortgage from will have so much value protecting its money (after all, what banker doesn't like to lend at 30 to 50 percent loan-to-value), this is a fairly easy mortgage to secure. This strategy is a way for you to get the seller a large chunk of money at closing, but having that money be borrowed rather than your own.

Using this strategy, it is important to note that the seller will need to be willing to carry a *second* mortgage for the balance of their equity. This is because you will be getting a new first mortgage to give the seller money at closing. To do this you need the seller to agree to subordinate his mortgage to second position *behind* the new financing you are bringing in from a conventional lender.

Here is exactly how to word your offer: "Mr. Seller, what if I were to bring in new financing and get you $30,000 or so cash at closing, and then you were to carry back a small second for the balance. Obviously you wouldn't want to have to wait forever for the balance of your money, so we'd put a short-term balloon note of five to seven years on it."

Notice you use the term "bring in new financing," not "put $30,000 down." Technically, if you say you are going to put money down that means you are going to be using *your* money. That's not what you want to do. You'll be using the bank's money instead.

(continued)

21 Advanced Deal Structuring Strategies to Unstick Even the Toughest of Deals *(continued)*

Let's be clear on one critical item: Of course the seller will need to be very clear that their loan will be in second position. You are not trying to pull anything over their eyes. The language you use is very important so that you frame the offer in the seller's mind the right way from the very beginning. You need to make sure the idea creates a good first impression on the seller. Later you can go back over it to make sure the seller is totally aware of all the advantages and disadvantages of this type of deal.

Using this technique you are going to be 100 percent financing the property. The critical question on any 100 percent financed property is, does it cash flow? If you pay market interest rates for the second mortgage that the seller is carrying back, it probably won't. But when sellers carry back seconds they don't need high interest rates—at least, they don't if they are motivated, and if they're not motivated what are you doing wasting your time talking with them?

CHAPTER FIVE

Core Investor Skill Three: Negotiating Magic—Getting the Other Side to Say *Yes*

David looked out across the room. "We so often think about negotiation only in terms of buying a property and selling a property, as if the only real negotiating going on in real estate happens when we buy or sell. But the reality is that there are dozens of other situations that you'll face as an investor where your negotiation skills will mean the difference between hundreds, thousands, or even hundreds of thousands of dollars in profits—or losses."

David paused for a moment. "Remember this: Any one real estate deal can be broken down into hundreds of smaller, 'micro' negotiations. Each of these micro negotiations has a huge cumulative impact on the overall profitability of your investing business. That makes mastering the skill of negotiation a *huge* profit leverage point. The time and effort you invest to master this skill gets rewarded hundreds of times in any deal, resulting in magnified profits. When you learn this skill, it's easy to increase your profits in a deal by $5,000 to $50,000 to $500,000 or more! For example, I remember a Mentorship student of ours who used a simple negotiating technique he had learned at the Advanced Negotiating Workshop during a negotiation for a small apartment complex he was buying. That one technique got the seller to reduce the price by $85,000! And it took less than five minutes to use the technique. I don't know what that skill paid him on an hourly basis, but I'm pretty sure it was a wealthy person's wage!

"We are going to take the rest of the afternoon to focus on the core skill of negotiation. First I'll go through the foundational negotiating techniques. Then we'll move on and cover the 14 Advanced Negotiating Secrets. Finally, you'll get the chance to ask your most challenging negotiating questions so that you'll be able to tie all this information together. In the end, it's not about knowing techniques just to impress your friends at parties. It's about knowing how to *apply* all these lessons so you will be more successful in your investing.

"So let's start with the foundational negotiating skills. For most of you this will be a review, but for some of you it will be new."

SUMMARY

The Instant Offer System: A Simple Five-Step System for Closing Deals*

Step One: Build Rapport

One of the most important requirements in any negotiation is to build an emotional connection with the other side. People like to do business with people they like. And what's more, when you're working with a motivated seller, you need to help them feel comfortable opening up and sharing their *emotional* reasons for selling and their *emotional* needs for any solution you offer. This means you need to build and maintain a high level of trust and rapport with the seller. The time to do this is both at the start of your meeting with a seller, and also throughout the entire duration of your negotiation. Look for common bonds and build bridges of connection with the seller wherever you can.

Step Two: Set an Up-Front Agreement

An up-front agreement is simply an agreement between you and the seller where you each agree to make a decision at the end of your time together. In essence, you both agree that, in fairness to both of you, you will each clearly let the other know where you stand so that you both know what, if any, next step is most appropriate. Using the up-front agreement language pattern will save you from hearing the seller tell you, "I'll think about it and get back with you."

*For more detailed training on the Instant Offer System, make sure to read *Buying Real Estate without Cash or Credit* (pp. 93–116). Also, for more free training on negotiating profitable deals, go to **www.InvestorFasttrack.com**!

(continued)

The Instant Offer System: A Simple Five-Step System for Closing Deals (continued)

Step Three: Build the Seller's Motivation

As an investor, you create value in the deal by helping to solve a seller's problem. If you can't get the seller to tell you about the real problems they are facing, then this is almost impossible. That's why uncovering a seller's true motivation and helping the seller to *feel* that motivation is the key step to getting a great deal. Most motivated sellers live in denial. It's your responsibility to help them break through that denial and face the tough choices they are going to have to make.

Step Four: Talk about the Money

After you have worked with the seller to build their motivation, it's time for you to talk through the money. *What were they asking for the property? What did they realistically think they would get? What are the details of the underlying financing on the property?* As an investor it's critical that you master the money step because it's here that you prenegotiate the money in a deal so that later, when you "officially" talk about money, you've already got some or all of the discounts you need to make the deal work for you.

Step Five: Make Your "What If" Offer

I recommend that you never make a formal offer to a seller. When you make a formal offer you are giving all the power over to the seller. They can either accept or reject or, what's worse, ignore your offer. Instead, make them a "what if" offer and get them to accept it before you ever formally make that offer. Say something like, *"Here's a crazy idea, Mr. Seller, but what if I were to get you a chunk of cash up front, and then pay you the balance down the road. Is that something we should even talk about, or probably not?"* Only if the seller says yes to your generalized "what if" offer should you move by degrees to pin that general offer down in concrete terms and numbers. By doing it this way *you* stay in control.

The Three Foundational Negotiating Strategies Every Investor Must Know

Foundational Negotiating Strategy One: Negative Phrasing

"What do you think really drives people who are motivated sellers? Do you think it's the desire to make a profit? Or the fear of making a mistake and getting taken advantage of?" David paused a moment and let the group determine their answer.

"In my experience it is almost always the latter. Motivated sellers, most sellers really, are more motivated by the fear of making a mistake and getting taken advantage of than the desire to make a profit. How does this fundamental understanding help you when you are negotiating with a seller? Simple.

"When people are driven by a fear of making a mistake or being taken advantage of, they will protect themselves as best they can by looking for what's wrong in a given situation. In a negotiation, when the other side is looking for what's wrong with something, they will usually mismatch anything you say, which is a term from psychology that means they will say something contrary to you. For example, if you tell the seller the price is too high, she'll argue back that it's too low. If you tell her the house is run down, she'll argue that it really is in fine condition and only needs minor work.

"In any negotiation, whenever you are able to anticipate the pattern of how the other side will interact with you, you can use this knowledge to shape a strategy to harness that other side's predictable behavior to your advantage. The way you do this in a real estate negotiation is through something Peter and I developed years ago called *negative phrasing*. Negative phrasing is a way to intentionally use statements to allow the seller to mismatch themselves into agreement with what you want.

"Here is an example of negative phrasing." David asked Emily, one of the Mentorship Program coaches, to come up front to help him in the role playing.

"Imagine you are an investor negotiating with a seller like Emily here. You might say something like, 'Emily, you mentioned you had listed the property with a real estate agent for three months, and that worked out really well?'"

Emily answered, "No, it didn't work out well at all."

"Really? I'm sure your real estate agent must have had a ton of prospective buyers out looking at the house for each of the open houses they held every weekend. Why didn't you like any of the written offers you got?"

"We didn't get any offers! In fact, the agent only did two open houses all that time."

David continued, "Oh, but what about all the advertising your agent was paying for? That must have generated a lot of traffic to see the house, right?"

"What advertising? As far as I can tell he just put it into the MLS and sat on the listing."

"I think you all get the idea now. Negative phrasing makes it easy for the seller to verbally take the position in the negotiation that you want them to take. There are two keys to using negative phrasing. First, understand that often the point of negative phrasing isn't to elicit information so much as it is to get the seller *themselves* to voice an emotional reality that they may have been hiding from previously. In the role play Emily and I just did, had you simply said to Emily that the agent she hired did a lousy job, Emily would have gotten very defensive and argued with you. But using negative phrasing made it comfortable and natural for Emily to argue for exactly what you wanted her to see. In a sense, you let the seller comfortably back into the very position you wanted her to occupy to begin with.

"The second key with using negative phrasing is to make sure you avoid sounding sarcastic or patronizing. Instead, cultivate the ability to be genuinely confused or optimistic. The best way to way to do this is to master two facial expressions.

"The first expression is called 'scrunchy face,' which is produced by furrowing your brow, creating tension on the inside corners of your cheeks underneath your eyes, and cocking your head slightly to one side. This is the expression to use any-time you want to be 'confused' and draw out more information or clarification from the seller.

"Whenever you use scrunchy face, make sure you drop your voice tone and volume lower and give the seller time to respond. This will literally draw out the seller in the conversation to fill the intimate space you have created.

"The second expression is called 'big eyes,' and you make it by opening your eyes wide in your best Forrest Gump naiveté and softening your voice. You use big eyes when you ask a question of the seller using negative phrasing.

"You can even use negative phrasing to get a seller to be more open-minded about an offer you want to make them. For example, you might precede a 'what if' offer you are about to make with a statement like, *'You'll probably hate this idea, but what if . . .'* Or you could use the negative phrasing at the end of your what if like, *'What if we were to pay you $450,000 for the house? Is that something we should even spend any time talking about, or probably not?'* By adding that short negative phrasing tag to the end of your 'what if' offer, you are increasing the odds that the seller will actually be willing to talk about your offer rather than merely dismiss it out of hat."

David got each of the students to turn to a partner and practice using this powerful language pattern.

Foundational Negotiating Strategy Two: Being a Reluctant Buyer

Bringing the group back together, David continued, "In every negotiation, you want to be perceived as someone who is willing to walk away from the deal if it is not a fit, without any hard feelings. In fact, you always want the other side to perceive you as being in the deal more reluctantly than they are. I call this dynamic 'being a reluctant buyer.' The reluctant buyer dynamic works whether you are the seller, the buyer, the borrower, the lender, the landlord, or the tenant. It just means that you are perceived to be almost doing the deal against your better judgment or with a great deal of internal struggle.

"Now while it is common knowledge that you should be a reluctant buyer in any negotiation, it's a little known art *how* to actually behave like a reluctant buyer. What you are about to learn is that reluctant buyers use specific language patterns over and over, and that just by your adopting these language patterns you can instantly transform yourself, in the eyes of the other side, into the most reluctant of buyers, even if inside your heart is screaming at you to take the deal.

"The single biggest pattern that reluctant buyers use is how they consistently qualify everything they say with dampening statements like, *'I don't know if this will even be a fit for me or not, but what if . . .'* Or, *'I'm not sure if that much will really work for me or not yet, but let's assume it will for the moment . . .'* Or even, *'My partner will probably have a fit when she hears this, but what if I could get her to go along with . . .'*

"You can even combine the reluctant buyer technique with negative phrasing and say something like, *'I'm not sure if I could get you the full $575,000 we've been talking about, but if I could somehow manage to pull it off, or at least get real close to it, is that something we should even talk about, or you probably think it's a crazy idea, huh?'*

"The key is that as a negotiator you want to avoid making unqualified commitments of what you can do until the very end of the negotiation when you are reviewing the terms that you and the seller have agreed to." David paused for a moment, and then added, "Even then, it never hurts to shake your head a little and ask the seller, using scrunchy face, *'Tell me again why this is such a good deal for me?'*

"The biggest benefit you'll get out of mastering the art and science of being a reluctant buyer is that instead of convincing sellers to sell to you, you'll get sellers selling *you* on buying their properties!

"Enough talk, time for you all to try it out." With that, David matched them into groups and had them do the role-playing exercise.

Foundational Negotiating Strategy Three: Building Motivation

David gathered everyone's attention and then continued with the final foundational technique. "Without question the single biggest negotiating mistake I see beginning investors make is rushing in and talking about price and terms with the other side before clearly establishing why it is that the other side wants to put together the deal. To negotiate a great deal, whether you are buying or selling, it's critical that you get the other side to emotionally connect with their drive to get a deal done. I call this process 'building motivation.'

"Probably the easiest way to really understand building motivation is to show you. Scott," David said, turning to one of the Mentorship Program coaches, "would you be willing to help me out with this?"

"Sure David."

Looking back out at the class, David continued, "I'll do a few examples—one with a motivated seller whose house I want to buy, the second with a buyer I'm trying to sell a rent-to-own house to. I want you to pay attention to how I use both negative phrasing and the reluctant buyer techniques to get the other side hungrier to do a deal.

"All right Scott, let's get into it. In our first example you'll be a seller of a property and I'll be the investor working to buy your house."

Getting into the role-play, David asked, "So what else have you tried to sell your house, Scott?"

"I had the house listed for a while, and then I tried selling it for sale by owner."

"You mentioned you had the house listed for a while with an agent, and that worked really well?" As David used this negative phrasing technique he used big eyes to make sure his tonality and nonverbal expression reinforced the effect he wanted.

Scott shook his head, "No, it didn't work out too well. The agent just sat on the listing and didn't do much to advertise or market the property."

"Hmm, had you thought about just giving this agent a second chance?" David said with his most innocent of big eye expressions. "I'm sure that if you explained what you really expected of them they'd do a much better job the second time around?"

Scott's replied forcefully, "No way! I'm not going to list the property with that agent, or any other agent again."

David stepped out of the role-play and said to the group, "I think you all get the idea here. If this were you in a real negotiation with Scott, you would spend the next 20 or 30 minutes or longer building Scott's motivation to sell fast and be done with things. Let's try another situation. This time I'll role-play an investor looking to sell one of my houses to a tenant buyer on a rent-to-own basis. Scott will be the prospective buyer at the showing for the house. Imagine Scott has just gone through the house and is now coming back to talk with me about price and terms. Go ahead and start us off, Scott."

"Well, how much is it?" Scott asked.

"Actually, before we get into the numbers, it's really important to me that I choose a future buyer who loves this house, because that way I know they'll not only care for the house, but that they'll also be happy here. This probably seems crazy to you—negative phrasing—but it's really important to me. So may I ask you, did you love the house when you walked through it?"

Scott replied, "I thought it was very nice. So how much is it?"

"Did you just think it was nice or did you love it, because if you just thought it was nice I don't think this house is going to be for you," David said using the reluctant seller technique.

Scott answered, "I loved it."

"Great! What specifically about the house did you love, Scott?"

"I thought the kitchen layout was great. It had a great view out into the yard."

"What about the kitchen layout was so important to you?" At this point David stepped out of the role-play and turned to the group. "Did you all notice that even when my buyer wanted to jump ahead and talk about price, I resisted this and instead focused the conversation on Scott's reasons for wanting this specific house. By doing this I make it much harder for Scott to come back later and try to negotiate a lower price because he's already verbally committed not only that he loves the house, but what specifically he loves, and why that was so important to him. In fact, if there is one thing to remember in any negotiation that will do the most to help you negotiate the best deal, it is this." David turned to the board and wrote:

Always build motivation BEFORE ever getting into the money!

"Always, always, always spend time on the other side's emotional reasons for doing a deal with you before you talk about the money. This is true whether you are buying or selling. In fact, this is critical in any real estate negotiation. Any questions so far?"

"Yeah David," Nancy raised her hand. "I can see how this works when you are working with a seller or buyer, but how would it work with other situations? It just seems that if you were dealing with a contractor, for example, they just wouldn't get why you were asking them all these questions, and it wouldn't work."

"That's a fair comment Nancy. Let's put it to the test." David turned to Scott. "Are you willing to do one more role-play with me?" Scott nodded yes.

"Let's say Scott is a roofer you are negotiating with to replace a roof on one of your rental properties. Now the average investor asks straight out what the roof is going to cost. If you do this without building the roofer's motivation to get the job, you lose your biggest advantage to getting the best price and service possible. Here's how I would handle it if I were you." David turned to Scott. "Let's pretend that you've already gone up on the roof and done your calculations and now you've come to me with your bid."

Scott hiked up his pants, getting into the role-play. "Well Mr. Finkel, let's talk about the pricing options for your new roof."

"Scott, please call me David. You say 'Mr. Finkel' and I start looking around for my dad! Actually, before we talk about the money part, I'm a bit hesitant to even bother going through pricing with you. I get a sense that you won't even have time to really focus on this project." As David used this reluctant buyer technique he combined it with scrunchy face. "You're probably so busy right now with other jobs that there is no way you could even squeeze in this job, huh?" David said this last part with the negative phrasing with big eyes.

"No, I have time to do this job. In fact, now's a slow time for me and I can focus on this roof and get it done fast."

David used scrunchy face. "Now's a slow time for you?"

"Yeah, for some reason we are having a bit of a lull right now."

David used big eyes, "Yeah, but you probably still have your guys spread over two or three jobs right now, huh? I mean there is no way you could get to my roof right away, is there?"

Scott replied, "I could get to it right away. My guys are sitting at home waiting for me to give them a call that I have a job for them to come in for."

David turned to Nancy and asked, "What do you think, Nancy? Do you think Scott is more likely to give you, the investor, a better price and better service on this roof because you spent the extra few minutes building his motivation, or probably not?"

Nancy answered, "I can totally see that now that Scott's told you about how he needs the job you'll get a much better price and he'll do the work faster. You make it look so easy though."

"It will become easy and natural for you too, *if* you just work on using these techniques over the next three to six months until they are internalized. Then you'll find yourself using them without even trying to. It will just happen. All right, on to the advanced negotiation techniques!"

14 Advanced Negotiating Secrets*

Advanced Negotiating Secret 1: Bilateral Negotiation—Dancing with Both Halves of the Other Party's Brains

In any decision-making process there is both an emotional and a rational element. It's critical in your negotiations that you understand this need and feed it accordingly. It is a deadly mistake to think that we negotiate with our rational brains. Usually most people will make the real decision *emotionally*, and then rationalize their decision with the "thinking" half of their brain. When you understand this, you can focus first on the emotional level of the negotiation. What needs are you satisfying? What fears are you either tapping into or helping the other side avoid? To touch the other side's emotional brain, speak in the language of pain and pleasure, of desire and fear. When speaking to their rational brain, understand that it's not actually driven by logic so much as by the need to look good and avoid embarrassment. So feed the rational brain sincere compliments about its thinking process and the questions it asks. Remember, the rational brain is actually driven by emotion too, the emotions of vanity and insecurity.

Advanced Negotiating Secret 2: The Power of Labels

The labels that are used in a negotiation control the context of that negotiation. The context of the negotiation controls both sides' expectations. The parties' expectations control the course of the negotiation. Therefore, a master negotiator must be a master labeler.

*See Appendix A for details on the FREE online negotiating workshop you get as part of the Investor Fast Track Program™ at **www.InvestorFasttrack.com.**

(continued)

14 Advanced Negotiating Secrets *(continued)*

For example, imagine you are buying a $500,000 house with owner-carry financing but the sticking point is that the seller wants a down payment. With the proper use of labeling, you can shrink the amount of down payment you'll need to do the deal.

Investor: "I understand that you need some money up front [the labeling has begun—notice you do not say "down payment" but rather have already made the shift to "money up front"] so that you know I am serious [you just labeled the reason why the seller needed that money up front, which further sets the context within which you'll negotiate this up-front payment] and that you can feel secure in the deal [shift is occurring from money up front to security, the *real* reason the seller would want that money up front]. Now if you needed some huge amount of money up front [notice the label "huge" here] like $20,000 or $30,000 it's probably not going to be a fit for me. But at the same time I want to respect your need to feel good about this too [notice how you are again defining the seller's needs in the deal with your own label]. What's the least amount of money [label] you need up front so that, while it wasn't perfect, at least you could feel whole about it?"

Advanced Negotiating Secret 3: The Most Powerful Shift to Guarantee Positive Cash Flow Negotiating an Owner-Carry Deal

Imagine you are negotiating with a seller on an owner-carry deal when the seller starts to ask you what interest rate you will pay them. Any discussion of "interest rates" with the seller favors the seller. Use the following language pattern to shift the context of the negotiation in such a way that it is a given that the property must cash flow.

Example: Seller just asked you what interest you'll pay them on the owner-carry deal.

"Well, I'm not sure what the *property* can afford to pay."

Notice the critical shift here is to talk not about what you are willing to pay (which opens up several cans of worms) but about how much the property can afford. The implied given is that of course the property will need to pay for itself. After all, it's an investment. This shift will make it much easier for you to negotiate your payment amount with the seller to guarantee you get positive cash flow from the deal.

Advanced Negotiating Secret 4: Create Competition in the Negotiation

The fear of loss is the single biggest driver to spark the other side to say yes. Wherever you can in a negotiation, subtly and organically inject a little scarcity and competition into the mix. It's like baking powder and yeast, it causes your profit margin to rise.

(continued)

14 Advanced Negotiating Secrets *(continued)*

Example One: When you are buying a property.

> "Remind me again Mr. Seller, how many bedrooms does your house have? I've been talking with so many home owners this week that sometimes all these houses start to run together."

Example Two: When you are hiring a contractor to do a repair.

> "May I ask you a question? If you were me and were looking at all the companies and contractors out there who are scrambling to get this job, why would you choose you over all these other companies?"

Advanced Negotiating Secret 5: Getting the Deal to Stick—Why You Need Friction to Close the Deal

Many investors mistakenly assume that any friction in their negotiation with a seller will kill the deal. Nothing could be further from the truth. In fact, friction is the traction that helps you close a deal. And it's the sticking force that keeps the deal closed once you do get it done.

You need the other side to struggle with some of your requests, and they need to see you struggle and hem and haw at their requests so that they feel satisfied with the deal they got. If there is no friction it's like walking on ice, so smooth that you're likely to slip on your backside. So always help the other side feel like they had to work for the deal you orchestrate, so that the deal you close stays that way.

Advanced Negotiating Secret 6: The Principal of Momentum

Imagine a big funnel. At the top end it's wide and open, with sloping sides that get closer towards the bottom. In your negotiation your goal is to get early agreement from the other party using broad, nonspecific language, and then as you pick up some momentum guiding them down the funnel, you get more and more definite in what you are agreeing to.

The key is to create motion in the direction you want, no matter how small. Once you have that motion it is 10 times easier to direct the other side further into your funnel. If you can get the other party headed in the direction you want, you are much more likely to keep them going that way. The way that you apply this theory is by getting agreement on the big picture *first*, and then and only then narrowing down the conversation and dealing with the tougher issues.

For example, you could ask a seller:

> "I don't know if we could do this Mr. Seller, but what if we were able to get you a chunk of money up front, and then pay you the rest as monthly payments over time. Is that something we should even talk about, or probably not?"

(continued)

14 Advanced Negotiating Secrets *(continued)*

Notice how broad that "what if" statement is. If the seller agrees you should talk more about it, then gradually start to narrow down to the specifics, slowly and incrementally. It's like clamping down a vise one turn at a time.

Example: Negotiating with a rent-to-own buyer.

> *Investor:* Now tell me again about where you are living now?
> *Prospective Buyer:* I'm renting over on Oak Avenue. It's a small house there.
> *Investor:* Okay, and why is it you're wanting to move out of such a nice area? [scrunchy face]
> *Prospective Buyer:* The owner I'm renting from is selling the house.
> *Investor:* Would you share with me what it was about my property that had you so excited to have me show it to you? [Notice how the questions are building the buyer's motivation to buy, which is one form of gathering momentum into the negotiation.]

Advanced Negotiating Secret 7: Be Generous with Psychological Currency
In just about any negotiation there is one party who gets the financial payoff and another party who gets the psychological payoff. You've already learned the importance of slow and simple. One very important way you can let your seller win is to give them all the psychological feel-good for being smarter, brighter, more articulate, and more worldly than you are. Gosh, I guess you'll just have to settle for making a ton of money. I bet you're probably disappointed with that notion, huh? (You can inject some scrunchy faces and big eyes where they belong in the preceding two sentences.)

Advanced Negotiating Secret 8: Don't Outsmart Yourself—Slow and Simple Gets Paid
Wouldn't you agree that you'd much prefer to sell your property to someone who you didn't fear was smarter than you, so that you could relax and feel that this person wouldn't take advantage of you? Of course. Just about any seller you ever work with will feel more at ease if you allow them to feel a bit sharper and a bit faster than you are. And when a seller is at ease, he is a thousand times more likely to give you a great deal on the property. So remember *not* to have all the answers. Instead of persuasive and sophisticated answers use simple questions and a little bit of old fashioned naiveté, with a healthy dose of scrunchy face and big eyes, to get the results you want.

(continued)

14 Advanced Negotiating Secrets *(continued)*

Advanced Negotiating Secret 9: Whenever You Give, Make Sure You Get
Never make a concession in a negotiation without getting something in return.
No matter how small the value you get in return, it's critical to stop the other
side from continually asking you for more, and to clearly establish that every
time they ask you for something you are going to expect something in return.
This is your way of conditioning the other side to always expect that they will
have to give you something to get anything.

Example: You have negotiated a great price on a property, but the seller is
asking to close 30 days faster than you wanted. You're willing to do this, but
you know you need to make sure to get something in return so that the
concession give-and-take is consistent.

> *Seller:* I need you to close 30 days faster than that.
> *Investor:* Hmm. That may be a problem . . . [pausing to create doubt and
> friction]. I may be able to agree to that, but if I do, I'm going to ask that
> you include the patio set as part of the sale, is that fair? [The patio set
> isn't critical for you to get, you just need to get something in return so that
> the seller doesn't keep asking for more and more.]

Advanced Negotiating Secret 10: Shrink Your Concessions over Time
A concession is just a fancy name for any time in a negotiation where you give
the other side something that they want that you did not previously include in
your offer or counteroffer. Think of making a concession like putting a poker
chip into the pot. That chip might be more money, a lower price, a longer
term, or lower interest, or any of an infinite number of possibilities. The
pattern with which you make concessions subconsciously trains the other
side as to what to expect if they hold out for more. This means that savvy
negotiators always shrink the units of concessions they make so that it *feels*
to the other party that if they hold out for more they are only going to get less
and less.

Example: You are negotiating an owner-carry deal with a seller and you are
working to reduce your down payment.

(continued)

---

14 Advanced Negotiating Secrets *(continued)*

> *Seller:* I'd need at least $40,000 up front.
> *Investor:* Whoa! That much! I may be able to get my partner to go along with a payment up front of $10,000 or $15,000* [$5,000 unit of concession], but $30,000 to $40,000 is a huge amount of money to put up front.
> *Seller:* No way I'd take anything less than $30,000 up front.
> *Investor:* I can understand that you want to know I'm serious, which is why you want to get a huge chunk up front like $20,000 to $30,000, and who knows, maybe that will be what kills this deal. Look, I want to be fair here, but I've also got my partner to deal with. What if we gave you $16,000 or $17,000 up front? [Notice how the units of concession went from $5,000 down to a $1,000 unit.]

Advanced Negotiating Secret 11: Hypnotic Negotiating Patterns™
You may already be aware that there are certain word combinations that, by their very structure, work below conscious awareness to effect powerful negotiation results. I call these combinations Hypnotic Negotiating Patterns™. Here are some potent examples.

Example One: As you may have already been aware . . .

> "Mr. Buyer, as you may have already been aware, this area has been appreciating at 10 percent a year."

This phrase makes it very likely that the other party will just accept your statement that the area has been appreciating at 10 percent.

Example Two: At least you don't have to be worried about . . .

> "Well Mr. Seller, I know you are living two hours away from the house now, but at least you don't have to worry about vandalism or damage to the empty house. I mean, with an area as nice as this, at least no one would ever break into the place when no one's there and cause major damage."

*I threw in the "Range Technique" in this example. For more details on this powerful negotiating technique, see *Buying Real Estate without Cash or Credit* (pp. 108–109), and go to the Investor Fast Track Program™ where you'll find a complete online training course on negotiating profitable deals. Details in Appendix A or at **www.InvestorFasttrack.com**.

(continued)

14 Advanced Negotiating Secrets *(continued)*

This pattern directs the other party's attention to think and worry about the very thing you tell them they don't have to worry about. It's an advanced form of negative phrasing.

Example Three: Obviously . . .

"Obviously, Mr. Contractor, we'll need to establish what happens in the event you don't finish the work on time . . ."

This is one of my favorites. Whenever you hear the "O" word in a negotiation, know that something that may not be obvious is coming your way!

Advanced Negotiating Secret 12: Use the Power of Imagination to *Instantly* Make Money!

In your next negotiation, think about how you can guide the other party's imagination to help make a better deal for you the investor. Here are two quick examples of what I mean.

Example One: You are selling to a buyer.

"Imagine you found the perfect house. I mean it was *exactly* what you were looking for. But it required a larger up-front payment. Should I even bring the house to your attention [notice the funnel going on here?] or should I go ahead and give your house [label] to someone else?"

Example Two: You are working with a seller.

"A thought just occurs to me. If a realtor came to you and said they could get the house sold for you in 30 days' time, and you *knew* they could do it—and heck, let's say they could even get you your full $280,000 or so. You'd probably turn that down, huh? Or maybe not . . ."

Advanced Negotiating Secret 13: Turn the Tables on Them—Getting the Other Side to See the Deal from *Your* Perspective

Here is another tangible way to use the other party's imagination to help you close a deal. The Hypnotic Negotiating Pattern™ for this one is, "Imagine you were me . . ."

Here are some examples of exactly how this works.

(continued)

14 Advanced Negotiating Secrets *(continued)*

Example One: With a seller.

> "If you were an investor like me who was looking at several houses each week to buy, what would you think would need to happen to make this a deal you would even want to take over another one?"

Example Two: With a real estate agent.

> "If you were an investor like me who was looking at several houses each week to buy [see the embedded presupposition that you are in fact looking at several houses each week], what would you think would need to happen to make this a deal you would even want to take over another one?" (A bit of competition thrown in to light the fear-of-loss fires in the realtor's emotions.)

Example Three: With a buyer who is balking at giving you an up-front deposit to hold the property.

> "Imagine you were me and you met someone who said they loved the house and that they really wanted it, but they hesitated for a moment before they gave you a deposit to hold the property, what would you be thinking about saving the house for this couple versus giving it to another family?"

Advanced Negotiating Secret 14: Using Negotiating Markers™
Negotiating Markers™ are a way of nonverbally influencing the other side. It's a way in which you link up a nonverbal cue with the words you are saying. You can use a gesture or a tone of voice or an expression as a Negotiating Marker™. The key is to practice a few key Negotiating Markers™ so that you can do it effortlessly and naturally in the flow of your conversation with the other party.

Example One: You use an auditory marker like lowering your voice to prompt the seller to lower her price.

> "Tell me Ms. Seller, what did you [voice dropping lower now] *realistically* expect to get for the property?"

Example Two: You can use a gesture as a marker to subconsciously label yourself as a "good" investor, and to label those other investors out there as "bad."

> "Why Ms. Seller, it sure sounds like some of the investors you've talked with [pointing away to the side] really weren't too up front with you. But I'm guessing that if you're open to it, you'll eventually find a buyer you can trust and feel good about selling your property to [gesturing towards yourself as you say this].

"Now that we've just spent the last few hours talking about the Advanced Negotiating Secrets, let's shift and talk about how you can handle some of the other most important negotiations as an investor.

"I'll put it out to you as a group. What situations have you faced that are the most challenging when you are negotiating? What can I share with you that you feel would give you the greatest value about how to handle a specific negotiating situation?" David asked.

Tim raised his hand. "For me, I love the Instant Offer System when I'm sitting face-to-face with a seller, but what I'm struggling with is that many of the deals I'm looking at are for properties listed with a real estate agent. How do I negotiate through a real estate agent when I'm trying to buy a property they have listed?"

As David looked around the room he could see that many of the other students were nodding their heads, showing that they too had felt stuck with how to handle this. "I'll give you two answers to your question Tim. And then I'll role-play how I'd do the negotiation through the real estate agent.

"The first answer is that if you are working with an agent of your own and making a ton of offers on multiple properties and playing the numbers game, then it's not essential that you worry about negotiating using the Instant Offer System at the start. You'll simply have your agent make all your offers as quickly as she can so that you get the law of large numbers working in your favor. Once one of your offers has been accepted, however, at that point I think it makes sense for you to meet the owner and agent together at the property you made the offer on. I'll go through exactly how to do that in just a minute. The key for now with my first answer is that if your strategy is to flood the market with quick cash offers on multiple properties, the real leverage point is the speed and accuracy with which your buyer's agent can find properties to put offers on, help you figure out the right price to offer, and get the offer in fast to the listing agent. Does that make sense? When you are playing a numbers game, it's less about negotiating skill—initially—and more about speed and volume."

"Yeah," Tim replied, "that makes sense to me."

"Good. Now let me give you my second answer. This is for situations where you are either looking at a handful of deals versus a bucketful, or you have one of your initial 'volume' offers accepted and you are looking to go back and renegotiate the deal. I think it's critical that you get yourself face-to-face with the seller so that you can transform the dialog from an intellectual conversation about price into an emotional connection dealing with personal circumstances and real needs. If you stay at arm's length from the seller and the emotional and relational components to the deal, then it's very difficult to get the best deals. You still can make money that way, but you'll be forced to make a whole lot more offers until you get one accepted that way. Plus, if your only contact with the seller is through a written offer handed to the seller by the agent, there is very little you can do to differentiate yourself from the other investors out there. Now some of you may be thinking that all a seller cares about is your offer. Well, if you do your job right and meet with the seller, you can help expand the context of conversation so that the seller sees the bigger picture in terms of their personal situation, you as a person and investor, and finally the relief, rewards, and certain solutions you can give them. The key is to get yourself face-to-face with the seller."

"But David," Tim blurted out, "How do I get past the agent?"

"What a great question. Rather than answer that, let's look at what that question reveals. 'How do I get past the agent' presupposes that the agent is some blocking factor that is in your way in the deal and who you need to find some way around, either through sneaky back roads or through powerfully pushing past. But what if instead you could convert the agent into your *ally* in getting the deal done? What if you could actually ethically co-opt the agent to be on your team, working to get the seller to say yes to your offer? Wouldn't this make your job negotiating a win-win deal that much easier?"

"That sounds great David, but how am I supposed to do that?" Tim asked.

"First you need to understand the three forces that drive a listing agent to keep you at arm's length from her client. The first and biggest force is fear. The listing agent is afraid that you are going to try an end run to get past her and deal directly with her client in a way that will cut her out of her commission. The reason why she is afraid of this is probably because she's either had that happen or heard of that happening to other agents in her office, or down deep she is afraid she isn't bringing enough value to the table and that if you and the seller met and dealt directly, she wouldn't be bringing enough value to the table to warrant her earning her commission.

"Stop for a moment and think. How does just identifying the listing agent's biggest fear help you as an investor?" David asked the class.

"It lets us know we need to reassure the agent," Vicki answered.

"That's right, but how do you go about doing that?"

"Can't we just tell her that we won't go around her and that we're happy to make sure she'll get her commission?" Tim chimed in.

"You tell me. If you were the agent and an investor said to you, 'Hey, trust me. I'll see to it that you'll get your commission. I really am a man of my word,' what would you be thinking?" David asked.

Tim's voice was soft as he said, "I'd be thinking that I better cover myself because this guy is going to try something on me."

"Exactly! Rarely does it work to directly tell people you're honest or that you're credible, because the very fact that you say that is a warning sign in their mind that calls it into question. Instead you need to be more subtle about it, yet still accomplish the same goal. I'll role-play how to do this in just a moment.

"Let's talk about the second force that pushes the agent to keep you at arm's length from the seller—the agent's desire to save the seller's time. Isn't one of the reasons a seller lists the property in the first place so that they can have the agent do all the work? So it makes sense that the agent wants you to go through her. Also, they've probably learned from experience that many so-called investors aren't really credible or that they just want to make some lowball offer on the property. The agent is afraid that if she lets an investor get direct access to the seller, somehow the agent will be embarrassed or look unprofessional to the seller.

"Which brings us to the final force that pushes an agent to keep you at arm's length from her seller—she's afraid that it will end up damaging her reputation in the community. One of the most valuable things any real estate agent has is his or her reputation and goodwill in a particular community or area. They will guard and protect this reputation from any perceived threats.

"Okay, now that we've identified the three forces that push the listing agent to keep you away from the seller and only working through her as the conduit, let's role-play how I'd handle that situation. Tim, will you be my listing agent?"

"Sure," Tim answered.

"To set the stage, imagine Tim is the listing agent on a four-bedroom house I want to buy. From things the agent has said over the phone and from the listing information, I get the sense that the seller is a motivated seller. First I'll call up the agent and find a way to meet with the seller directly in such a way that I *indirectly* reassure the agent that I won't try an end run, and then I'll role-play part of the negotiation with the seller and the agent together."

David turned back to Tim. "So Tim, can you help me with the listing on Granny Avenue?"

"Yes I can."

"Great, my agent told me about that property and a few others in the subdivision and I am very interested in buying one or two of them. May I ask you some questions about the property?" David asked.

"Sure."

Stepping back from the role-play, David said to the class, "To put the agent at ease, I ask a few harmless questions about the property. Then I tell him that I'll drive by it or have my agent check it out later that day and give him a call back. Later that day I call him and continue my conversation."

Now David stepped back into the role-play. "So Tim, my agent Pam did go past the house and she said it fits my criteria. I'd like to set up a time to meet with you and the owner so that if I'm comfortable I can make my offer to buy the property. Now if for some reason you *can't* make the time to be there then, to be frank, I'm not interested in the house. I've learned through experience that as the listing agent, you'll have some key information that the seller and I will need to rely on to find a win-win fit on the property, and if you can't be there then it's a waste of my time too. What time later tonight or tomorrow would work for you and the seller to meet me at the property?"

"Well," Tim said, trying to make things tougher on David, "Why don't you just put together your offer and I'll present it to my seller and we'll let you know if we want to accept it."

"I could do that, Tim, but as old-fashioned as it sounds in today's world, I'm just not comfortable buying a property from an owner I haven't been able to meet in person. It's important to me to shake their hand and get to know them a little bit so that I can get a sense of what they are like as a person. I'm just not comfortable buying properties blindly without ever having met the previous owners and feeling that they are good people. And I've found over the years that the properties I end up buying are the ones where the listing agent, the owner, and I sit down and go through the property and the numbers to find a fair and reasonable fit. It probably seems crazy to you that I'm such an old-fashioned person to actually want to meet with the people I am doing business with, huh?" David asked, using negative phrasing.

"Wow!" Tim responded, who in his excitement forget his part in the role-play. "Can you say that again so I can write it down word for word? I know I was the agent, but all I could think when you asked me that last part was no, it wasn't crazy that you wanted to meet the people you are doing business with. I felt very comfortable with the idea when you put it that way."

David repeated the scripting for the class, then continued. "Let's move to the actual face-to-face with the seller and the listing agent at the property. First, I don't think you should bring your buyer's agent with you because chances are they'll butt in and say something that will hurt the flow of negotiation. But if you do want to bring them with you, make sure you plan with them exactly what role you want them to take. If it's me, I'd let them know I want them to be totally quiet and maybe later on in the deal, once the seller and seller's agent can taste the deal going through, your listing agent can play the 'bad cop' role—gently—of introducing a little doubt into your negotiation to help you close the deal. But that's just me. I feel that I'm a much better negotiator for me than any agent ever could be. You have to decide on how you want your buyer's agent to play it. Just make sure you clarify this with them before you meet with the seller and listing agent.

"Ready to get back into the role-play, Tim?" David asked. "We'll need a seller to do this too. Nancy, would you be our seller? Thanks.

"So imagine we've walked through the house, built rapport with both the seller and the listing agent, and now we are ready to move into Step Two of the Instant Offer System—setting an up-front agreement."

David stepped forward into the role-play, "So Nancy, you're really lucky to have found an agent as good as Tim to work with. Not only is he well respected in the community, but I have to tell you, he's really impressed me with his professionalism. Every time I had a question about the property, he was really quick to get me the information I needed and always promptly got back to me. I have to tell you, that hasn't always been my experience with *other* agents. May I ask, how did you first meet?"

David stepped out of the role-play and turned to the room. "Never underestimate the power of a third-party compliment like this to help begin the process of getting the listing agent on your side emotionally.

Nancy said, "I actually met Tim through my daughter's soccer team."

David stepped back and turned to the class. "I think you all spot the opportunity to build on this personal connection by asking both the seller and the agent about their daughters. I'll jump ahead in the negotiation," David said, turning back to the role-play.

"Tim, Nancy, I don't know if we'll be able to find a fit or not. But I am going to ask that if you think the ideas we talk through here are obviously not a fit for you, would you both be willing to tell me that?"

Both Tim and Nancy nodded their agreement.

"Great, I appreciate that and promise you won't be hurting my feelings. I've been buying houses long enough to learn that sometimes it's just not a good match." As David said the words "good match" he tapped the center of his chest. "On the other hand, if what we talk through looks like a good fit for you, are you both willing to let me know that here today too?"

Again both Tim and Nancy said yes.

"I appreciate that. I'll be doing the same thing. If I don't think I can buy the property in a way that meets your needs and still makes me a conservative profit as an investor, then I'll let you know that today. On the other hand, if I think I can meet your needs and feel good that I'll be able to make a fair profit for my effort, then I'll let you know that too. Only if we both feel it's a good fit will we take any next step, okay?"

David stepped out of the role-play and said, "How many of you recognized that the scripting of that up-front agreement was just a slightly modified version of the one you have been using for a while now as part of the Instant Offer System? The key difference is to involve the listing agent in the dialog as soon as possible."

"But David," Leon asked, "How in the world do you do the Motivation Step of the Instant Offer System with the agent there?"*

"Good question. Let's demo it here." David turned to Tim and Nancy.

"Nancy, may I ask you a question? What was it that initially prompted you to even want to sell your house?" The class instantly spotted that when David asked this question he scrunched up his face to get that uncertain, questioning tonality into his voice.

"Well, when I came to the decision to sell my house, I thought about the different agents I knew and decided to call Tim," Nancy answered.

Nodding his head, David said, "That makes a lot of sense. I would hope that if I were you I would have had the good sense to call an agent like Tim, too. May I ask

---

*For the exact languaging of the entire Instant Offer System, see *Buying Real Estate without Cash or Credit* (pp. 93–116).

you," David paused and his voice pitch and volume dropped, "why would you ever decide to sell a beautiful home like this?"

"On just one income this home was just too big for me to support," Nancy said.

"On just one income?" David asked, letting the question hang in the air, drawing the seller forward to explain.

"My ex-husband and I lived here for almost five years. Last June, after he and I split, I did my best to manage staying here on my own, but the property is just unfeasible for me on my single income."

"Oh, that makes sense. I think this makes it even more important for you to work with a top-notch agent like Tim," David said, nodding his head up and down.

Turning to Tim, David asked, "Tim, are you also then helping Nancy find a smaller house to buy in the area?"

"Actually," Tim answered, "We've already found her a beautiful two-bedroom house near the park district."

"Wow! That's great," David responded. "Congratulations on finding that next house, it isn't always so easy. May I ask, when is it you close on that other house?"

Nancy chimed in, "Oh, as soon as we find a buyer for this one."

"As soon as you find a buyer for this one?" David asked using the scrunchy face expression and looking at Tim.

"The sales contract on that house is contingent on Nancy selling this one," Tim explained.

"Oh, that makes sense." The class now saw David's eyes open wide and his face take on the simplistic expression they had previously learned was called "big eyes." "So whenever this house sells, this month, or next month, or a few months down the road, then at that point, in a month or in six months, you'll just close on that other house and move in." When David said this last part he was looking at Nancy.

"No, we can't wait that long. We need to have this one close so that my lender on the next one will let us close in the next month, or I lose the house to another buyer."

"Oh, well that makes sense." David turned to the class and stopped the role-play. "I hope you all noticed how critical it is that you involve the listing agent in the conversation on your side. How do you do this? You make sure to reinforce your third-party compliments of the agent to the seller. After all, if you are complimenting the agent, there is a subtle pressure on the agent to agree with your ideas, at least initially, since one of your ideas is that he is a great agent. Once the agent starts down this road, the principle of consistency will keep him on it. Remember, each time the agent shows himself to be agreeing with you or listening to you is another small step carrying him and the seller down the road to being open to your later offer, whether it be a cash offer or a terms offer. And that's all you really can ask for—for them to be open-minded and have a positive frame when you get to the 'what if' step of the Instant Offer System."

Five Questions Your Real Estate Agent Will Ask That You Should *Never* Answer

Remember, your agent, while he wants to do his best for you, is fundamentally incentivized to make sure the deal gets closed, any deal. Most agents have learned that part of their job is managing their client to help them complete the deal. I recommend that you never tell your agent anything you wouldn't want him to convey to the other side of the negotiation. While your agent would never intentionally tell the other side confidential or costly information, very often your agent will inadvertently give away a crucial piece of data, either by directly saying something foolish, or indirectly through body language or tone of voice. The key is to share information with your agent on a need-to-know basis. If you don't tell, neither can he!

Here are the five questions your real estate agent will probably ask you that you should never answer, along with your scripted response to handle each question.

One: Your buyer's agent asks you, "How do you feel about the house?"
"I'm not really sure yet how I feel about this house. The most important thing for me as an investor is to make sure the numbers work out so I am making a smart business decision when I choose to buy. I won't ever fall in love with a property like other people you work with might. For me, it's just a matter of will I make a conservative profit if I buy the house or not."

Two: Your listing agent asks you, "Why is it you wanted to sell your property?"
"I'm not totally convinced yet that I do want to sell it. I would like to see what you can get me for the house in a reasonable period of time looking for the right buyer. I guess I'm lucky because I don't *have* to sell the house, so if we don't find someone who is willing to pay what we are asking for it, then we can either keep it on the market longer, or maybe I'll just take it off the market."

(continued)

Five Questions Your Real Estate Agent Will Ask That You Should *Never* Answer *(continued)*

Three: Your buyer's agent asks you, "What's the most you'd be willing to pay for the house?"

"That's a great question. I'm not really sure what would make sense as an investment property. Rather than give you an amount to work with as the most I'll pay, I'd rather you take this offer we just wrote up to them and do your best to get them to agree with it. I think it's a real reasonable offer, and if for some reason they feel they need it to be different, you do the best you can do to get the lowest counteroffer you can. Then I'll make a decision of whether it's even worth spending more time on it or not. If they accept our offer like I am hoping, then we'll close on the property right away because it's a fair deal all around."

Four: Your listing agent asks you, "What's the lowest offer you would accept?"

"That's a great question. Rather than even thinking about that right now, what I'd prefer you do is to use all your skill and talent to get me the very best offers you can, and I'll talk with my partner and see if we're willing to accept one of them or if the buyer will have to do better before we'll consider accepting."

Five: Your listing agent asks you, "What concessions are you willing to give to a buyer to make the house sell faster?"

"I'm not sure I'd be willing to make any concessions. Quite frankly, I don't think I'll need to, considering how fairly we've priced the house. If you find a serious buyer who asks you about this, get her specific request down in writing, and also get very clear on what she is willing to give me in return for these concessions, and I'll certainly be willing to consider it."

"What other situations do you find most challenging to negotiate?" David asked the class.

"What if they ask me for references and I've never done a deal before?" Nancy asked.

"Great question. I have a simple answer for you—just tell the truth. Which in your case would sound something like, 'This will be the first property I've bought as an investment property. I've been working for the past 20 years doing

IT management. When I made the decision to start real estate investing six months ago, I went out and did all my research to do it the right way. Since that time I've taken the classes, been meeting with the sellers to find and identify the right house for me to buy, and have been working with my mentor who's been doing this for years. I understand that you want to know people I've done business with over time so that you can feel comfortable about my character and the type of person that I am. I'd be happy to put that together for you if we find a mutual fit here. That way anything we put together here will be subject to you checking through my references, getting comfortable with me as a person, just like from my end I'll have to do my checking to make sure of things like you have clear title to the property, and that there's no big surprise with the house when we buy it.'

"Then sign up the deal subject to their approval on your references, allowing the seller to cancel in, say, 72 hours with written notice if she's not happy with your references. Understand that *no one* has references when they get started, and that is okay.

"We have time for a few more questions before we need to take a break."

"David, I do great negotiating with sellers," Leon said. "But when it comes time to talk with a lender about getting financing on my properties, I get nervous and find myself feeling powerless. Can you help me find a way to be the one in control of that situation, just like the Instant Offer System puts me in control when I'm negotiating with sellers?"

David nodded his head. "I can sure identify with that challenge. In fact, I bet there aren't many people here who have worked to get conventional financing who haven't found the process to be intimidating and mysterious. Let me share with you the single most important shift to make in your negotiating frame when dealing with lenders. If you can make this switch, it will instantly move the power in the situation from your lender to you.

"Leon, imagine you are a lender who I want a loan from. Let's role-play this powerful technique I'm about to share with you. What I do is call you up and say, 'Hi, my name is David Finkel. I'm an investor who lives in the area and I wanted to talk with the best person in your bank who can help answer my questions about lending programs you have. Can you tell me who I should talk with?'"

"That would be me," Leon said.

"Oh, great. I'm sorry, I didn't catch your name."

"I'm Leon."

"Nice to meet you, Leon. As I said, my name is David. I'm an investor in the area who is considering financing several of my properties. What I'm in the process of doing is interviewing several local lenders to see which one I'm most comfortable with to select to give my business to. May I ask you several questions about what your bank offers investors like myself?"

David turned back to the class. "The key is to make the shift from you pleading for a loan into forcing the lender to sell themselves to you in order to earn your business."

"David, that's great!" Leon shouted. "I can already see how the problem was that I had been looking at the situation like I needed them desperately, but what you helped me see is that the lender is really like any other business. The lender needs people like me to lend to if they want to stay in business."

"It even gets better than that when you understand how the game is really played," said David. "Your lender is really several units in one. There is the 'originator' unit. These are the people who hunt up the business for the bank to lend money too. Think of them as the sales and marketing division of the bank. Most of the people are incentivized in some way, whether by commissions or by bonuses or even by quarterly or annual evaluations, to get more loans originated. So here is the key in all your dealings with these people." David turned and wrote on the board:

When dealing with loan "originators," make *them* sell you on working with them.

"Anytime you have a lender or mortgage broker fighting to sell you on working with them, they are becoming more and more committed to having you choose them. They will be much more likely to get you lower fees or better rates, or to tell you about the 'hidden' programs they don't tell everyone about. In a way, this is just an extension of the reluctant buyer negotiating fundamental we've already talked about.

Three Questions to Ask Every Lender or Mortgage Broker You Work With

It's essential that you shift every front-end "originating" lender or mortgage broker you work with to be scrambling to earn your business. It's also key to convert them in the process to being your champion within their organization so that your loan sails through the approval and underwriting process much easier. This means befriending them, but it also means cultivating within them a deep commitment to seeing that you get your loan. Notice how these three questions each layer in another key shift or commitment step on the part of the mortgage lender or broker you are dealing with.

Question One: "As you know, I'm in the process of interviewing several lenders to see which of them I want to select for me to give my business to. If you were an investor like me, why do you think your company is the one you would choose to work with out of all the hundreds of lenders in town and through the Internet? What lending programs and services do you have that would make you a dream for me to work with?"

Question Two: "If I do end up working with you, I'd want to be one of your preferred clients who does business with you again and again. Would you mind sharing with me what extra incentives or perks you give to your preferred lending clients? What are the preferred rates you give them or the lowered fee scale you give them to keep your preferred clients coming back to you again and again?"

Question Three: "One last question for you,   [Insert their name] . If I do choose you to work with, are you going to be willing to commit to do what it takes on your side to be my champion within your organization to make sure I get a great deal on my financing package? It's really important to me that I establish a partnership with my lender so I feel comfortable and have fun working with them over time. You are? Great. Well, as someone who's really savvy as to how your company works with its approval and underwriting process, I'm going to rely on your help to make sure that my preliminary documents are presented in just the right way so that my loan sails through. Can I count on your help and experience to help me do things the right way? I thought I could. Let's take a moment and brainstorm out the pieces of your company's approval process so that together we can make sure we make it easy for them to pass the loan through. After all, your time is valuable too, so let's make sure we get it right the first time. Are you up for it?"

"Now in addition to the originating unit, your lender has some form of 'approval' or 'underwriting' unit too. When working with this unit, the key is to befriend the person you are talking with and let them feel important for being the powerful and knowledgeable insider they are. That way you set up the dynamic so they feel powerful not by opposing you, but by magnanimously helping little, old you." With that David smiled out at the room in his most innocent of big eyes expressions.

"I think you all are getting how effective this will be in turning the underwriter you talk with into your expert guide through the process. Ask them exactly what they need from you and in what format to make it easy for them to approve your loan. If you plan on doing more business with this lender, and I think you should, make sure you thank them with a card when the deal is done for all their help on the loan.

"Okay, enough on negotiating with lenders, let's move on to the next Core Investor Skill, doing your due diligence to decide if you want to keep the deal."

CHAPTER SIX

Core Investor Skill Four: Running the Numbers—How to Know You've Got the Right Deal—*Fast!*

"Once you've found your motivated seller, negotiated and structured a potentially winning deal, next you'll have to run the numbers on the deal to make sure it really is a deal worth closing on. This is the due diligence and deal evaluation stage.

"This means doing all your checking and inspecting and number crunching to make sure the deal really is good for you. I know I've stressed this over and over, but it's too important to only say once: When you find a good deal, you've got to act fast. If you even *think* you have a good deal, act fast to put the property under contract and *then* do your checking and due diligence. **Remember, doing due diligence on a property you do not have under contract is like doing extra-credit homework for a class you aren't even enrolled in—it might be fun, but it isn't going to get you a higher grade.**

"The most successful investors all act fast in locking a property under contract, but they make sure they act just as fast to sort through the deal afterward to ensure it is a keeper. If it isn't, then the best investors are all very quick to go back and talk through the deal with the seller. Best case, they renegotiate the deal to make it a win-win. Worst case, they exercise one of their escape clauses in the contract and back out of the deal. The key is speed. The quick get paid, and the slow fall by the wayside.

"The heart of the skill of analyzing the deal is to follow a proven process so that you get consistently accurate results with which to intelligently make your final investing decisions. It's too easy to get caught up in the excitement of the moment. This is why the powerful three-step process I'm going to be sharing with you will be so important. It took me close to a decade to refine this process so that it's fast and easy, yet incredibly reliable and effective. This process that I developed is called the Deal Evaluation Wizard™.

"The first stage of the process is your Deal Quick View™. When do you think you'll do your Deal Quick View™?" David asked.

"After we've signed up the deal?" Vicki tentatively answered.

"Exactly, *after* you have the deal under contract."

"But David," Leon interrupted, "what if we sign up a bad deal? How are we going to know what price to even offer when we meet with the seller if we haven't done our homework before we meet with the seller?"

"That's a great question, Leon. The truth is that you *won't* know if the deal you sign up initially is the right deal or not—at least, not at first. You'll do your best to negotiate the best deal you can, sign up that deal, and then tell the seller that you'll get right on your checking and due diligence and that you should have feedback for them on the numbers in the next week. Which brings us back to the Deal Quick View™.

"Your goal is to complete the Deal Quick View™ within 72 hours of signing up the deal so that you can immediately go back to renegotiate the deal with the seller if you need to. Worst case, you will turn the property back to the seller at that time.

"The Deal Quick View™ has three main questions to it." David turned and wrote on the board.

Question 1: What is the REAL market value of the house?

Question 2: Is your price right?

Question 3: If you are planning on holding on to the property long term, will it cash flow?

"A property really has two values—the resale value and the rental value. In the Deal Quick View™ you want to see how the price and terms match up with the market. If your numbers are good, keep moving ahead with the deal. If the numbers are out of whack, make sure you immediately go back and talk with the seller."

"David, won't the seller be upset with us?" Mary asked.

"Maybe, but if you are tactful when you talk with them and do it right away, it's been my experience that the seller will understand. Call them up and say, 'Mr. Seller, I've just finished my initial checking of the market value of the house and it seems I was mistaken when I thought the house would rent for $2,000 a month. I had a rent survey done and it showed that the rents in the area are actually only $1,700 to $1,800 a month. In fact, there are two rental houses on your street of similar size and construction that only rent for $1,700 a month. Like I told you when we put this together, the property has to be able to pay for itself, so I don't see how I can pay you $1,900 a month. What do you think we should do about it?'

"Notice how you are honest with the seller and involve them in finding a solution. If the seller refuses to budge on the payment, maybe they'll drop the price or throw in another sweetener to offset the cash flow. If not, you have no choice but to walk from the deal. At least you've been respectful not to tie up the seller's property for months on end only to cancel. You raced through your Deal Quick View™ to find any glaring problems right away.

"Step two is the Due Diligence View™. This is where you inspect the property, check out the neighborhood, and examine the title to the property. This step will take you between two and four weeks.

"The Due Diligence View™ is the time to look at the deal fresh and make sure the numbers really do make sense and that, after the first blush of initial excitement has worn off, the deal really is a keeper.

"The single biggest key in this step is to neutralize your emotions and check your assumptions. You neutralize your emotions by realizing that *everyone* makes decisions emotionally—everyone. I do. You do. We all do. There is nothing wrong with this, only it's dangerous when you are unaware of how your emotions of desire and fear are coloring your judgment. You just need to put your emotional biases onto the table so you are aware of them. Now look at the deal alongside these biases. You'll make a much better decision this way.

"The bottom line is that the Due Diligence View™ is your chance to check your assumptions and to make sure the deal doesn't have any hidden snags or red flags.

"Which brings us to the third step in the deal evaluation process—the Closing View™. The Closing View™ is actually happening alongside the Due Diligence View™. It's your chance to think through the merits of the deal along with your plans for the property once you buy it. Remember, you will always know your way out of any deal you decide to step into.

"As an aside," David asked the class. "What do you think is the single best way to know you have a winning deal?"

"If your numbers all check out," Mark answered.

"If you have a great price," Tim shouted out.

"These are both good answers. But how do you know if the numbers really check out? How do you know if you have a great price—I mean *really* know?" David asked.

"Because you've done your checking," Vicki answered.

"Okay, but where is the best place to check to really guarantee you have accurate numbers?" David was really pushing the group to go past the comfortable textbook answers.

"By marketing the property?" Nancy tentatively answered.

"Exactly! The very best way to know you have a great deal is to have presold the property to your end user. Now this could mean you have an earnest money deposit from a retail buyer. Or it could mean you have a rental deposit from a tenant, or a deposit to hold the property from a tenant buyer. The best way you can know you'll make money is to have already found your end user for the property before you close on the property yourself. What one thing have you collected from a buyer or renter or tenant buyer that lets you know you that they are for real?"

"Money!" This time the class knew the answer and shouted it out.

"Look," David said in earnest. "I know this isn't how most investors think. The average investor would never dream of marketing the property before they had closed on it, but that's dumb! Even if you aren't able to sell or lease the property prior to closing, the feedback you get from the pool of prospective buyers or tenants is incredibly valuable. After all, who really determines the market value? It's these very same people you are asking by showing them the property and seeing if they are willing to put up money and say yes to the price or rent."

The Deal Evaluation Wizard™*

Step One: The Deal Quick View™—Determining the Property's *Real* Market Value and Making Sure Your Price and Terms Make Financial Sense

A. (Sales Comparables) Check the Resale Value—Get at Least Five True "Comps"

Comp #1 _____ # Bed _____ # Bath _____ Sq Ft _____

Sale Date _____ Sale Price _____ Features _____

❏ Sale within 3 months ❏ within 6 months ❏ Same # Bedrooms

❏ Sq Ft within 20%

Property determined to be <u>similar construction and similar location</u> to subject
 property by:

❏ Info from owner of subject property ❏ Info from real estate agent

❏ Personal visit by investor to exterior of comparable property on
 (date) _____

❏ Other:_____

Comp #2_____ # Bed _____ # Bath _____ Sq Ft _____

Sale Date _____ Sale Price _____ Features _____

❏ Sale within 3 months ❏ within 6 months ❏ Same # Bedrooms

❏ Sq Ft within 20%

Property determined to be <u>similar construction and similar location</u> to subject
 property by:

❏ Info from owner of subject property ❏ Info from real estate agent

❏ Personal visit by investor to exterior of comparable property on
 (date) _____

❏ Other:_____

*For a FREE online workshop on using the Deal Evaluation Wizard™ go to
www.InvestorFasttrack.com.

(continued)

The Deal Evaluation Wizard™ *(continued)*

Comp #3 _____ # Bed _____ # Bath _____ Sq Ft _____

Sale Date _____ Sale Price _____ Features _____

❑ Sale within 3 months ❑ within 6 months ❑ Same # Bedrooms

❑ Sq Ft within 20%

Property determined to be <u>similar construction and similar location</u> to subject property by:

❑ Info from owner of subject property ❑ Info from real estate agent

❑ Personal visit by investor to exterior of comparable property on
  (date) _____

❑ Other:_____
_____

Comp #4 _____ # Bed _____ # Bath _____ Sq Ft _____

Sale Date _____ Sale Price _____ Features _____

❑ Sale within 3 months ❑ within 6 months ❑ Same # Bedrooms

❑ Sq Ft within 20%

Property determined to be <u>similar construction and similar location</u> to subject property by:

❑ Info from owner of subject property ❑ Info from real estate agent

❑ Personal visit by investor to exterior of comparable property on
  (date) _____

❑ Other:_____
_____

Comp #5 _____ # Bed _____ # Bath _____ Sq Ft _____

Sale Date _____ Sale Price _____ Features _____

❑ Sale within 3 months ❑ within 6 months ❑ Same # Bedrooms

❑ Sq Ft within 20%

Property determined to be <u>similar construction and similar location</u> to subject property by:

❑ Info from owner of subject property ❑ Info from real estate agent

❑ Personal visit by investor to exterior of comparable property on
  (date) _____

❑ Other:_____

(continued)

The Deal Evaluation Wizard™ *(continued)*

B. Check the Rental Value—Get at Least Five True "Market Rent Comps"

	Address	# Bedrooms	# Baths	Rents For
Rental Comp #1	_____	_____	_____	_____
Rental Comp #2	_____	_____	_____	_____
Rental Comp #3	_____	_____	_____	_____
Rental Comp #4	_____	_____	_____	_____
Rental Comp #5	_____	_____	_____	_____

Question: How do your price and terms match up to the *real* property value? Is your price right? If it's a terms deal, will it cash flow?

_____

Step Two: The Due Diligence View™—Inspect the Property, Neighborhood, and Title

A. Inspect the Property

❑ Professional inspection?

❑ Thorough personal inspection?

❑ Talk with the neighbors for hidden defects, unusual circumstances, and to uncover the property's history?

B. Inspect the Neighborhood

❑ Is it in demand?

❑ Perception in marketplace as to desirability?

❑ Who most wants to live in area?

❑ Market trends—current rates and projected trends

    ❑ Appreciation rates?

    ❑ Vacancy factor?

❑ Development projects, rezoning, or infrastructure changes that impact value?

(continued)

The Deal Evaluation Wizard™ *(continued)*

C. Check the Title

❏ Who owns the property?

❏ Liens?

❏ Judgments?

❏ Current loan status, terms, balance?

❏ Taxes current?

❏ If home owners association, how much are fees? Are they current?

❏ Pending bankruptcy of seller?

❏ Personal liens against seller not yet recorded against property?

❏ Mechanic's liens?

❏ Credit check on seller?

❏ Community property state?

❏ Accurate legal description of property?

❏ *Letter-for-letter* double check of name and spelling on your paperwork?

Step Three: The Closing View™

Closing Considerations:

❏ How much time are you going to give yourself to close?

❏ Should you rush to close or take your time?

❏ What is the risk of the seller backing out of the deal?

❏ What is the cost to delay the closing?

❏ What advantages accrue to you by waiting?

Up-Front Money:

❏ How much money will it take you to close?

❏ Where else can you get this money?

❏ What's the cost of this money? (Remember there is *always* a cost, even if it's your own money.)

❏ How long before you get this money back?

(continued)

The Deal Evaluation Wizard™ *(continued)*

Exit Strategy:

❏ What is your exit strategy going to be?

❏ Is this a realistic match with the time you have to close?

❏ What could go wrong with your exit strategy?

❏ How will you deal if these things do go wrong?

❏ What's your backup exit strategy?

Mitigating Risks:

❏ Are you personally liable for the money in the deal?

❏ What is the condition of the property, especially if you are going to keep it long term?

❏ What are the market conditions and trends where the property is located?

❏ How much money are you risking in the deal before you get a cash deposit from a buyer or end user for the property?

❏ Are there any fraudulent conveyance risks to consider? (If the seller is in foreclosure, bankruptcy, or pending bankruptcy.)

❏ Did you *read* carefully through the exclusions to the title insurance policy?

Final Question: Taking this all into consideration, is this a deal you want to take?

The Ten Deadly Deal Analysis Disasters

Mistake 1: Taking too long

Good deals don't wait around for indecisive people. Many people "think a deal to death." The best way I know to lower your anxiety level with a deal is to move forward provisionally (i.e., with a subject-to clause or liquidated damages clause of some sort—you'll learn more about this in the next chapter).

Mistake 2: Trusting seller's numbers

Even if they have only good intentions, most sellers just aren't knowledgeable and all of them are inherently biased at least a bit. The most common problems with a seller's numbers are pretty obvious—they overestimate the value (often confusing listing prices of local homes with actual selling prices), and they underestimate the cost to fix it up.

Mistake 3: Trusting appraisals

An appraisal really isn't meaningful, unless *you* hired the appraiser, *you* gave them the instructions, and *you* are handing the appraiser the check. I can influence an appraiser to appraise a so-called $100,000 house for as little as $80,000 and as high as $120,000 (or more). That's close to a 40 percent variance on the two appraisals of the same property! So take any appraisal the seller hands you in the spirit that it was intended, as a *marketing* piece! The best appraisals are ones where you hire the appraiser and give them their instructions. If I really want an appraisal to be accurate, then I choose a reliable appraiser I've used before and ask her, "What would this house need to be priced at to sell in 90 days or less in its current condition?" This should give you a conservative estimation of value.

Mistake 4: Doing your math in pencil

The next time you catch yourself thinking it's okay to fudge your numbers a little to make the deal cash flow or the rehab pay off on paper, beware! Some investors have a tendency to play with the numbers a little to make them show that a marginal deal is better than it really is. Remember, just because the deal makes a profit on paper doesn't mean you'll make money in the real world.

Mistake 5: Overestimating the market rents

This one happens all the time. The way you know what a house will rent for is to do a market rent survey. The rents listed in the paper or that a real estate agent told you may or may not be accurate.

(continued)

The Ten Deadly Deal Analysis Disasters *(continued)*

Mistake 6: Overestimating the "as is" value

So many investors forget that to turn a house in 90 days or less requires the price to be *real*, not pie in the sky. What would it really take to get the house into top showing condition? Be careful to be conservative in your estimate of value going into the deal. The worst case then is that you make more money than you anticipated!

Mistake 7: Getting bogged down in process

Use the three-step process you just learned about so that you incrementally invest more time in the deal only as it proves it is warranted. Learn to trust your due diligence and evaluation process and make sure it is checklist driven. This is your best insurance that you'll do it the right way every time.

Mistake 8: Worrying about the house on the Quick View step

On your first pass, you are only concerned about three things: (1) What is the real market value of the house? (2) Is your price right? (3) If you are planning on holding on to the property long term, will it cash flow?

Mistake 9: Underestimating the time it will take to flip/fix/fill/sell

I've bought a lot of houses from investors who got stuck with holding costs being too much for them to handle. Be careful here. If your exit strategy is to sell the house to a retail cash buyer, it will need to be in showing condition or you'll struggle to find a quality retail cash buyer. Always be conservative with how long it will take you to execute your exit strategy and, if possible, build in a healthy cushion of extra time.

Mistake 10: (The biggest deadly deal disaster of all) Hiding behind analysis because you are afraid to pull the trigger on the deal

At a certain point, as an investor you will need to step forward in the deal and commit.

CHAPTER SEVEN

Core Investor Skill Five: Writing Up the Deal—Understanding the Language of Real Estate

Learning the Language of Real Estate

GO ONLINE

While you don't have to become a real estate attorney or even a title company nerd, it is important that you understand the language of real estate so that you can intelligently move through the world of real estate safely and profitably. It's been said that the language of science is math. Well, the language of real estate is the language of contracts and industry-specific jargon. It's terms like *deeds* and *mortgages* and *encumbrances* and *conveyances*. Don't let any of this intimidate you.

Anyone, and I do mean anyone, can learn the language of real estate. All it takes is a little patience and a willingness to spend enough time exploring the world of real estate and you cannot help but acquire the language of real estate.

Rather than let this book bog down in a glossary of real estate terms, I've included a special online training course on the language of real estate, including the 10 real estate terms you *must* know, as part of your FREE Investor Fast Track Program™. To access this free primer course just go to **www.InvestorFasttrack.com**. You'll get a chance to master these key terms and learn how to use them in your investing business.

(continued)

Learning the Language of Real Estate *(continued)*

After all these years helping new investors make a lot of money buying homes without cash or credit, I've got it boiled down so that in one—and I do mean one—quick crash course you will be up to speed on the "Big Ten" as I like to call them, and well on your way to becoming fluent in the language of real estate. Make sure you go to Appendix A for instructions about how to get your free Investor Fast Track Program™ so you get instant access to this powerful online workshop. Or for immediate access go to **www.InvestorFasttrack.com**.

After everyone took their seats from the break, David began again. "Let's talk about the final core skill—understanding the language of real estate. I understand that a lot of this terminology can be intimidating at first. I sure felt that way when I got started investing, and I recognize that every new investor goes through that learning curve over the first year of investing as he or she learns the ropes.

"Many of you are probably scared to death that you have to become an expert in how to write up agreements and know real estate law. The good news is you don't. But you do need to know enough to effectively write up your initial agreements with buyers and sellers so that you can tie up a deal. Then you need to know how to intelligently use your attorney to put the finishing touches on your paperwork. And you need to know the basics so when it comes to papering your tail, I mean trail, with tenants or lenders or contractors, you keep yourself clearly in control. I'd like to cover the most important aspects of contracts and agreements first."

BRIGHT IDEA

The Seven Essential Contract Basics

Essential One: Relax, and put it in writing.
A contract is just an agreement between two or more parties in which one party makes an offer, the other party accepts the offer, and something of value (called consideration) changes hands. While a contract doesn't need to be in writing to be valid, with real estate in order to be enforceable a contract typically needs to be in writing. But even if this wasn't the case, if you get nothing else from this part of the book take this one key home—*always* put things in writing. The key phrase to remember is: *"If you dare it, document it!"*

(continued)

The Seven Essential Contract Basics (continued)

Essential Two: Clearly and accurately identify all the parties to the agreement.
It's really important in any of your agreements to accurately lay out who are all the parties involved in the agreement. Now this seems obvious, but you'd be surprised at the number of students I've seen write up paperwork on a deal where they used vague language as to who exactly the parties were in the agreement.

If it's a purchase contract where you are buying a property, make sure you list the seller's full name exactly how they have it on the deed with which they took title. Do they use a middle initial? Or do they spell out their middle name? Maybe they hold title as the trustee on behalf of a Revocable Living Trust? Make sure you get it right.

If you are leasing a property to a family, make sure you list all adults who are party to the lease as "Tenants" and not just one person.

Are you requiring a co-signer to a loan agreement? If so make sure you accurately identify the co-signer and get their signature.

Are you selling a four-unit property to a corporation? If so, make sure you identify the legal name of the corporation and the state in which it is incorporated. Did you remember to get the title of the person signing clearly listed? (As a side note, the title company will probably want to see a corporate resolution as well as a certified copy of the bylaws empowering the corporation and the individual signing on behalf of the corporation with the authority to enter into the deal.)

I think you are getting the point. You can't be too careful when it comes to accurately identifying and clarifying the parties to the deal.

Essential Three: Define acronyms and shortcuts.
If the contract uses an acronym or other special label as a shortcut to reference a proper noun, make sure these shortcuts are clearly defined and consistently used. This is just a fancy way of saying that if you use a proper noun like "Closing Agent" in your agreement, make sure somewhere in the agreement you have a clause that says, "The 'Closing Agent' shall be XYZ Title Company, located at 2211 Main Street, Anytown, CA 91960."

When you're reading through a contract, sometimes it helps to have a cheat sheet listing all the acronyms and defined terms and parties so that you can easily translate the legal gobbledy gook into plain English.

(continued)

The Seven Essential Contract Basics *(continued)*

Example:

Trustor: John Homeowner
Trustee: ACME Title Company, LLC
Beneficiary: Big Bucks Bank, Inc.

Essential Four: Accurately describe the property being discussed.
I think you're probably spotting the trend with contract basics—half the battle is just being crystal clear as to who or what you are actually talking about. In the case of identifying a property, while a street address can be enough for things like a lease agreement, or a repair contract with a roofer, make sure that for any purchase and sales contract or any document you plan on recording (see later in this chapter for more on "recording" documents) you use the "legal description" of the property. This is the official description of the property, found in the public land records at the county recorder's office or county courthouse.

Here's an example of a legal description:

"Lot 3, Block 24 of the High Hopes Subdivision as recorded on Map No. 322 recorded in the County Recorder's Office on May 1st, 2009, in the County of Glorified, State of . . ."

The easiest place to get the legal description is from the Preliminary Title Report you get on the property from the title company as part of your due diligence work. This is a simple report the title company will generate for you which will have in it the legal description of the property. If the legal description is really long, like for a condo, I just photocopy the legal description section and attach it to my document. You can also get it from the loan documents the property owner has in her files from when she bought the place, or from an old copy of her title insurance policy, or even from a copy of her deed if she has that handy.

(continued)

The Seven Essential Contract Basics *(continued)*

Since you probably won't have any of this handy when you are meeting with the motivated seller to put the property under contract at the start, just sign the deal using the street address, and in the blank space in your purchase contract where it asks you for the "legal description" simply write, "To be provided later."Never let the fear of not having the right answer stop you from signing a deal. Provided you use investor-friendly forms and contracts, you will have powerful protections in place that let you safely sign up a deal fast; then, after you have it under contract, go back and do your due diligence.*

Essential Five: Lay out in plain language what both parties are agreeing to. State things plainly so that a neutral third party (read "judge") who is reading the contract without explanation would interpret your agreement in the way you want them to.

I want to make sure I am making something absolutely clear. I am not looking for you to act as your own attorney, nor am I asking you to become a real estate law expert. I think you will need to have a sharp attorney look over and write up many of your real estate contracts. It's just critical for you to understand the basics for three reasons.

First, there will be many times when you are ready to strike a deal and you won't have your attorney handy and with you. If you wait until your attorney draws up any needed agreements, you might as well kiss most deals goodbye. For example, imagine you're meeting with the owner of a six-plex that you'd really like to buy. Because he is highly motivated, he's verbally agreed to sell you this $1.2 million property for $700,000. What do you think would happen to this deal if you said to the seller, "Gee Mr. Seller, I'm glad we could come to agreement on price and terms for a cash sale. I'll go meet with my attorney to get all the paperwork written up. It should take three or four days for me to get it back for you and I to sign . . ."

What do you think would happen to your great deal in those three or four days? Hint: Look for the other investor walking out of the house with a silly grin on her face and a signed contract in her pocket. The key is to lock up the property, and then later you can have your attorney draft the more involved closing documents for the actual closing on the property.

*For more information on getting a CD-ROM or downloading the 78 forms and contracts that I personally developed and have used in my investing over the past 10 years, just go to **www.InvestorFasttrack.com** and click on the "Investor Resources" tab.

(continued)

The Seven Essential Contract Basics *(continued)*

The **second** reason for you to become fluent with the basics of real estate agreements is because there are going to be many times when you need an important "contract" to immediately use in your investing but you won't have your attorney draft the document. Instead you'll need to get the agreement in writing on your own. For example, once you get your attorney to go through your "standard" lease you'll use with renters, you will need to be able to know the basics so you can correctly *use* that contract in your management of your properties. One goal of building your successful investing *business* is to build a library of approved contracts for your business to use in its day-to-day operation. This will include documents like lease agreements, purchase contracts, rent-to-own paperwork, and standard releases from your contractors once they've been paid.

The **third** and final reason you need to understand the basics of contracts is because this is the language of real estate. Just like math is the language of physics and money is the language of accounting, contracts are the language of real estate.

You'll be training your brain to get good at agreements by following this simple rule. Remember, a contract doesn't need to be in fancy language with "whereases" and "ipso factos" and "pepto-bismos." Rather, it just needs to clearly lay out who agrees to do what, by when, to what standard, with what consequences, with what warranties, and for what payment.

Essential Six: Always be the one who drafts, or pays for the attorney to draft, the agreement.
Why? Because in any deal, for every deal point you talk through and agree to orally, there will be two more that never came up, but will when you get it onto paper. Because you're the one controlling the document you control the context, the terrain, of the deal. And in doing this you will be in the driver's seat on the deal.

For example, let's say you agreed in a purchase and sales agreement to buy a house for $600,000 with a down payment of 10 percent ($60,000) and the seller to carry back the balance at 5 percent interest. Actually this is a real deal I did on a nice house in San Diego a few years back. Because I volunteered to write up the paperwork, I made sure to include things in the deal like the fact that the loan was for "interest only," which lowered my monthly payments considerably; that I had a "first right of refusal" to buy the note if the seller ever tried to sell it to a third party; that I got the washer/dryer, drapes, yard furniture, and a few other sundries with the sale, like the refrigerator.

(continued)

The Seven Essential Contract Basics (continued)

Now while I did end up paying the seller a few hundred dollars for the refrigerator, I got all the rest because I had included them in the agreement. Understand there is a subtle yet strong pressure to accept any written contract the way it is written. And it takes a strong will to change every point of it. That's why you want to be the one who is in control of the paperwork.

As an aside, what do you do if the other party insists in writing up the paperwork? My suggestion is that you then go to the effort of getting paperwork written up on your side anyway. That way at least you'll have your clear, authoritative contract to compare side-by-side with the other party's document. The lazy path of least resistance is to let them do the paperwork. Is it any wonder that most lazy investors go broke!

Essential Seven: If you ever use a fancy formula or hard-to-describe condition in your contract, give an example or two of how you want that clause interpreted. Here's an example of what I mean. I once bought a two-bedroom condo from a motivated seller who was in the military and had been transferred. In order to sweeten the deal for the seller, I agreed to an equity split where a portion of the profits I earned when I resold the property would be paid back to the sellers (of course, I built in a "base profit" of $25,000 first, just like I told you earlier in the book—called a "hybrid equity split"). To make the paperwork clear, I made sure to list in the agreement an example of how this split would work. It said something like, "For example, if the Buyer resells the property for $200,000 then the Seller shall get paid the Option Price of $105,000 plus 12% of the amount over $130,000. In this case the Seller will get $105,000 plus 12% of $70,000." I think you get the idea. The key is to make it easy for a third party to understand how the deal works.

Protecting Yourself with Corporations and LLCs

"One very important thing to talk about," Dave continued, "is how you can make sure you protect yourself from liability as an investor. For better or for worse, as an investor you are a high-profile target in the eyes of the world."* David paused as he said this, letting the gravity of situation sink in.

---

*To learn the five most important asset protection strategies for real estate investors, log onto **www.InvestorFasttrack.com.**

"Whether it be from a tenant getting hurt in one of your rental units or from a contractor who falls off a ladder and wants to sue you, as the owner of a real estate investing business you want to make sure you operate your business behind the liability shield of a properly set up and maintained entity like a corporation or limited liability company."

"I think it's important that you get good legal and accounting help to get the right entity set up for your situation.* If you were to ask me which is the best entity for the average investor, I would give you two simple answers. In fact, I'm about to share the bottom-line distillation of the past 10 years of my investing, mixed with the experiences of our 100,000 investor clients. While this won't be perfect for everyone and every situation, it will work for 90 percent of you 90 percent of the time, which makes it a pretty darn useful starting point for now.

"First, if you plan on buying and holding for the long term, then the entity for 90-plus percent of you is a limited liability company (LLC). Most of you have heard about LLCs. They are the simplest and most effective way for most investors to structure their investing business. The key advantage you get with an LLC is great liability protection. To get this protection it's important that you have more than one member of the LLC. A member is simply the equivalent of a stockholder of a corporation. The members are the owners of the LLC. While you can have a single-member LLC, I advise you to have at least two owners of the LLC, because there have been recent court decisions that have let creditors pierce the liability shield of single-member LLCs. In essence a two-member LLC is a partnership, and this leads to the next advantage— you can have your LLC taxed as a partnership. This means that profits and losses flow through to you and each year the partnership files a simple tax return. I don't want to get caught up in the tax implications; for the moment, just know that being taxed as a partnership for an investing business that buys and holds is a good thing.

"If you are planning to buy and then immediately resell, then you may be better off with a corporation. The reason to create a corporation for an investment business that buys and immediately resells property rather than an LLC is to best

---

*For a great book on the basics of tax strategy for real estate investors, make sure you read my good friend and mastermind partner Diane Kennedy's outstanding book, *Insider's Guide to Real Estate Investing Loopholes*. Also, listen to a special interview with me and Diane where I pick her brain on the "Seven Most Powerful Real Estate Loopholes." To get instant access to this unique interview, just go to **www.InvestorFasttrack.com**.

handle a few serious tax consequences of buying and immediately reselling. This is one to have a long heart-to-heart with your CPA about over lunch to get her counsel, but make sure you ask her about the tax advantages of a corporation over an LLC when quickly turning the real estate you are acquiring.

"Now it might seem like a lot of effort to set up an LLC or a corporation, or for some of you even both, and having to observe certain formalities, but the liability protection of doing business in the name of a corporation or LLC is more than worth the effort. It will impact how you draw up agreements with buyers, sellers, and tenants. For example, when you're drafting a promissory note for an owner-carry deal you are buying, make sure you don't list your name as the borrower. Instead list the corporation or LLC as the borrower, and make sure that on the signature line you sign as a corporate officer and not as an individual. Here's what the signature line will look like." David turned and wrote on the board:

John Smith, Manager of Action Homes, LLC

"For those of you who have more questions about what entities are best for you or how you can layer in more protection, make sure you ask them during the question-and-answer session later tonight."

The Eight Key Contract Clauses When Buying an Investment Property

In real estate you need a set of "standard" contracts to use when you are buying and a second set to use when you are selling. Your contracts should be carefully prepared by your attorney to cover you as the buyer when you are buying and to cover you as the seller when you are selling.

Here are eight key clauses you need in your purchase agreement when you are buying a property. Make sure you go over this list before you sit down and meet with a seller so that you understand what you are asking for. You can also use this list as a checklist when you are having your attorney draft your contracts, so that you save lots of money and protect yourself when you are buying.

(continued)

The Eight Key Contract Clauses When Buying an Investment Property *(continued)*

Clause One: Liquidated Damages Clause

A liquidated damages clause is critical to minimizing your risk because it lets you contain the cost of walking away from a deal. When you enter into a contract with another party, you both have the right to expect the other party to perform everything that was mutually agreed to in the contract. If one party doesn't do what they agreed to do, the other party may sue for *"specific performance."* This means that they ask a court to make the defaulting party live up to the terms in the contract.

When you are buying real estate and you sign an agreement to buy a property, you want to be able to walk away from the deal if, after doing your due diligence, you discover something wrong with the deal. Now the way many investors give themselves this freedom is by using all sorts of "subject to" clauses in their agreements with the seller. For example, "This agreement is subject to Buyer's inspection and approval of the property." Or, "This agreement is subject to Buyer obtaining satisfactory financing." You get the picture.

If you were a seller and your buyer showed you paperwork with all kinds of these overt escape clauses, would you feel confident that you had a real buyer? That's where a liquidated damages clause comes into play. It accomplishes the same thing as an escape clause, provided it's used correctly, without arousing seller concerns about your commitment as a buyer.

A liquidated damages clause merely spells out the exact payment one party must make to the other party in a contract should a default occur. When you're buying a property, you use a liquidated damages clause that spells out that if you as the buyer default (i.e., don't buy the property) then the seller gets to keep all the money you've paid to the seller so far as "full and complete liquidated damages." This sounds pretty strong and sellers like that, but remember, you are only giving the seller a token up-front payment.

Normally I use a single dollar. Some investors use up to $500. The key is to delay the payment of any serious up-front money until the point that you have done your due diligence and are sure you want the deal. (Preferably you will have already found your end user for the property before you ever give the seller any serious money, whether you put a tenant buyer in the property or are selling to a retail buyer for all cash.)

(continued)

The Eight Key Contract Clauses When Buying an Investment Property *(continued)*

Here's what the legalese version of a liquidated damages clause sounds like: *"In the event of default of Buyer, all money paid to Seller by Buyer shall be retained by the Seller as consideration for the execution of this contract and as agreed liquidated damages and in full settlement of any and all claims for damages."*

Clause Two: ". . . Or Assigns, Buyer"

Anytime you sign a deal to buy a property, you want to maintain maximum flexibility. You may want to buy and hold the property or you may decide to quickly resell the property for a fast cash profit. One important component to this flexibility to sell fast is the ability to assign your interests in the deal over to another party for a quick cash payment. While any contract is always assignable unless there is a clause in the contract limiting or forbidding the assignment of the contract, it still makes sense to clearly put in your agreement the fact that you can may assign the contract.

The best way to do this is to preprint into the contract the words "or assigns" right after the blank where you fill in who is the buyer. The reason you preprint it into the contract is because if you write it in by hand into the line of who the buyer is (e.g., "John Smith or assigns, Buyer") it calls it to the attention of the seller. Anything that is printed directly into the agreement flows smoothly past the seller and is usually accepted without comment.

If the contract that your seller wants you to use has a nonassignment clause, make sure you cross out this clause and both you and the seller initial the change.

Clause Three: The Closing Date and Closing Agent

Controlling the closing is critical for your success when buying (or selling for that matter). You always want to be the one who gets to control who will be doing the closing so that you can make sure they do it in a way you are comfortable with. That's why I recommend you always reserve the right to be able to choose who the closing agent will be. Also, when you are buying, you want to be able to have a degree of flexibility in case you need a little extra time to finish getting your financing together, find your renter for the property, or just to do other preparation for the closing. You can accomplish both these things by using the following clause:

"Closing shall be held on or about _____ unless extended by no more than 60 days by either party in writing. Closing shall be at a time and place designated by Buyer, who shall choose the escrow, title, and/or closing agent."

(continued)

The Eight Key Contract Clauses When Buying an Investment Property *(continued)*

Clause Four: Get Access to the Property and Permission to Start Your Marketing *Before* You Close

Why wait to get started on marketing the property to your end user? Maybe you'll want to rent out the place, or even sell it on a rent-to-own basis. Either way, one of the best ways to reduce your risk in any deal is to have a nonrefundable earnest money or rental deposit from your end user before you ever close on the property. But to do this you need access to show the property and ideally permission to put your marketing sign in the front yard while you are waiting to close. Now I can hear some of you saying that the seller will get upset that you are selling it for more than they sold it to you for. Of course you are selling it for more! I sit down and make sure every seller understands that the reason I am willing to buy their property is because I want to make a profit. I also tell them that if they don't feel the deal we've agreed to is a real win-win for them, then we shouldn't do it. If you are up front with the seller, they will be happy when you win too. Remember, you aren't buying from just any seller. You are buying from a *motivated* seller who has a specific need or problem you are helping to solve.

Here's what the legalese version of this clause looks like:

"Buyer shall be entitled to a key and access to the property prior to closing to show partners, lenders, inspectors, contractors, and other interested parties prior to closing. Buyer may place a sign on the property prior to closing to help Buyer find end user for the property." (Be aware, if the seller still lives in the house and it's not empty, then usually, rather than him giving you a key, you simply arrange to bring any interested parties, whether they be prospective buyers or renters or contractors, over at a time when he can leave the house for a few hours and take the kids to a movie or to the park.)

Clause Five: Execution in Counterparts—How to Sign Together Even When You're Miles Apart

Let's say you are working with an out-of-town owner who really wants to dump their property. Do they have to fly out to sign the purchase contract with you? Not if you are smart enough to use a clause like this one that lets you lock up the property with a signature signed on a separate copy of the agreement that you can fax, e-mail, or overnight to the seller and that they fax or overnight (preferably both) back to you.

"Execution in Counterparts: This agreement may be executed in counterparts and by facsimile signatures. This agreement becomes effective as of the date of the last signature."

(continued)

The Eight Key Contract Clauses When Buying an Investment Property (continued)

Clause Six: The World's Best Inspection Clause

Check out this inspection clause. It not only clarifies that everything should be working in the property and that the seller will pay for any needed repairs prior to closing, but it also says that unless otherwise noted you get all the personal property—read curtains and appliances and such things, too. It also comes with a guarantee from the seller that survives the closing that everything is in working order when you buy. Now I know I'm getting pretty excited over this clause, but after using it for close to a decade now I am very partial to it. (One thing to be clear on is that if you are buying a fixer-upper for a low, low cash price, then you are going to have to modify this clause in most cases, since part of the reason you are getting a great cash price is the fact that you are going to be responsible to do the repairs to fix the place up.)

Here's the clause: *"Buyer or his agent may inspect all appliances, air conditioning and heating systems, electrical systems, plumbing, machinery, sprinklers, and pool system included in the sale. Seller shall pay for repairs necessary to place such items in working order at the time of closing. Within 48 hours before closing, Buyer shall be entitled, upon reasonable notice to Seller, to inspect the premises to determine that said items are in working order. Unless specifically excluded in this agreement, all other items of personal property located in or on the property shall be included in the sale and shall be transferred by Bill of Sale with warranty of title. Seller expressly warrants that property, improvements, buildings or structures, the appliances, roof, plumbing, heating and/or ventilation/air conditioning systems are in good and working order. This clause shall survive closing of title."*

Clause Seven: Automatic Renewal or Extension of Note

Many times when you are structuring owner-carry deals, the seller won't want to have to wait for 30 years to get all of his money. In these cases using a balloon note works wonders. A balloon note is a loan that has a clause saying that the unpaid balance all becomes due at some future date. For example, I recently bought a four-bedroom house where the seller carried back the financing with a five-year balloon due for the balance of the note. This meant that I paid the seller monthly interest payments and at some point within five years of closing I must pay off the balance of the loan. This is called a balloon payment. Typically it's paid by either reselling or refinancing the property.

(continued)

The Eight Key Contract Clauses When Buying an Investment Property *(continued)*

Obviously, as an investor, the more time you have before that balloon note comes due the more flexibility you have. But there are situations where the seller won't give you as much time as you would like. The best way to handle these types of sellers is *indirectly*. Don't argue with them and butt heads; instead, agree to go along with them. Then later in the negotiations, simply ask for either a one-time or two-time renewal of the term of the loan, or for an extension if you need it.

Here's the way to ask the seller for this. "Mr. Seller, I'm okay with a balloon note of four years. That should be enough time for me to still conservatively make a profit here. But I would like to have as a worst-case scenario the ability to renew the loan one time. Obviously I'd have to have paid you on time every month and all that. Does this seem fair with you?" If the seller won't give you a renewal, ask for the right to extend for 24 to 36 months. (Use months here, not years—it seems much shorter to most sellers.) Even if you only get the seller to agree to a one-time extension of 12 months, that is still one year more on the note than you had before! If worse comes to worst, offer to pay the seller a payment of a few thousand dollars to extend the note. If you do use this idea make sure you spell out that this payment is of principal (i.e., it counts toward the money you would have had to pay the seller anyway!). The time to ask and to get it in writing is up front, *not* at the end of the loan.

Here's an example of what the legalese version could look like: *"Borrower may renew this note for __ additional terms by paying to Note Holder $_____ of principal on or before 30 days prior to the date all sums in this promissory note are due to be paid in full."*

Clause Eight: Substitution of Collateral

Another clause you should consider asking for in your seller-carry deals is called "substitution of collateral." Imagine you are buying a $200,000 house and the seller carries a second mortgage of $50,000 at 7.5 percent interest. You want to sell that house but don't want to want to lose out on the low-interest use of the $50,000. If you have a substitution of collateral clause in your loan agreement with the seller, you can move that low-interest second mortgage of $50,000 over and secure it against another property you have that has enough equity in it to be fair to the seller. Again, you don't have to use this clause, but it does give you maximum flexibility.

(continued)

The Eight Key Contract Clauses When Buying an Investment Property (continued)

Here's the legalese version: *"Note Holder agrees to allow Borrower to substitute any property(ies) in which the Borrower has a total amount of equity equal to or greater than the amount of equity as existed to secure this note at the time this note was created, as collateral for this promissory note and accompanying Deed of Trust. Furthermore, Note Holder agrees to execute in a timely manner any documents necessary for the implementation of this substitution of collateral."* *

*To download a free ebook with 7 more key contract clauses I didn't have room to include in the book, just log onto **www.InvestorFasttrack.com** and click on the "FREE eBooks" button.

The Ten Paperwork Pitfalls

Pitfall One: Signing Naked

Signing naked means investing without the liability protection of a corporation or limited liability company. For better or for worse, investors have a high-profile bull's-eye painted on their financial chests that is a tempting target for a slew of potential litigants to try to take some of your hard-earned wealth. The most important step you can take to protect yourself is to always do your investing behind the financial shield of a properly maintained incorporated company or limited liability company.

The key is to make sure that you always list your company's name in any official paperwork, and when you sign make sure you sign on behalf of the company, either as an officer, member, or manager of that company. As I like to say at my workshops, "Never sign naked!"

Pitfall Two: Taking Title with a Quit Claim Deed

A deed is simply the piece of paper that says who owns a property. It's the document used to transfer title (i.e., ownership) of a property from one party to another party. Depending on what type of deed you get when buying a property, you either get a big, little, or no warranty with your purchase.

(continued)

The Ten Paperwork Pitfalls *(continued)*

It's kind of like buying a car. You can either buy it with a full-blown maintenance protection plan, with a limited warranty, or with no warranty at all. When you buy a property and get title transferred to you, you want to use the form of the deed that gives you the maximum warranties possible as to the quality of title you are getting with that property. In most states this means using a "warranty" deed or "general warranty" deed. Or, if you live in the western half of the United States, this typically will mean using a "Grant" deed or "Grant, Bargain, and Sale" deed. These types of deeds come with some useful protections that you are in fact getting clear title to the property you are buying. (More on this in a moment.)

A "Quit Claim Deed" is the weakest form of a deed you can use. In effect it says, "Hey, I may or may not actually have an interest in this property . . . but if I do have an interest, and I'm not saying I do, then I am transferring that interest over to you." Doesn't exactly inspire you with confidence, does it?

The bottom line is, whenever you are getting title to a property, make sure you use the best form of deed your state will allow, and usually this will be a warranty or grant deed.*

Pitfall Three: Missing the Exclusions to the Title Insurance Policies

Title insurance is a form of protection buyers and lenders use to make sure that they are covered when buying or lending on a property. Title insurance protects you or your lender from past breaks in the chain of title, or other problems that may prevent you from actually having clean, unchallenged ownership rights to a property. In effect, it's an insurance against any past event that may in fact cause you (or the seller who sold the property to you) not to have clear ownership to the property you just bought. In essence, the title insurance company researched at the land records office to make sure you are in fact getting clear title to the property, and they are giving a limited guarantee that you are in fact getting "marketable" title to that property.

As with *any* insurance policy, the single most important place to look at with careful attention is the "exclusions." These are the listed exceptions that are not covered by the title insurance policy. Basically what the title insurance company does is research the chain of title and then list out any potential problems they spot as "exceptions" to the policy. It's almost like a health insurance company doing an exhaustive physical on you and then saying they'll cover you, except for heart disease, cancer, or random car accidents.

*Not sure which type of deed to use in your state? Just log onto **www.InvestorFasttrack.com** for a FREE state-by-state listing of which deed to use.

(continued)

The Ten Paperwork Pitfalls *(continued)*

The exclusions are where the title insurance company does its best to cover all its risk for things being wrong with the title.

Now you may wonder what good this does you then, since none of these exclusions are covered under the title policy. Well, you are really paying the title insurance company to do accurate and detailed research of the chain of title so that they can spot any potential problem areas that you need to examine closely. Common items you'll see in the exclusions section of your title insurance policy are things like property taxes for the current tax year, or previously recorded mortgages. You just want to make sure you are comfortable with everything they list as an exception to the policy.

For example, on one house I bought several years ago, there was a $5,000 judgment recorded against the property from a car accident the seller had gotten into years earlier. The seller wasn't even aware (at least that's what they told me) that this judgment had been recorded against their property. When I saw this on the Preliminary Title Report, I made sure to clarify in our closing paperwork that this lien was to be paid off at closing from the money I was paying and that I was to get a signed release from the person the seller owed this money to showing that it was in fact paid off.

If there is some exclusion that you are not comfortable with listed on the Preliminary Title Report, then you'll either have to make sure to get the seller to take care of that problem prior to or at closing, or you may decide you need to back out of the deal altogether.*

Pitfall Four: Name Problems—Incorrect Spellings, Wrong Parties, and Missing Parties
Believe it or not, one of the most common contract pitfalls is getting the other party's name wrong in your agreements. Whether it be a purchase contract with a buyer in which you misspell their name or even forget to list a spouse on the contract, or a contract with a seller in which you list his name but didn't realize he holds title in a company or trust, it's critical that you check—letter by letter—that you have clearly listed the correct party you are intending to do business with on any and all agreements.

*Would you like me to *personally* walk you through step-by-step how to get a Preliminary Title Report for FREE and how to actually read the darn thing when you get it? Then just log onto **www.InvestorFasttrack.com** right away and click on the "Investor Training" button. This is just one of several free online training workshops available for a limited time to readers like you. For more details, see Appendix A.

(continued)

The Ten Paperwork Pitfalls (continued)

While usually any mistake can easily be corrected later, sometimes a simple oversight can be incredibly costly. I remember one 10-year lease option on a two-bedroom condo where I only had the husband sign the "Residential Lease Option Agreement" and not his wife. Months later, after I had already found a tenant buyer for the property, this seller said his wife never agreed to the deal and that he wanted to back out. We ended up settling out of court, but the whole mess could have been avoided if I had simply made sure to have triple-checked that all the parties I needed to sign did. Ultimately that one mistake cost me over $125,000 in lost profits!

Pitfall Five: Ignoring or Procrastinating Doing the Paperwork
Without question, the single biggest reason that investors get sloppy or lazy in their paperwork is because they are either time challenged or fearful.

Time-challenged investors claim they don't have the time to accurately paper their trail in their real estate deal. They foolishly say to themselves that they'll remember all the details of the deal. I used to think so, too. And for deal one and two and three it was easy to keep things straight. But when I got to deal 20 and then to deal 30 it got to be much harder to remember what I had agreed to unless it was meticulously documented in my files. Oh sure, I saved precious minutes in those early years trusting to my memory, but I ultimately lost days and days trying to re-create the agreements and track down third parties and get them to sign necessary documentation later.

In the early years, the real reason I didn't always do all the needed paperwork was because I was scared. I was afraid that by asking the other party to sign all those detailed follow-up documents, I would kill the deal. But now I know that when it's done properly, people respect you for being someone who looks after the details. Anyway, if carefully clarifying a deal on paper is going to kill the deal, trust me when I tell you that you are better off with that deal dead *up front*, versus after you've put a year or two or more of work and potentially money into it.

I've also seen many new investors skip paperwork and documentation because they're scared of not knowing how to do it, or even uncertain about exactly what paperwork needs to be done. I know that in the past, with our Mentorship Program students who had deals, before we teamed up with a private deal servicing company to help our students get all the correct paperwork done for any real estate deal and facilitate the closing with local title companies, most of our students buried their heads in the sand and ignored the need for the documents that we coached them to get filled out.

(continued)

The Ten Paperwork Pitfalls *(continued)*

It was only when we started having this amazing company actually *do* the bulk of the work organizing and taking the lead with the deal paperwork that students began to consistently get it done—accurately and timely. This simple relationship made our students millions of dollars. It may very well be a smart move on your part to pay a third party to facilitate your deal paperwork. The costs are nominal in comparison to the savings of time and energy, as well as the added protection you get in your deals when you properly prepare all your paperwork.*

Whether you do all your own deal paperwork, or pay a third party to help you get it done, I have learned one very crucial lesson in all my years of investing, namely, that the time to take care of *all* the paperwork is at the beginning of the deal. Sure, it may take a few days or even a few weeks to organize and finalize it all, but the peace of mind and security it will give you is worth every effort.

I've always believed that the best way to learn is from other people's pain, so hear me out on this one. I have made millions of dollars with real estate. Yet I've also lost out on millions of dollars of profits over the years from deals that fell apart because I got too busy or too scared to properly take care of the paperwork. But hey, what do I know, right? Paperwork, schmaper-work, who needs it!

Pitfall Six: Not Knowing When to Record Documents and When to Keep Documents from Being Recorded

Recording a document on the public record is a way to "stake your claim" on a property. It means to take a notarized signed copy with the accurate legal description of the property down to your local county recorder's or land records office and get a copy of the document onto the public records. This process, called *recording* a document, is a simple and cheap way to protect yourself in many real estate deals. But many naive investors make mistakes because they don't understand when to record and when not to record a document relevant to a deal they are working on.

When to Record: Whenever you want to tie up a property or lock in your interest in a deal, make sure you record a document against the property. For example, if you have just had a motivated seller agree to sell you a $500,000 property for $275,000 in an all-cash closing, make sure you record a Memorandum of Agreement against the property so that the seller doesn't turn around and try to sell the property to a second investor for more money.

*To learn more about using a deal servicing company like the one Mentorship students do, just go to **www.InvestorFasttrack.com** and click on the "Investor Resources" button.

(continued)

The Ten Paperwork Pitfalls *(continued)*

Or if you sell a house and carry back a second mortgage, make sure you record your lien against the property so that you establish the priority of your mortgage on the chain of title. Any later lien against the property that the seller gets, either intentionally or unintentionally, will now fall after your lien of the recorded second mortgage. (The rule is "first to record is first in line on the priority on the chain of title.")

When *Not* to Record: Anytime you do *not* want to create a cloud or lien on the title. For example, when you allow a tenant buyer to rent with the option to buy one of your houses, your option paperwork with your tenant buyer should specifically prohibit your tenant buyer from recording the option and clouding title to your property. This way if you have to evict your tenant for not paying his rent, you don't have to go through a court action to get clear title back to your property. (That's why the option agreement that Mentorship students use specifically *prohibits* a tenant buyer from recording it.)

Pitfall Seven: Forgetting Common Sense. Be Clear, Be Reasonable, and *Always* Write for the Judge!
The **three most important "commonsense" investor rules** are as follows.

One: Be clear in your agreements. Who is agreeing to do what? By when? What standards are you agreeing to so that you will know if the actions each party takes really do meet the commitments? What happens if one side defaults? Have you clearly identified the key terms and people in the agreement?

Two: Be reasonable in your agreements. Sure, you can put everything and the kitchen sink in your contracts, but if your real estate agreements are too one-sided most judges will not allow you to enforce the contract, determining that the contract is "unconscionable," which is a fancy term that means way too unfair. While you should make sure you the investor are covered in all your agreements, make sure you don't get carried away gaining concessions from the other party. Here are some examples of unreasonable terms in an agreement:

- If you sold a house and carried back part of the purchase price as a second mortgage, it would be unreasonable to double the loan payment if your borrower was late making her payment. (It *would* be fair to charge a 6 percent late payment penalty if she was more than 10 or 15 days late.)

- If you are buying a "junker" house for 50 cents on the dollar of the as-is price, it would not be reasonable to make the seller pay for all the repairs for the property. Just about any judge who looked at an agreement like that would find it too one-sided.

(continued)

The Ten Paperwork Pitfalls (continued)

Bottom-line reasonability test: Is the deal fair and a win-win to both parties? It is perfectly reasonable to have you make a lot of money on a deal just as long as you really are taking care of the main need or needs of the other party at the same time.

Three: Always remember you are writing for the judge. It's a mistake to think that you are writing your real estate agreements to remind yourself what you agreed to. The real person you should write all your paper trail for is for a judge who is looking at the paperwork to determine exactly what you and the other party agreed to, without you or the other party being able to explain your side of things. If you keep this firmly in mind you'll develop some powerful long-term "papering" skills that will help increase your peace of mind and minimize misunderstandings with people you do business with.

Pitfall Eight: Thinking the Legal System Runs on Common Sense
I know this one is 180 degrees opposite to pitfall seven, but such is the life of a real estate investor. The legal system plays by its own rules, many of which are arbitrary and fly in the face of common sense. Early on, one of the things I had to learn the hard way was just because two parties had agreed to a contract in writing didn't mean that was the way a contract would actually work in the real world. For example, when I first got started with my investing I thought that just because the lease said that if my tenant didn't pay me by 5 P.M. on the first of the month I could start an eviction, that that's the way it would work. Well, I remember when I learned that in some states by law you are required to wait five days before you start your eviction proceedings, regardless of what your lease agreement with your tenant says.

Or, just because a seller says he will sell you a house he has that is in foreclosure doesn't mean you can buy it. In some states there are laws that require you to give sellers a 5- or 10-day right of recision (i.e., a chance to change their minds) even if they end up losing the house to a sale at auction as a result of this waiting period. This is all just part of the game.

Pitfall Nine: Thinking a Real Estate Closing Will Go Perfectly (Ha!)
It's tempting to think that the closing will go just the way you planned it, but rarely will it! I've learned that no matter how many times I ask the title company or lender if they have everything they need from me, there is almost always at least one other document that I will need to rush to them at the last minute to keep a real estate closing on track.

(continued)

The Ten Paperwork Pitfalls *(continued)*

I used to let this stress me because I thought it wasn't supposed to be that way. Now I just laugh it off because I know that most real estate closings will take one to four weeks longer than I expected and require a little finesse and effort to make them close. This includes closings when you are buying or selling or even when you are simply refinancing a property. Sure, I'm pleasantly surprised from time to time, but rarely.

My advice to you? Expect that it will take longer to close than you thought and that you'll need to set aside a few hours to get last-minute paperwork over to the closing to make sure it stays on track. Nine times out of ten you won't be disappointed. And remember, it's all a game anyway! Which brings us to our final pitfall . . .

Pitfall Ten: Thinking You'll Never Be Fluent in the "Real Estate Speak"
For those of you who think you'll never be able to actually get all this investing terminology or paperwork, just relax. Here's my belief—if you are capable of learning the rules of baseball (or any other sport or game), then you can become competent in real estate vocabulary and contracts.

The key is to remember that the rules are arbitrary. There is no absolute source of legal doctrine. It's nothing more than the accumulated combination of laws plus the way the courts have interpreted those laws over the years.

Some of those things are easy to understand, like "after three strikes you're out." This might be the equivalent of a real estate contract needing three elements—an offer, acceptance of that offer, and something of value (aka "consideration") changing hands.

Sometimes the rule may be a bit hard to understand at first, like if a foul tip is counted as a strike, why can't you strike out with a foul tip? For example, in states that have "community property" rights, even if a spouse of your seller is not on the deed, he or she still most likely has an interest in the property and will need to agree to the sale of the property to make the deal go through.

The point I'm trying to make is, don't waste effort looking for "why" the rules are the way they are, or, even worse, waste energy moaning that the laws *shouldn't* be that way. Leave that one to the legal scholars. Just accept that the rules are what they are, and you'll find they're not too hard to pick up and understand. Just by spending time around the game of real estate you can't help but learn the jargon and rules fairly quickly.

Middle Stage Level Two Investing— Fine-Tuning Skills and Leveraging Your Time

CHAPTER EIGHT

First Steps to Building a Profitable Investing Business

In the next segment of the workshop, David began, "I want to give you a snapshot of what it's like when you're a Middle Stage Level Two investor. First, you'll probably notice that you feel a sense of energy and well-being. We call this the 'investor's high.' This feeling is familiar to those of you who work out regularly. It's the feeling of energy you get after putting in a good day's work because you are now fluent and competent as an investor. You find a real satisfaction from doing your investing because it finally all makes sense. You know how to work with sellers in a variety of situations. You're able to deal with a problem tenant without it spoiling your day. You're comfortable collecting big checks from real estate closings and the large amounts don't intimidate you anymore.

"As a Middle Stage Level Two investor you are fluent in all five of the core investor skills. You can take a deal and work it smoothly from start to finish, troubleshooting as needed. With this competence comes the confidence to jump on good deals fast.

"At the front edge of Middle Stage Level Two investing you are still working to fine-tune your five core investor skills, but at this point it is much more about making small *refinements* than it is about developing these skills from scratch. As you transition through Middle Stage Level Two investing, you develop ways to leverage yourself in your investing business by building systems and growing your investing team. You tentatively let go of pieces of your investing business to free your time to focus on those parts of your business that earn you the greatest return for your time and energy invested. You hire on a full- or part-time assistant, outsource your bookkeeping, and perhaps even hire someone to show your properties for you, ideally on a commission basis where you only pay for results.

"It's at this point that you either make the crucial shift to begin to leverage yourself by growing your investing business or you get caught in the daily grind of being the sole producer for the business. Over the years I've met many mom-and-pop investors who have gotten caught in this trap. Granted, it's still worlds better for them than for the average noninvestor who ends up financially dependent on others, but still, it's a far cry from the true financial freedom that sparked their investing to begin with. I call this trap the 'Small Time Bubble.'

"The reason that many Middle Stage Level Two investors get trapped by the Small Time Bubble is that they never learn to separate their business from themselves. Refining your skills and leveraging your time can make you an extremely successful Middle Stage Level Two investor, but ultimately to break out of the Small Time Bubble you will need to build an investing business that has a life beyond just you.

"We'll be talking about how to grow your investing business and break out of the Small Time Bubble later, but for the moment it is critical for you to understand that if your business is dependent on you then you'll always be required to show up. Also, unless you break out of the Small Time Bubble and build a successful investing business that extends beyond you, you will be limiting both the volume and size of the deals you can handle.

"Now I know I am really emphasizing that point, but it's also important to recognize that it takes time to grow and develop your investing business. It is healthy and necessary to go through the Middle Stage Level Two investing period as you develop and grow as an investor. This stage will actually help you develop the business-building and investing muscles that you'll need as you move on your way to being a Level Three investor.

"As a Middle Stage Level Two investor you are the central hub around which you are beginning to build the pieces of a viable real estate investing business. Chances are you are the one driving the business, negotiating the deals, and directing who does what. The biggest difference between a Middle Stage Level Two and an Advanced Stage Level Two investor is that in the Middle Stage you are building the business to complement *your* skills and to leverage *your* investing efforts. But because you are the hub around which your investing business revolves, if you aren't there to actively work, your Middle Stage Level Two business will grind to a halt. Later, when you transition to Advanced Stage Level Two investing, you will work to replace yourself in your investing business altogether. At that point your focus will fundamentally shift from inward focus on yourself to outward focus on your investing business. But we'll talk more about the Advanced Stage later. For the moment, let's focus on Middle Stage Level Two investing."

The Four Biggest Pitfalls for Middle Stage Level Two Investors

Pitfall One: "I can do it better than anyone else."

One of the biggest barriers to your successfully leveraging yourself by getting staff and outside vendors to take ownership of parts of your investing business is the myth that you can do it better than anyone else. You could hire someone to do your bookkeeping, *but* no one does it as well as you. You could hire someone to do the minor repairs on the Baker Street property, *but* the last time you did the guy messed up the job so you better just do it yourself this time. You could hire an assistant to help you around the office, *but* no assistant would ever be able to do things just the way you like best.

Hanging on to the belief that you can do it better than anyone else is just too expensive. Not only does it strictly limit the amount of business you can handle, but it *guarantees* that you'll never earn the freedom from having to actively participate in your investing business. Sure, you may be able to do much of the business better than most other people, but if you can't learn to cultivate the ability to intelligently let go, piece by piece, you'll never truly be financially free since your business will require that you show up to work each day. Plus, do you really have the time to do all those parts of your business as well as you think you can? Or do you really let many of them slide because you just don't feel like you have the time to do them?

Personally, I believe that when you learn to build simple yet powerful business systems, then other people *can* do it as well as you, and many times even better than you. Also, when you hire team members whose skills and natural aptitudes complement your own, you find niche players who are better suited to give all of their attention to their specialty area. Besides, even if you could do everything better, many parts of your investing business don't need to be done to perfection. Sometimes "good enough" really is.

The Four Biggest Pitfalls for Middle Stage Level Two Investors
(continued)

Ultimately, if you're not willing to let go of parts of your investing business so you can incrementally build a business that stands alone and works better without you there every day doing the work, then you'll never become a Level Three investor, nor will you enjoy a Level Three life.

Pitfall Two: "I can't afford to hire help or outside services."
If you are constantly being pulled back to do $10 to $30 an hour work like organizing your property files or cleaning a house to prepare it for a showing, how can you earn the big money that you really desire? The only way to earn $100 an hour, or $1,000 an hour, is for you to consistently let go of the lower-value work to staff or outside vendors so that you free up more of your time to invest in the highest-payoff pieces of your business.

When you meet with a motivated seller about buying their property and in two hours you sign a contract on a house with a $100,000 profit, you are making thousands of dollars an hour with your time. This is where you need to be spending your time as a Middle Stage Level Two investor—signing deals with motivated sellers, sitting down with qualified buyers, collecting hefty option payments or earnest money deposits, and cultivating relationships with sources of private money to fund your deals or people to refer you deals. But the only way you'll make the time to spend on these high-leverage activities is by building systems and handing off the lower-level work that right now is flowing to you by default.

Pitfall Three: "I'm too busy to build systems."
When I first began to build business systems to make my real estate businesses run more smoothly, I struggled with the frustration that to systematize a repeated activity in the business meant that I had to take three to five times longer to do that task. I made excuses, saying that I was just too busy. But eventually I learned that it was worth it to take the time to build business systems up front in order to get the repeated activities of my real estate business done in a consistently excellent fashion. Peter was a great influence on me here. He's always been committed to building business systems that get results, even at times when I wanted to skip this step in my urgency to "just get things done." The real payoff comes over the course of time because this simple focus on building business systems will save you hundreds of hours of effort and make the biggest difference in helping you transition to become a Level Three investor.

(continued)

The Four Biggest Pitfalls for Middle Stage Level Two Investors
(continued)

Pitfall Four: "I'm too scared to build a hugely successful investing business." If you are truly being honest with yourself, for most people the real root of all three of the earlier pitfalls is fear. Whether it's the fear of letting go and trusting someone else to own a part of your business, or the fear that you can't afford to hire someone, or even the fear that you just don't have the time or ability to build business systems, the bottom line is that the first three pitfalls happen when you let fear stop you from taking your investing business to the next level.

Remember that control is really an illusion anyway. Control is a chain that anchors you to your business day in and day out. Unless you intelligently find a way to leverage yourself through outside vendors, business systems, and a skilled team, you will never be free from your business's insatiable demands that you show up to work each day.

Or maybe for you the deeper fear is the fear of failure. You ask yourself, what if your success to date was a fluke and it stops working for you so you don't have enough money to afford to hire out and build an investing business? Or maybe you're scared that if you let go of parts of your business you won't really be able to find higher-value activities and projects to focus your energy on. Or that while you could find these activities, they scare you and you'd rather hide behind lower-value tasks.

So what's the cure to all this fear? It is simple. The antidote to fear is faith, and the way to develop faith is to repeatedly get yourself to take the steps you are scared to take, even though you can't help but be terrified as you are taking those steps! Learn to take action in the presence of your fears.

CHAPTER NINE

How to Leverage Your Time as an Investor for Maximum Profit

"**A**s a Middle Stage Level Two investor, leveraging yourself is critical," David said. "Since you are the key driver to your investing business at this stage, the more production you can get out of yourself for your investing business, the more profitable your investing will be and the faster your investing business will grow.

"The first leverage point for your investing business is your individual skills. It's the shortcuts you've learned and the known pitfalls you are able to avoid. And the fastest way to build your knowledge base is to combine the best input and coaching from outside mentors with consistent action on your part implementing your mentors' ideas and strategies. What have you all found to be the most effective learning strategies for your investing skills so far in your investing?" David asked the class.

Mary raised her hand and said, "For me it's been the weekly feedback from the Mentorship coaching call sessions. I've found it so helpful to be able to get fast answers to my questions plus learn from all the other questions and experiences from other students on the coaching calls." Mary paused for a moment, then continued, "But I don't think these calls would have made such a huge impact for me if it wasn't for the fact that I was immersed in this stuff every day. It made the learning so much more real to actually be out in the field doing it. Plus I was so much more motivated to learn because I knew I'd be in a situation where I'd have to know the information."

"Great point," David said. "Anybody else have something to share on this?"

"For me David," Mark said, "it was the role-playing at the Intensive Training. It gave me the initial boost I needed, almost like using a flight simulator when I was first getting trained as a pilot. And now, I find the weekly mastermind meetings* I attend are the essential piece. I get held accountable for my actions and get weekly feedback from outside partners who I respect and listen to. It's really hard to see myself and my business accurately, and they can give me the objective feedback I need."

"What a critical piece," David said. "To really refine your investor skills you need not only consistent practice, but objective feedback. This can come from a mentor or from a mastermind team. Ideally you'll have both.

"Speaking of mastermind groups and mentors, another key leverage point for you to get more from less is by leveraging the contacts and efforts of other people. For example, you could leverage the work that your mastermind partner has already put in to find the best price on marketing materials for your business. Or you could leverage your mentor's contact list to find the best accountants or attorneys to work with.

"So just what investor skills are the most powerful for you to leverage as a Middle Stage Level Two investor? In my opinion it's the five core investor skills, because they are the hardest skills to hire out and the skills you'll use over and over in every real estate deal. Also, a weakness in any one of these five core areas will cost your investing business big-time.

"If I had to pick just one of the five core skills that is the most valuable to master, it's the skill of negotiation that will ultimately earn you the most money. In my opinion, it's the highest paid skill you have as an investor."

Nancy raised her hand, "But David, I love the numbers part of real estate. Why can't I just find someone to go out and do all the negotiating with buyers and sellers for me? Why do I have to get good at it at all?"

---

*For a Three-Step Power Format to run your real estate mastermind groups, see *Buying Real Estate without Cash or Credit* (pp. 153–154). Also, download the FREE ebook, *How to Build a Successful Mastermind Team*, available at **www.InvestorFasttrack.com.**

David shook his head. "Of all the skills that your investing business will need, negotiation is probably the very hardest skill for you to hire out. Why? Well, if you are doing many of your deals without your cash or credit, and you had someone else negotiating all your deals, what do you think this person would quickly do?" David asked.

Nancy answered, "Do the deals themselves."

"Exactly. Look, as an Advanced Stage Level Two investor you'll eventually have other people and systems find your deals. And you'll have systems and teams to oversee the management of the deals. You'll even be able to get the people to handle the sale or leasing of your deals fairly easily. But one of the toughest challenges you'll have is to find someone to negotiate your deals up front with sellers. Eventually you'll be able to do that by incentivizing the right person with a stake in the profits or with the right bonus incentives, but as a Middle Stage Level Two investor, it will be you doing the negotiating, so you might as well master the skill."

"David," Tim asked, "I can understand why I need to learn to be a master negotiator. I get that. But I hate all the back-office paperwork and organization stuff, especially the due diligence nitty-gritty details. Why should I even bother learning it, why not just pay someone else to do it for me?"

David answered, "Over time you shouldn't be doing it yourself. It makes a ton of sense to get other people to do it for you. It's just important for you to have a clear grasp of the basics so that you can intelligently hire and manage this part of your business. The idea here is that as a Middle Stage Level Two investor, you want to build your business so that you are only doing those parts that you love and are best at, with teams, systems, and outsourced solutions handling all the rest. This is exactly what I meant when I said that you want to leverage yourself as a Middle Stage Level Two investor. You do this first by leveraging your investor skills, then by leveraging your contacts, and finally by leveraging your team and business systems.

"But to effectively hire and train someone to take over a part of your business, or to outsource a part of your business, you still need to speak the language of that area of your business to make sure that the transition happens the right way. Also, to effectively manage the person or company that's managing that part of your business, you will need to have a clear, fundamental understanding of that area of your investing business. And when we talk about building a business system, it's even more important for you to know the basics about these 'forgotten' areas of your business."

Leveraging Your Time as an Investor for Maximum Profit

The key to leveraging your time as an investor is to focus with absolute clarity on the areas of your business that give you the highest return for your investment of time and energy. Constantly ask yourself, "What's the best and highest use of my time right now?"

If you find yourself doing tasks that you could pay someone else $10 or $20 per hour to do, how in the world are you going to earn $100 or $200 per hour, let alone $1,000 or $2,000 per hour?

Look at where your time goes each day and each week. Every day, find a way to delegate, delete, delay, or outsource one more of the repetitive activities you find yourself focused on doing.

Delegate It! Let one of your team members take over this activity. For example, let your assistant organize your files of property documents. Let your bookkeeper keep track of rental deposits.

Delete It! Don't do it at all. Why return that call from a vendor who you never asked to call you? Why tell your tenant that you would help them find a moving company to buy boxes from? You get the idea. If the activity doesn't move you toward your goals, then remember the magic word is *no*!

Delay It! If it's a low-priority item then maybe just let it go for a few days or weeks while you focus on more important things. You could always keep it on your "someday" list. Learning to procrastinate the *right* activities is a prime success skill.

Outsource It! Can an outside vender do it for you cheaper, faster, simpler, better? If the answer is yes, let them take it on (and let your assistant manage the outsourced relationship for you). For example, turn over the pre-showing preparation of a property to a cleaning company, or maintenance to an outside contractor.

23 Advanced Techniques to Leverage Yourself as an Investor

Technique 1: Only spend time with qualified sellers who have both motivation and situation.

- *Motivation:* A compelling reason to sell with a time crunch to do it in.

- *Situation:* There is a way to structure a profitable deal—either the seller has the equity to take a deep discount in price or the financing is such that you can structure a terms deal where you make a profit.

Technique 2: A deal is only a deal once you have it *signed*.

Technique 3: Use "standardized" forms and contracts that you know how to use fast.

Technique 4: Only perform your due diligence *after* you have the property under contract.

Technique 5: You don't need to see the house before you put it under contract.

Technique 6: Always use group appointments when selling or renting a property.

Technique 7: Never stop marketing a property until you have *nonrefundable* cash in hand.

Technique 8: When doing the paperwork with your buyer or renter, *always* collect the money *first*, then do the paperwork.

Technique 9: Value your time—hire an assistant.

Technique 10: Get an assistant to take all your front-line calls.

Technique 11: Have your assistant set up 15-minute phone appointments to eliminate "phone tag" and compress your conversations.

Technique 12: Train your assistant how to qualify buyers, renters, and sellers while *not* giving away information you don't want them to have.

Technique 13: Get a private "back office" phone line. If you have a high-volume business (e.g., you deal in rentals or you buy and resell lots of properties, etc.) then get a hidden "back office" line and build a screening system to sort out the important calls from the low-level urgent calls.

(continued)

23 Advanced Techniques to Leverage Yourself as an Investor *(continued)*

Technique 14: Only give your back-office number to those people whose calls are most important to you.

Technique 15: Be willing to request that someone *not* use your back-office line.

Technique 16: Get and use caller ID.

Technique 17: Get and use mandatory phone number disclosure on your back-office line (if available).

Technique 18: Let it go to voice mail and only call back the people you want to speak with.

Technique 19: Turn off the ringer when you are working on a high-importance project.

Technique 20: Choose *not* to return some calls.

Technique 21: Outsource to high-quality vendors in a way that lowers your real cost and provides greater results for you.

Technique 22: Build relationships with these vendors so that you know you can trust them and they know they can count on you over time. Switching back and forth and picking vendors solely on price is the *costliest* mistake you can make.

Technique 23: Use technology to make it easy to get paid.

- Direct deposit
- Auto draft
- Payroll deduction

ADVANCED STAGE LEVEL TWO INVESTING— BUILDING A PROFITABLE REAL ESTATE INVESTING BUSINESS

CHAPTER TEN

The Key Perspective Shift That Will Make You Wealthy

As everyone gathered back in the room from the break, David began. "Let's shift our discussion to talk about *Advanced Stage Level Two* investing. This is when you begin building your real estate investing business in earnest. In fact, as an Advanced Stage Level Two investor, you will spend a growing proportion of your time working *on* your business rather than working *in* it.

"**The critical perspective shift that leads to true financial freedom and security, and ultimately to a Level Three lifestyle, is to see yourself not as an investor, but rather as a business builder who is growing a real estate investing business that will work without you needing to be there to run it.** You are only a temporary producer until you can build the business systems that can replace you. In essence, you are the engineer, designing and building a profit machine that consistently kicks out cash flow each and every month."

David turned and wrote on the board:

Target of Advanced Stage Level Two

To build an investing business that consistently makes you money without you needing to be there to run the business.

"Keep this goal firmly in mind and let it influence all the decisions you make and the actions you take. When you are successful in doing this, what will it mean for you?"

"That we'll be financially free?" Mark offered.

"Yes, it will mean you'll be financially free. But which of the three investor levels will you be at when you build your business to this point?" David asked.

"We'll be Level Three investors," several students shouted out at the same time.*

"Exactly! Remember, the real reason you are putting in all the energy and time to build an investing business isn't so you can make more money, although that will happen. The real reason to go to the effort of building your investing business is so that you can gain your freedom. You don't want to spend all your time stuck managing and running your investing business. Yes, you can make a ton of money doing this, but why not make the money and have a ton of freedom too? Personally, I think that the only way you can really be secure and know that your income streams are secure is to have the business infrastructure in place to run it over time, whether this infrastructure be in-house or intelligently outsourced.

"In many ways, building your investing business is the most exciting time of all because not only is your investing business working to consistently make you money, but you're starting to reap the benefits of having reliable systems and team members to handle the parts of the business that either stress you or don't interest you. This means it is easier for you to take time away from the business because you have reliable teams and systems to ensure that the business gets done while you are away. It also makes the business more fun as you're able to let go of the work that you find mundane or unpleasant and instead focus your time on growing your business. Can you imagine how satisfying it is to watch your fledgling real estate mini empire grow and blossom? Each day as you enter your office you feel a directed sense of energy, of purpose, which guides your efforts as you build your business for you and your family, not for some faceless corporation or conglomerate.

---

*Would you like to make that transition to Level Three investing? Would you like to someday be doing big deals on larger properties? Then make sure you get your copy of book three of the *Creating Cash Flow* series, which will focus on exactly that. For more information see Appendix B.

"I think the most amazing transformation that I observe with Advanced Stage Level Two investors is how close they are to making the final transition into Level Three investing. Most Advanced Stage Level Two investors are just 12 to 36 months away from being able to go passive in their investing. Can you imagine how good it will feel when you make this transition and are fully financially free—forever!

"The thing I love most about working with our Advanced Stage Level Two students is how they super-size their investing dreams because they have grown so much as individuals over the few years it took for them to get this close to their final objective. They push back the walls of their dreams and start to expand what they know is possible. They grow the size of their dreams while they grow as people. They start doing bigger deals like buying apartment buildings, shopping malls, office complexes, self storage centers, and mobile home parks. How many of you here aspire to be a Level Three investor doing big deals?" David asked.

Every hand went up.

The Three Pitfalls of Advanced Stage Level Two Investors

Pitfall One: They struggle to let go of the control of the details.
As you empower your team to take over whole sections of your investing business, you may find that you struggle with the desire to keep control. You are going to need to develop the "delegation muscles" that allow you to let go of your business—piece by piece—as you bring in key team members to take over. As long as you build in simple scorecards that let you track your team's performance on a daily, weekly, and monthly basis as you hand off areas of your business, you'll be able to accurately watch the performance of each business area to celebrate your team members' successes and coach them through any rough spots.

Pitfall Two: They are great investors, but lousy leaders.
At a certain point, the only way your investing business can make the jump to the next level is for you to have key staff that you have groomed and developed to take on the responsibility and challenge of running your business. But how do you empower talented people to run your business if you don't understand the difference between managing and leading team members?

(continued)

The Three Pitfalls of Advanced Stage Level Two Investors *(continued)*

Managers focus only on executing for bottom-line results. They are focused on effective ways to get their team to perform. The problem is that most managers don't grow their team's abilities to self-manage. And what is worse, very few managers ever develop the next generation of leaders on their team or the know-how to set the big-picture vision and direction for a company.

Leaders have their focus not just on getting results, but on getting results in a way that develops and grows other leaders on the team who can lead and get results. The ultimate form of leverage is to develop leaders on your investing team who are committed, capable, and utterly reliable. It's not just about making a leader better, but about upgrading the knowledge base of your entire investing team and unifying the vision they hold of exactly what you are all working to accomplish.

Pitfall Three: They grow impatient to get to Level Three and let go of key areas too early.

Now this pitfall probably sounds like a direct contradiction to pitfalls one and two. And it is. Yet that's life for you, full of seemingly unsolvable paradoxes. I want to caution you against leadership by abdication, which is an all too common, costly mistake that I regularly watch investors make. Leadership by abdication is not the same thing as strategically developing your business systems and team to take over and own parts of your business. It usually happens when an investor grows impatient with the slow pace of growing their business systems and teams, and tries to speed up the process. But some things take time, and developing people and systems are two of those things. Most investors who rush this don't delegate, they dump. That is, they walk into the office of the new team member and dump projects and responsibilities on his desk. It just doesn't work to throw the keys to a part of your business to new team members who haven't been trained or where no real business system exists. That's a recipe to set them up for failure.

Instead, hand off small pieces of the business to your team one at a time, making sure to arrange the time to coach them during the transition and check in on them regularly over time until they are truly ready to take complete ownership.

It's a delicate balance, this incremental handoff of your investing business. On the one hand, many investors hold on too tight, and on the other hand other investors let go too soon. You'll have to feel your way across this dynamic balancing act as you go.

What Stops Most Investors from Putting Their Investing Profits on Autopilot

"I'm sure you've flown on an airplane before. Just think about how amazing those planes are nowadays. As they take off, they have a highly trained pilot getting the plane up into the air and on course. Then they turn on the autopilot system. This system maintains their course and manages long stretches of the flight, with the pilot keeping an eye on the instrument panel to troubleshoot any problems that might be identified. And when the plane gets close to the destination airport, the pilot again takes over and lands the plane.

"I think this is a lot like how you'll build your investing business. You'll have systems that generate leads for you to meet and sign deals, which is like the takeoff of the airplane. Once you get the deal going, your investing business's systems and team will manage and control those deals, with you there just to keep an eye on their progress. This is like the autopilot on the plane. And finally, when you come in for a landing and sell the property, you will take a more active role in the decisions and monitoring of the closing process to make sure it happens the right way.

"Now you don't need an autopilot to fly a plane, just like you don't need a business infrastructure of teams and systems to make money investing in real estate. But you need to understand that without an autopilot, flying long-distance is exhausting and pretty uncomfortable. Can you imagine the strain of having to focus on flying the plane for four to six hours at a stretch? It's not like you can just pull off the road for a quick pit stop!

"It's the same way with your investing. When you don't have the systems and team, your investing business autopilot, then while you can make a ton of money, the strain and lifestyle cost is too great. I've seen many investors who make $500,000 or more each year with their investing, but they live, breathe, and die by their investing. They can't get away from their business for more than a long weekend here or there. That doesn't feel like success and wealth to me.

"I remember one past Mentorship student from the early days. She had a Middle Stage Level Two business with about 50 properties in her portfolio. She was earning a great living, but all the key business systems were totally dependent on her. She worked 18-hour days and hadn't taken a vacation in over two years! She understood that she needed to make a change. Peter and I consulted with her and mentored her to build the systems and team to earn her freedom from the business. Within 18 months she had a hugely successful business that made her more money, she had reduced her working hours by 30 percent, and she took a six-week vacation to Australia and New Zealand! That's starting to create wealth—when you have the freedom of time *and* the money."

David paused for a moment. "It all sounds so easy, doesn't it, when I talk about it that way? But you've got to ask yourself what things put you at the greatest risk of not being able to successfully do this. What's really stopping you from achieving all you want with real estate? After all, if it really is so easy to build a profitable investing business, why don't more people do it?

"The reason more investors don't build profitable investing businesses to turn their profits on autopilot is that there are three half-truths that stop most real estate investors cold."

David turned to the board and wrote:

Half-Truth 1: "My goal is to become a great investor."

"Many investors mistakenly believe their real goal is just to become a skilled real estate investor. It's not. Your real goal is to build a profitable investing business that makes you money without you being there to actively work the business.

"Becoming a skilled investor will only take you so far. It will help you turn your time into profits on deals. This sounds pretty good—however, if you ever want to truly create the freedom and time to do what matters most to you, then you need to build the infrastructure that supports and cares for your investing business without you needing to be there. The world is full of skilled landlords who spend their days dealing with leaky faucets and late-paying tenants. And the world is full of skilled investors who frantically move from one deal to the next in the chaotic game of real estate investing. The former may make consistent money with their investing but they are chained to the obligations of managing their rental portfolio. The latter may make a lot of money by doing deals, but they are usually stuck on the treadmill of having to find, close, and turn their next deal to keep the money flowing.

"You are not out to make yourself indispensable. **The only reason for you to become a highly skilled investor is so that you are able to transfer your skills, experience, and decision-making ability into your investing business so that the business produces without your needing to be there each day to oversee it.**

"This brings us to the next half-truth that stops most investors." Again David turned and wrote on the board.

Half-Truth 2: "I am investing to build equity."

"Equity is important, but it is only a means to an end. The reason to build equity is so that you can tap into that equity to create cash flow. Never forget that the end goal of your investing business is *not* to just have equity, but to convert that equity into cash flow. You can convert equity into cash flow by selling, leasing, refinancing, or leveraging your real estate portfolio. Still, it's cash flow, not equity, that is the ultimate goal. In fact, it's not just cash flow but passive streams of income that you want. It's the golden eggs your goose produces each month.

"Of course, you don't want to ignore building equity, especially in the early years of your investing where you are looking to grow your net worth, skill level, and investing business infrastructure so that in later years you can convert that equity into cash flow. Cash flow is what pays for your current lifestyle and day-to-day money needs. Net worth—equity—is what gives you a tool to create more cash flow and a buffer for your future security.

"Passive cash flow gives you the time to step back and intelligently invest portions of your net worth to create even more cash flow and net worth. For this formula to work, you have to build an investing business that allows you to step away from it so that you're not drowning in the details of the day-to-day running of the business.

"This takes us to our final half-truth." David turned and wrote on the board.

Half-Truth 3: "I am the key person of my investing business."

"Nothing keeps investors trapped like this half-truth. Many investors mistakenly believe that they're supposed to build their investing business around themselves. **But the more you structure the business where you are indispensible to it, the harder it will be for you to ever become truly financially free.** While it's tempting to think of yourself as the only one who can do key pieces of your business, the truth is that if you structure it correctly, you can and in fact must build an investing business that works best without you in it day to day.

"I used to fight this one a lot. I thought, how could anyone negotiate better than me? How could anyone handle the closing paperwork better than me? How could anyone oversee the reselling of the property better than me? The truth is that once I built the investing business that freed me up from all of these areas, where I was just an adviser and coach to the people and systems that actually did all the steps in the deal, my income skyrocketed. It allowed me to step back from my investing far enough to strategically sort through the bigger-picture decisions about which project to take on next.

"I make many times more money from my investing today than I ever did, and I spend on average less than 10 hours per month actively engaged in managing each of my investing businesses. My role is now to point the businesses in the right direction, help make the decision to pull the trigger on the next deal, and then to check in from time to time to help coach my team to make the deals go even better, or to improve the systems to run even more smoothly. I've found this to be the most fulfilling part of building my investing business—this freedom to be able to make a leveraged difference in the running of the business by having the time and space to see the entire business from the outside looking in.

"This new perspective has sharpened my moneymaking capacity and become one of my most joyous areas of self-expression. Imagine what it will feel like to you when you reach the place where, having built your investing business the right way, you are able to do the exact same thing.

"Now that we've gotten clear on the key perspective shift from working on your investing to working on your investing *business*, it's time to talk about how you actually go about building systems in the five key areas of your investing business."

CHAPTER ELEVEN

How to Build Business Systems That Work So You Don't Have To

"It's time for us to turn our attention to how to build the business systems you will need for your successful investing business. Let's start off by reminding ourselves exactly what a *system* is." David turned and wrote on the board.

A <u>system</u> is any repeatable business process that allows your business to get a consistently great result.

"The key words are *repeatable* and *consistent*. The systems you build need to reliably get you a predictable result. The very best business systems can be used by any member of your investing team who has undergone the proper training, and ideally that training is also a systematized part of your business.

"Who can name a few business systems you've learned either at the Intensive

Training* you first attended as a Mentorship student, or from this Advanced Investor Workshop?" David asked the class.

"The techniques for finding motivated sellers we learned about," Mark offered.

"Which ones specifically were systematized for you? Name one technique that we systematized for you so I can make sure the distinction of what a business system really is is clear."

Mark paused for a moment as he thought, then answered, "The four-step plan for using classified advertising to get motivated sellers to call us. You showed us which ads to test, where to place the ads, and how to track and evaluate the results of those ads over time."

"Good! What's another system you've learned?"

"Well, the tracking system you gave us yesterday that included the worksheets we can use to evaluate all our marketing lead sources," Tim answered.

"Another great answer. Someone tell me another system you've learned."

Vicki tentatively raised her hand and said, "Well, isn't the Instant Offer System a system for negotiating deals?"

"You tell me," David responded. "Is it a system?"

"Yes."

"What makes it a system? In fact, what are the common elements to all business systems?" David pushed Vicki and the class to think deeper.

"Well, you told us exactly how to do it." Vicki said. "I mean, you gave us the exact steps to take and the order to take them in. You even gave us the exact words to say."

David started writing elements up on the board. "What are the other common elements to the systems we've already talked about? In other words, what makes a system work? What are its component pieces?"

"How about instructions?" Leon offered.

"Good. What else?"

Now the answers really started to flow from the group. Within a few minutes David had the following list up on the board.

---

*To get an insider seat at the "Intensive Training" that Mentorship students attend as the launching point to their investing, read *Buying Real Estate without Cash or Credit* (pp. 1–139).

Building Blocks to Great Systems

- Scripts
- Worksheets
- Spreadsheets with built-in formulas
- Other software that automatically does steps or processes information for you
- Databases of key information
- Templates and samples
- Common question and answer sheets
- Step-by-step instructions
- Predictable problem areas and how to deal with them
- Camera-ready artwork ready to use
- Approved investor forms and contracts
- A timeline or master calendar

"Okay," David said. "We now have a list of the building blocks of successful business systems. Again, remember the goal of any business system is to allow you to produce a consistently great result in some area of your business. Let's talk about how you build a business system for your investing business."

ACTION STEP

The Seven Steps to Building Business Systems

Step One: Clearly define the outcome or desired result for the system under construction.
What do you want the business system to do? What is the result you want it to consistently produce?

Step Two: Find the best person in your business (or outside your business if you have access to someone better) to model your business system on.
Who is the very best of the best at consistently producing the result you want to achieve? For example, when it came to negotiating with motivated sellers, I used Peter as the model from which to build the Instant Offer System. Why? Because he's the best real estate negotiator I've ever seen. Who do you know who is world class in some area of your investing business that you can model?

(continued)

The Seven Steps to Building Business Systems *(continued)*

Step Three: Observe them producing the result and freeze their process to write down each of the steps they take and the order in which they take them.
Whether it's yourself or some other person, follow the process as a highly skilled person produces the result you want your business system to produce, and list the steps this person takes and the order in which they take them.

Step Four: Repeat step three a few times to make sure you have all the steps and the exact order.
With complicated business processes that involve interactions with other people, it will usually take several times through for you to get a draft of all the steps down accurately. Each time you go through the process you are fine-tuning your documentation of the process and procedure.

Step Five: Teach the system to someone new and see if they can use the system to get the desired outcome.
Nothing shows the weaknesses and holes of a system better than getting a new person to try out the system. As you watch the new person use the system, it is very easy for you to spot the steps that you didn't notice and write down earlier. You'll also be able to spot the steps that need more explanation. One of the reasons that the investor business systems Peter and I created as part of the Mentorship Program work so well is that over the past 10 years we've leveraged our observations of how thousands of students used the systems to make it easier and easier to replicate our success. For example, we had to change a lot of the negotiating language of the Instant Offer System because many of the things that Peter could do average students couldn't. Over time, through trial and error, we got the mix just right. Now *any* investor can use the system to close deals.

Step Six: Make the system even easier to use by filling in the gaps with checklists, instructions, worksheets, scripts, samples, and so on.
The best way to see where the gaps really are is to pay attention to the questions and struggles of the team members you are training to use the system. It's their fresh, new perspective that will give you the most accurate feedback on where you need to beef up the system.

Step Seven: Simplify the system and refine it over time.
See what steps of the system could be automated by building the right software or worksheet. How could you eliminate or combine steps? Is there a better way to get the desired result that is simpler? You should not only be building systems over time, but you should also be *pruning* your existing systems over time so that they stay fresh, healthy, and vibrant. Your goal is to get more from less.

The Five Key Areas of Your Investing Business

"All businesses have five key areas. First there is the **operational** area. This is the part of your business that produces whatever the business is selling. Next is the **sales and marketing** area, which is responsible for generating sales. Third is the **financial** area that deals with the accounting and collection of money and payment of bills. The fourth area is the **human resources** (**HR**) part of the business that deals with the hiring and development of new staff members. And finally there is the **leadership** area of the business, which is responsible for the big-picture vision and strategy of the business.

"Your investing business has all five of these key areas too. In fact, as an Advanced Stage Level Two investor, you'll be building an investing business that grows teams and systems in each of these five areas so that your business becomes bigger, stronger, and more profitable."

The Five Key Areas of Your Investing Business

One: Operations

- Rent collection
- Maintenance and fix-up
- Deal paperwork to finish a closing
- Tenant management
- Office oversight
- Arranging financing

Two: Sales and Marketing

- Leasing empty units
- Finding buyers and tenant buyers
- Marketing systems to generate leads
- Closing more deals with sellers

Three: Finance

- Accounts payable
- Financial reporting
- Financial controls
- Payroll

(continued)

The Five Key Areas of Your Investing Business (continued)

Four: HR or "Team"

- Hiring new contractors and office help
- Compliance with labor laws
- Training of new team members
- Dealing with team issues and challenges

Five: Executive Leadership

- Big-picture decisions about the company
- Vision setting
- Leadership development

As an Advanced Stage Level Two investor, your job is to build a business with the right team who develops and uses systems to help your investing business create great value in the marketplace and consistently earn a profit. The key to make this transition smooth is to clearly define the outcomes for which a team member is responsible and incrementally grow their responsibilities. For example, if you are hiring an office manager to take over the operational aspects of your business, it's critical that you give them responsibility piece by piece as they show they have grown in their capacity. You may start off by having them step in and take over the rent collections system. With time, as they get fluent with the system, they will probably make many enhancements and upgrades to your old system. Maybe they'll set all your tenants up on auto-pay straight from the tenant's checking accounts to your checking accounts, or maybe they'll start sending official invoices with payment envelopes to each of your tenants each month.

Once they are settled in with this area, then give them one or two more pieces of the operational business to own. Within 12 months they will be in charge of 90-plus percent of your operational activities.

Sample Business Systems for Each of the Five Key Areas
Within each of these areas you'll be building systems to automate that part of your business so that you get high-quality results no matter who is the team member running that system. The goal is for your business to be systems reliant so that team members are empowered to own their areas of responsibility. A quality system clearly defines expectations and a known process for success in that area. With the right system, your business gains a high degree of stability and this in turn allows your team to focus on growing the business since the foundation upon which the business is built is strong and stable.

(continued)

The Five Key Areas of Your Investing Business *(continued)*

Here are some sample systems for each of the five key areas of your investing business:

Operations

Tenant Management System: The heart of this system is the step-by-step checklist for exactly how to bring on a new resident in your properties. The right checklist lays out the process to make sure:

- All the right paperwork is filled out correctly and signed.
  Tools: Blank-by-blank instructions and filled-out sample paperwork.

- The resident clearly understands your expectations and company policies.
  Tools: Boilerplate company "Resident Policies" form.

- Residents enjoy the move-in experience because you make things easy for them.
  Tools: "New Resident Information Guide" and "Utility Hook-up Shortcuts."

- Your resident pays on time or early—automatically.
  Tools: Auto deduction from their checking account form, or payroll deduction form.

- You have a clearly defined, written in stone, Eviction Procedure.
  Tools: Procedures manual, checklist, phone number for an outsourced flat fee eviction service.

- You have a Tenant Retention Program in place to lower tenant turnover.
  Tools: Templated letters to tenants, master calendar of when to send letters and when to approach to renew lease, scripts for staff to use when talking with tenants about renewing leases.

- You have a Tenant Move-Out Procedure for managing the tenant's departure and the reletting of the unit.
  Tools: Checklist for tenant, move-out form, checklist for management, checklist for handyman, process to notify sales and marketing that you'll have an empty unit for them to fill.

Sales and Marketing

Direct Mail System: The heart of this system is the detailed mailing campaign "Master Calendar" and user-friendly database that lets your team know:

- What mailing piece gets mailed on what date.
  Tools: Mailing worksheet or spreadsheet template.

(continued)

The Five Key Areas of Your Investing Business *(continued)*

- Where to get the mailers made for the best prices and the computer file of the artwork, along with a sample mailing piece to give the printer.
  Tools: Templated "Request for Bid" form, computer template for direct mail pieces, spreadsheet of printers from whom to invite bids.

- Exactly who your marketing pieces get mailed to.
  Tools: Spreadsheet or database of these contacts.

- Tracking system to make sure you get accurate and immediately useful feedback about how your direct mail campaign is producing.
  Tools: Voice-mail system set up to take calls, software or worksheet to record results as they come in.

In the two preceding systems I highlighted the specific tools you can use to build your business systems. See if you can spot the tools on your own in the sample systems for the "Finance" area of your business.

Finance

Financial Reporting System: The heart of this system is a properly set up bookkeeping system where key reports can be automatically generated in user-friendly formats to give you and your team immediate feedback on the financial success of your investing business. To ensure that you get quality and reliable information out of this system, you must make sure that:

- The architecture for the bookkeeping (i.e., your chart of accounts) is properly thought through and set up from the very start.

- Each property that you add to your portfolio is added to your bookkeeping system according to a "New Property Set-Up Checklist" that maximizes your team's success in accurately getting new properties into your accounting system.

- A "Deposit Guide" directs your team to correctly enter all money deposited to the correct place within your chart of accounts.

- An "Accounts Payable System" clearly correlates each expense to the correct place in the chart of accounts.

- Memorized reports within your bookkeeping software instantaneously generate useful information to guide your team's performance.

The Five Key Areas of Your Investing Business *(continued)*

In the final two areas of your business, HR and Leadership, I've purposefully not included the tools that could be used to build the needed systems. As you read through these sample systems, jot notes in the margins as to which tools you think would work best to build the needed systems. This is your chance to start to train your brain to see systems and the tools to build your systems everywhere you look. Ultimately it's by conditioning your brain to think in systems that you'll be best able to grow your investing business and reach Level Three success.

HR or Team

New Team Member Orientation System: This system helps an existing team member walk a new team member through the orientation process, helping all new hires to know:

- Clearly defined expectations of their roles and level of performance.

- Company policies about what is and is not acceptable behavior.

- How the new hire will be coached and evaluated.

- Payroll policies and paperwork.

- The big picture of the company history, vision, and goals.

- A feedback process to receive the new hires' feedback and improve the orientation process for the next new team member.

Executive Leadership

Leadership Development System: Any business is limited in its success by the caliber of leaders it is able to create or recruit. One of the most important roles of the executive leadership is to systematically develop the talent pool of leaders inside your investing business.

- How do you identify potential leaders?

- What steps do you take to help give them regular opportunities to take on new responsibilities and grow their leadership capacity?

- By what process do you give them regular and useful feedback to help them grow and develop?

- How do you create the environment that rewards them for stepping up and leading and makes it okay for them to make learning mistakes?

Taking Your Investing Business to the Next Level

David continued with the workshop, saying, "As an Advanced Stage Level Two investor you are engaged in full-out business building. This business building has **three powerful building blocks for you to use to build each of the five key areas** of your investing business.

"First there are **systems**. We've already spent a lot of time talking about this one. Second comes **team**. By building the staff that is fully responsible for parts of your business you are able to leverage your team's skills, time, energy, and commitment to grow your investing business. The third building block is **outsourced solutions**. Let's spend some time on this for a moment.

"In my opinion, the only thing better than leveraging your business by building systems and team is to leverage your business by tapping into the systems and teams available in outsourced solutions. For example, why should you do all your own employee paperwork and compliance? Instead, hire a specialized 'PEO' company (professional employment organization), which is a company that 'co-employs' your team and, in exchange for a small fee, usually based on the salary you are paying, will manage all the HR paperwork you need to comply with state and federal employment legislation. Sure, you could train a team member to handle this in-house, but this is not a good use of your time or resources.

"The best thing about outsourced solutions is that they allow you to get the benefit of economies of scale, such as lower costs and more specialized talent, without having any of the risks of building this for yourself. If you don't like your outsourced solution you can switch to another provider. As long as you pay attention and learn about your options as you go, market forces of competition will help you get great pricing and service. My philosophy is that if it isn't a core competence of my business, I always prefer to outsource it in such a way that it lowers my real cost and at the same time gives me an improved solution."

"David," Nancy asked, "can you give us another example of an outsource solution we can use to build our investing business?"

"Sure. Here are a few more quick examples. Why hire a bookkeeper when you can hire an outsourced bookkeeping company? Or why buy an expensive voice mail system when you can just 'rent' a voice mail system like the one most of our Mentorship students use for $15 per month plus a small usage charge? Or why master all the loan programs available and how to work with tenant buyers to improve their credit scores so they can qualify to buy your rent-to-own properties? Instead, just outsource this by matching your tenant buyers up with a great mortgage broker with whom you've developed a winning relationship. I think you are getting the idea. The bottom line is that you should constantly be on the lookout for ways you can pay an outside company to produce a valuable solution for your investing business in a way that saves you money and simplifies your business.

"You'll use all three of these powerful building blocks to grow your investing business so that ultimately you are able to transition into a Level Three business."

Three More Core Investor Skills of Advanced Stage Level Two Investors

1. Evaluating talent—whether it be in hiring team members or outsourced partners.

2. Intelligently letting go of parts of your business in an incremental way.

3. Building systems and coaching your team to build and manage business systems.

CHAPTER TWELVE

The Final Session of the Advanced Training

David looked out at all the smiling faces in the room. "It is hard to believe that this is the last session of our three days together," David said. "I am going miss spending time with you all and I wanted to take this final session to share the **three most important lessons** I can. You'll notice that the lessons aren't necessarily new, but they are so important that they need repetition to reinforce them.

"The **first lesson** is that you are all on track to be massively successful with your investing. It's now totally in your hands what you do with your knowledge and momentum. I ask that you be both kind and firm with yourselves. Be kind if you have a rough day with your investing. You'll still have moments where deals will fall apart right before your eyes, or days when buyers will back out at the last minute, or when loans will fall through. When these things happen, and they will, just remember to breathe, relax, and be kind to yourself. Beating yourself up will never help you progress as an investor to.

"One of the biggest mistakes I see Level Two investors make is to think things are supposed to be smooth and easy. They're not. Things are supposed to be challenging and worthwhile so that you earn the wealth you create and savor the journey because it helps promote your growth as a person. When you align your expectations to know that you'll have plenty of opportunities for growth along the way, you don't allow any one challenge to seem too big or grow too far out of proportion. And this is an essential key to the balanced, wealthy life you are committed to.

"When I see investors beating themselves up over a mistake or a shift in fortune, it lets me know that they are taking themselves and their investing too seriously. Yes, your actions and outcomes matter, but they are not the most important parts of your life. The greatest tool you have to see things in their proper context is laughter. Most of all, be willing to laugh at yourself when you notice you're getting too serious. This is a lesson I'm working on daily in my own investing life.

"But I also believe that you need to balance this kindness toward yourself with firmness. I ask you to be firm in keeping your commitments, both to yourself and to other people. While it's okay to have an off day here or there, or even to have an off week, never accept that week stretching into two weeks or four weeks. When you start to stray from your focus, pull yourself back on track. It's times like these when it's so important for you to get back to the basics—small actions you take daily that move your investing business forward one step at a time.

"The **second lesson** I want to share with you is the importance of using every tool at your disposal to learn and grow as an investor. When I look back at what made the biggest difference to my rapid success as an investor I realize it was my background as someone committed to learning from others. I read, and still read, over a hundred books a year. I took courses to learn along the way. I connected with a mentor, Peter, who showed me how to integrate all of this information I was learning and who let me borrow his faith that real estate would work for me when I didn't have any faith of my own. And finally, I reflected daily and weekly on how my investing was going and how I could improve bit by bit as I applied these lessons in my investing.

"I believe that you all can achieve anything you want in life if you just pay the price to learn and grow in that area. If you want to earn more, you've got to learn more. In our fast-moving world the key skill truly is the willingness and discipline to learn and unlearn—to unlearn what you know that is no longer accurate or relevant, and to learn what is critical to help you accomplish and enjoy what is most important to you.

"The **third and final lesson** I have for you is for you to savor the adventure of the next few years of your investing. Trust me on this one, there is something joyous about the years between when you first start succeeding in building your fortune and the time you realize that you have enough so that money will never be a legitimate worry for you and your family again.

"I look back and I wish I had given myself more permission to enjoy the journey and celebrate my little daily victories more along the way. I was so focused that I missed out on this. I once heard a famous poet say, 'Life is so fast, I must move very slow.' The early and middle years of your investing will happen in the blink of an eye, and if you don't move very slow—that is, if you don't pay attention and savor the journey—you risk missing it.

"I get asked all the time what I would do differently if I had it to do all over again with my investing and wealth creation. That's an easy question for me to answer. I would relax and trust more; I would have faith that things were moving exactly as they were supposed to. And from this quiet faith I would gaze out at the flowers I was tending, and smile, and smell and roll in them along the way. I'd take photos of myself in front of every house I ever bought (I wish I had done this one). I'd get photos of me with every family I ever sold a house to and with every seller I ever helped. I'd celebrate with my wife more the little things along the way like a deal I just closed, or a thank you card I just received from a tenant buyer.

"And I'd also take myself a lot less seriously. Too often in my years of Level Two investing I let my blood pressure rise and I allowed my thoughts to dwell on 'the end of my world.' Of course, none of those ends ever actually happened, anywhere outside of my imagination, that is. If I had it to do over, I'd relax and look at each of these moments as a big puzzle to lose myself in figuring out, not out of adult seriousness and fear, but in a childlike state of wonder and exploration.

"Maybe you were expecting my final lesson for you to be something else, something more serious. But I'm not sure if there is anything more profound than this lesson. Thank you all for being a light in the world, shining to show other people the way. The way you are living your lives and going after your dreams is important to the world. I wish you much growth, success, and enjoyment over the next few years. Good journey to you all!"

With those final words, the room was filled with music and the class stood and gave David a rousing ovation.

Later that night, when the room was empty and the students gone, David wandered back into the room and thought about the weekend and the people who had touched him during the three days. He smiled when he thought about the fun and challenges they would all have over the next year. He wondered how it would all work out. But most of all he just smiled, drinking in the memory and the moment.

PART TWO

THE REAL WORLD—
12 MONTHS BUILDING
YOUR INVESTING BUSINESS

CHAPTER THIRTEEN

Month 2—Tim Tests a Leveraged Deal Finding Strategy

Tim was more than a little nervous. He had the phone numbers of five real estate offices in his area in front of him. He almost regretted having committed to his mastermind team that by the end of this week he would have booked at least one 10-minute talk at a real estate office in the area to show the sales agents how they could make money working with investors like himself. It was one of the leveraged strategies that David had covered at the Advanced Investor Workshop, but it was really a stretch for Tim.

He had told his mastermind group that he felt he wasn't credible enough to go in and talk with the agents, but the group had been unanimous that he should go and do it anyway. Mark had commented that regardless of the outcome of the first few talks, Tim would gain valuable experience and couldn't help but make several useful connections with local real estate agents. Mary had pointed out that Tim and Nancy had actually done their first deal last month off of a lead that a real estate agent contact had brought them, giving Tim all the credibility he needed.

Tim thought about that deal now. He was so relieved that he and his wife Nancy had finally completed their first deal after almost five months of effort. A buddy of his, Bart, was a real estate agent who turned Tim on to a motivated seller who was going through a divorce and wanted a fast sale. It turned out that Tim was able to buy the $425,000 house subject to the existing financing. He gave the seller $28,000 to cash him out of his equity, and he got the house subject to the $360,000 first mortgage. Bart had just passed the lead on to Tim to help him out, but Tim had sent Bart and his wife out to dinner to say thank you. In addition, since that time, Tim had referred six other sellers to Bart as leads for Bart to get listings to sell their houses.

Currently Tim had put a tenant buyer into the house on a two-year rent to own. Tim collected a $15,000 option payment and had a $380 per month cash flow on the property. Tim hoped the tenant buyer wouldn't cash him out at the end of two years even though, at the tenant buyer's option price of $475,000, Tim stood to make about $85,000 on the back end. Tim knew the area was appreciating strongly and he wanted to hold on to the house over the long term.

Tim shook his head as he looked down at the phone numbers in front of him. How had he gotten himself into this, he thought. He knew the answer to that. When he had shared his success on the mastermind conference call his fellow mastermind partners had all said he should leverage this success by looking for a better way to network with more real estate agents. They had challenged him to call up and book himself to talk at a local real estate office's weekly sales agent meeting.

Tim took a deep breath, looked at his script, picked up the phone, and dialed.

"Hello, Prudential Realty, Sharon speaking. May I help you?"

"Hi Sharon, my name is Tim and I'm hoping you can help me. It's a little awkward for me because I don't know exactly who in your office I need to talk to." As Tim said this he used scrunchy face just like the script said to.

"I'll sure do my best."

"Thanks Sharon. I'm a local real estate investor and I wanted to know who in your office is the person responsible for organizing your weekly sales meetings. I'd like to talk with them about coming in for five or ten minutes to share with all the agents in your office my specific buying criteria of houses I'm looking to buy and to share with them how I often buy agents' hard-to-sell listings. Who do you think is the best person for me to talk to?"

As simple as that Tim got the name of the broker who ran the office and the weekly sales agent meetings. When Sharon transferred Tim to speak with the broker he was not only in, but turned out to be delighted to have Tim come in and speak with his agents next Monday.

When Tim hung up the phone he felt drained. He couldn't believe how easy it was to book the appointment, but he was still really intimidated about going in to give the talk. But at least he had five days to prepare for that part.

The five days went by in a blur. Tim arrived at the Prudential office about 15 minutes early and went in to find Larry, the broker in charge of the office.

Walking into the office, Tim recognized Larry immediately from his picture on his company web site. Larry was a medium-height bald man with a broad smile.

"Hi, Larry?" Tim said.

"Yes. You must be Tim. Welcome, and thanks for coming by today to talk with our agents."

"You bet Larry. I'm looking forward to it. Oh, I brought bagels and cream cheese for your team just in case they're hungry this morning," Tim said, lifting up the two bags he was carrying.

"How thoughtful of you Tim. I know they'll really appreciate the food. Let me show you around the office."

Tim spent the next 10 minutes walking around the office talking with Larry. Tim felt himself getting more and more comfortable with the whole idea of talking to the office agents the more he toured the office. Larry was great and introduced him to five or six of his sales agents as they walked around.

After the tour, Larry took Tim into the conference room, which was already packed with about 20 agents, many of whom were digging into the bagels and cream cheese. Larry got the meeting going fast. After he went through some of his regular business he introduced Tim.

"We have a special guest joining us this morning. Tim is a local investor in the area who is going to be talking with you about how you can sell more houses and make more money by working with local investors like himself. And he was also the generous soul who brought in all these bagels we're munching away on." If nothing else, Tim thought, it's obvious from the cheer that the food was a hit.

"Hi everyone. My name is Tim Dowling and I'm a local real estate investor. Thank you for inviting me in to visit for a short while this morning. I understand how busy successful agents like yourselves are, so I promise to be brief and to the point. And that point is to talk about how you can close one or two extra transactions each month by tapping into a fresh area of the market." Tim noticed several heads look up when he said this last part.

"I don't know if any of you have ever experienced the final few weeks of a listing that just isn't going right. Not only do you lose all the time and energy you put in with all the open houses and putting out and taking down signs, but you've lost a good deal of money since you've already spent money on advertising and color flyers and any of your staff you've paid along the way. And the biggest cost isn't the time or money, it's how not having this listing sell could be a real blow to your reputation in the area, because we all know bad news spreads fast.

"Well, I'd like to offer you a solution so that you never have to experience a loss like that again. How many of you in this room have a stable of investors on tap that are qualified to buy as many good investment properties as you can get them, including listings you have that just aren't going to sell any other way?" Tim looked around and saw only a few hands up.

"While I can't speak for other investors, I'd like to share with you my thoughts and buying criteria so that you can see how you could work with one serious investor, and this will give you insights on how to develop a buyers list of qualified investors who can close on a listing fast.

"I guess I'd like you to think of me as your 'Plan B.' Obviously we all know that if you can get a retail buyer to cash your seller out, that will be your first choice. However, if for some reason beyond your control that's not possible, why should you let the listing expire?

"As an investor, I can close quickly so that you get paid your full commission up front every time, no matter what. In fact, since I often buy properties with the seller participating in the financing in some way, many times I can pay close to the full asking price, which means a bigger commission check for you.

"So what are my buying criteria? I'm looking for properties where the seller is willing to take a fair discount of at least 20 to 25 percent for a fast, no hassle, all-cash closing. Or for properties where the seller wants a higher price, but is willing to significantly participate in the financing. I also specialize in helping sellers who are in various stages of foreclosure, even if the house is overfinanced."

At this point Tim handed out flyers and his business cards to everyone in the room.

"So whether you have a listing that is at risk of expiring, or if you can find a listing out there where the seller may fit my criteria, let me know. I'm very open to you representing me in the deal too, so you can get a double commission if it's your listing, or at least the full buyer's agent commission if it is a listing you found for me to buy.

"I like to think of this as a win-win-win. Your seller sells fast and is done with the property. As an investor, I get a solid buy on an investment property to add to my portfolio. And you get your full commission with none of the ordinary hassles of a finicky retail buyer.

"Oh, and one more thing. If you help me buy a property, not only will I make sure you get your full commission, but I'll also guarantee to get you 10 listing leads within the next 90 days, or I'll pay you up to an additional $1,000 cash. You'll get $100 for every lead I'm short. It's easy for me to make good on this promise since I talk with over 50 FSBOs each week, most of whom end up turning to qualified agents like yourselves to list and sell the property for them. Thank you for your time today." To Tim's surprise, the agents actually gave him a round of applause. As he was leaving, several of the agents huddled around him, asking questions and asking him to follow up with them later in the week.

When Tim got into his car he was so excited. The talk had gone great and he had business cards from six of the agents to follow up with later in the week. Tim knew he'd have to track the results over time, but he really felt proud that he had pushed himself to talk with the agents. He had already booked a second talk with another real estate office for later in the week. He couldn't wait to tell his mastermind partners about how it had gone and how he had successfully stepped up to the challenge.

If this worked as a marketing channel like he hoped, Tim figured he could meet with one or two real estate offices a month just spreading the word. He recognized that this would let him talk with over 200 real estate agents in the next twelve months without very much effort on his part. He bet David would agree with him that this was good leverage.

The Four Bottom Lines to Networking with Real Estate Offices

One: Understand that what you are offering has incredible appeal to the agents you talk with.

- Full commissions.
- Possibility to save a sale.
- Opportunity to earn a double commission.
- Protection for their reputation in the community.

Two: Bring food and flyers.

Three: Remember you are *not* selling anything, you are offering to *buy*.

Four: Reinforce the three biggest benefits you offer.

- You can close fast.
- You'll make sure they get paid a full commission.
- You can salvage any listing that is about to expire.

CHAPTER FOURTEEN

Month 3—Vicki Feels the Pressure

Sitting at the closing table in the title company's conference room, Vicki was scared. Four weeks ago she had signed her seventh deal to buy a small fixer home from a young couple who had run out of money to do the rehab. Vicki had agreed to a cash price of $185,000, which was about 65 percent of the as-is value of the house. After going back and forth she had decided to just flip the contract for a quick $10,000. She had found her buyer, a local investor named Gene who had agreed to pay her $8,000 to buy her contract on the house. The problem was that here she was at the closing, ready to flip the house to Gene, and the guy was trying to pressure her into a new deal.

"I just want to get this straight," Vicki said, working very hard to keep her temper. "You're telling me that you are no longer willing to pay me $8,000? That you want me to take $3,000 now? You've got to be joking!"

"Well," Gene said with a practiced tone to his voice. "It's not like you've had to do much work here. And $3,000 is a lot of money. Besides, you yourself told me that your contract on the house expires in one week. Surely $3,000 cash is a whole lot better than nothing."

Vicki turned to the title agent who was there to notarize the closing paperwork on the assignment of the contract. "There won't be any closing today." With that Vicki stood up, gathered her purse and coat, and started to walk out of the room.

Gene quickly moved to block her way and said, "Wait, where are you going? Let's sit down and talk about this like civil people."

Vicki firmly looked Gene in the eye. "Move out of my way. I will not ever do business with a person of so little integrity. Not today, not ever." With that Vicki walked out of the room.

When she got to her car she was shaking. She was so upset. She called Mark from her car in the parking lot. Over the past few months they had grown even closer and she really needed a friend right now.

Thankfully he was there and answered the call. Vicki quickly told him what had happened.

"You did the right thing Vicki. I can't believe what a jerk that guy was to go back on his word like that. Don't even waste any time thinking about the guy."

"It's just that he's right. I've only got one more week on my contract. I let him stall me on this closing for over two weeks. He kept saying how busy he was and like a fool I believed that he'd honor his word and close today. It's not the money. I just don't want to let the owners down. They really are a sweet couple and I want to do right by them. I knew I shouldn't have delayed the closing and I should have insisted that Gene give me a nonrefundable earnest money deposit of at least $2,000 for me to have agreed to sell him my contract. Stephen told me to ask for that much at least when he coached me on the conference call a few weeks ago."

Mark's voice was soft now. "Don't beat yourself up over it. You learned a lesson. You are a person of your word, that other guy wasn't. I promise you we'll figure out a way for you to take care of your sellers and make this deal work, okay?"

Vicki felt so much better just talking with Mark. Over the next half hour they brainstormed possible solutions about how to proceed. In the end they came up with a plan that they both agreed was best. After they hung up, Vicki quickly started making calls to put that plan into action. She felt a sense of determination. She knew that not only would she make this deal work, but she would make sure to send a thank you card to Gene when this was all over and she ended up making a much larger profit!

Nine days had passed and Vicki was on a coaching call led by Scott. When it was her turn Vicki quickly laid out what had happened nine days prior for the other students on the line.

"Well, what's happened since then?" Scott asked.

"Mark and I came up with a plan that called for me to get a quick hard money loan and close on the house myself. I spent all that afternoon and much of the next morning leaving messages with potential lenders until I finally found one who agreed to lend me the money I needed provided the house would appraise high enough. It took two days for the appraisal to happen and the loan to get approved. I ended up having to pay 5 points up front and 12 percent interest. But the lender not only lent me the money to buy the place and get me an extra $10,000 at the closing that I needed to finish the final repairs on the property, but he also lent me money for the first six months of payments to take the financial pressure off me. I closed on the house four days ago and the sellers were thrilled. I have a few contractors lined up to finish the repairs over the next two weeks and then I'll go ahead and list the property for sale. Conservatively I'll end up netting about $30,000 to $40,000."

"That's great Vicki," Scott said. "I really admire how you were able to recover from a blow. That really says something about you. The lesson for all of you who are on the call tonight is that while you will rarely meet someone as outright dishonest as this investor Vicki dealt with, still you have to be aware of how people can pressure you at a closing and how you can protect yourself.

"One thing that Vicki learned the hard way is that a buyer's word is not always something you can trust. It's really hard to force a buyer to go through with a sale just because they signed a piece of paper. Yes, you can sue for specific performance. But that will take time and cost money, and in the end it is rarely worth it. That's why it's so important to always have nonrefundable money in hand from your buyer before you stop marketing your property. I know the times I've broken this rule I've regretted it."

"Scott," Nancy asked, "Tim and I just sold a house and had something similar happen. It wasn't even close to what Vicki had to deal with, but we had a deal on a five-bedroom house and at the closing our buyer kept pressuring us for more and more discounts on the price. I felt trapped because by that point I didn't want to lose the sale. It had taken over three months to get this buyer to closing and I didn't want to have to carry an empty property for three more months. What should I do in the future?"

"There is nothing worse than that sickening feeling of anxiety of losing a deal you really don't want to lose, is there?" said Scott. "Let me share with you some of the techniques David and Peter have shared with me that have really worked wonders for me when I have to deal with buyers or sellers or real estate agents who push me to make last-minute concessions at the closing table.

"First, I like to make sure to preframe the negotiation to get agreement and commitment from the other parties involved that there won't be any last-minute nibbling. One way I do that is by always making sure I have some firm commitment on their part before I commit myself. If it's a seller, his commitment is a signature on the agreement. But if it's a buyer, I need something more committing him to the deal. With a buyer this means money. If my buyer isn't willing to give me a decent earnest money deposit then I know I don't have a committed buyer. Or if my buyer wants all kinds of contingencies in the purchase agreement so that he can back out without losing anything, I know I do not have a committed buyer."

"But what do you do if they're not willing to give you money unless they have a contingency like on the inspections and lender approvals?" Nancy asked.

"Simple," Scott answered, "I give my buyer a short but reasonable period of time to do his physical inspection, and clearly let him know that until he removes the contingencies the property stays on the market. Let's role-play this. Nancy, will you be my buyer?"

"Sure."

"Great. So let's say you and your agent just handed me an offer to purchase the property. We went through one counteroffer and agreed on the price and terms. Now we're about to agree on the purchase contract language itself. Let's start the role-play.

"Nancy, before we spend the time getting the agreement just right for both of us, may I ask you one simple question? And all I want is your honest, straight answer. Are you willing to give me your straight answer?"

"Sure."

"I appreciate that," Scott replied. "Over the years of doing real estate I've learned that your answer to this one question lets me know who is for real, and who is just faking it. And neither one of us has time for someone who is just pretending. So tell me Nancy, are you going to buy this house? Look, I know that you have to do your inspection, and check the chain of title and all. That's a given. But when all that comes out reasonable, are you going to buy my property?" As Scott asked Nancy this question, everyone on the phone could almost imagine Scott looking Nancy right in the eye as he waited for an answer.

"Yes I am Scott. I'm going to buy it."

Scott ended the role-play and said, "The key is to get the other party to commit out loud that they are serious. Once they've made this commitment, you can use it to make sure that you protect yourself from this other party not treating you fairly. For example, if you want to give Nancy 14 days to remove the inspection contingency, you can simply say, 'Of course you need to get the property professionally inspected. I think a week or so should be plenty of time for a serious buyer like yourself to make this happen, don't you think? But let's build in a little fudge factor, let's give you 14 days to get the inspection done. Look, when you have it completed I want to be reasonable about things. If there is something major wrong with the house that I wasn't aware of, then I will make it right for you or we'll adjust the price. But I also want to make sure you're not going to try to use the inspection report to nickel-and-dime me down in my price over the petty stuff. You're not going to do that, are you?'

"Did you all see how I preframed what would happen after they got the inspection report to make it very difficult for them to come back and nibble me for concessions?" Scott continued. "I am establishing a precedent that we will both follow that will also benefit you at the closing."

Scott went on to explain several other closing keys until the coaching call ended an hour later.

BRIGHT IDEA

The Three Keys to Protecting Yourself from a High-Pressure Closing

You are most vulnerable for the other party to nibble concessions from you at the closing table. After all, at this point you're psychologically committed to the deal. Here are the techniques to protect yourself at the closing table.

Technique One: Give them a strong, positive reputation up front at the closing to make them feel awkward going back on their word.
"I'm so glad that we were able to create a concrete win-win deal that we both could absolutely commit to. It really means a lot to me to do business with someone like you who stands by their word. You'd be surprised at the number of people I've met who've tried changing things at the end even though they'd already given me their word on things. It's really a treat to be doing business with someone I like and trust like you."

(continued)

The Three Keys to Protecting Yourself from a High-Pressure Closing (continued)

Technique Two: Always make sure you have more than enough time to review agreements and to feel slow, calm, and peaceful during the closing.
I suggest that you require that any closing document be given to you at least three working days in advance of the closing so that you have time to review it at leisure. If the other party gives you a new document at the closing table that you haven't seen or pressures you to sign the documents without reading them for a last time, simply say, "You know, I'm a little embarrassed to admit this, but I'm a really slow reader. I know I can trust you enough, which is why I was willing to share this with you, although it's a bit scary. Maybe I should take these documents to the waiting room and sit down with them for a while and read them through slowly, or if you want, you can give me an hour or two here alone to go through them. That way you can use your time productively and I don't feel pressed to read faster, which actually makes it harder for me. Which do you prefer?"

Also, always make sure you leave the entire day free to do the real estate closing and not just an hour or two. Bring food with you and something to drink. You settle in like you're happy for the closing to take all day. You'd be amazed how powerfully this counteracts a last-minute nibbler, since the longer you take going through documents and just chatting with them, the more they feel pressured to just close the deal like you agreed to. It's the Zen way to do a fair and honorable closing.

If the other side still tries to give you new documents right at the closing, then make sure you do *not* read them with the other party standing over your shoulder. If they're in the room while you are reading the new documents, then there is implicitly subtle pressure on you to hurry. You should ask for all the time you need to carefully read through the documents on your own.

If after reviewing them you are at all uncomfortable, I recommend that you have your attorney on call to help walk you through any questions and make any needed changes to the documents.

Technique Three: Learn to effectively deal with the unethical last-minute deal renegotiators.
Yes, it does happen, rarely but often enough that you need to know how to counteract an unsavory person who is trying to get you to tweak the deal at the closing table by pressuring you to do things that aren't fair to you. First, call them on their behavior in a nice way. Say something like, "Now Mr. Buyer, I think I must have misunderstood what you just asked me to do with the price.

(continued)

The Three Keys to Protecting Yourself from a High-Pressure Closing *(continued)*

I know we agreed in writing over four weeks ago that the price would be $469,000, and you are a man of your word who doesn't go back on his word. You didn't really mean it when you just hinted at me lowering the price, did you?"

Usually this will be enough to embarrass the person to play fair. If it isn't, then you know you are dealing with someone who has, shall we say, a flexible sense of integrity. With these people you have two choices. Choice one is to drag out the process as long as you can, knowing that you have all day and chances are the other party doesn't. In a high-pressure negotiation with a win-lose negotiator, the party with more time on their side has a big advantage. If you keep your calm, make them repeat their requests over and over again, and with an iron will keep repeating your clear commitment to do the deal only as written in the original agreement, over and over like a broken record, you have a good chance of getting your way.

If you're not willing to go through this ordeal (actually I find it fun, since I look at it like an intense workout at the negotiating gym, but admittedly I'm a strange person) then immediately call the other party on their behavior and bring the deal to a head. "Mr. Buyer, it almost feels to me like you are wanting to change the deal here in the last moment. I am hoping I'm wrong about that. Let me ask you direct and straight. Are you going to buy according to the terms of our written agreement without changes, yes or no?" If they equivocate or waffle, repeat your question until you get a clear yes or no.

If the answer is a no, simply stand up, and tell them that you aren't willing to do business that way. Make sure you document their answer and have the title company representative who is in the closing room initial your notation that the other party backed out of the written deal (so you have no problem keeping their earnest money deposit), and leave. This is a rare occurrence, but know that it just isn't worth it to do business with unethical people who don't honor their word. Life is too short.

CHAPTER FIFTEEN

Month 5—Mark Gets Coaching on How Best to Leverage His Time

Mark got back to his house around 5:30 in the evening. He felt tired from the day, but it was a good tired. He'd just finished a drawn-out meeting with two contractors about a house he was getting ready to sell that needed sprucing up first. They had spent over three hours at the house, walking through it, creating a punch list of things that needed to be done to make the house sell fast.

As Mark fixed himself dinner, he thought back over the last two months since he had made the leap and took a leave of absence from his job with the airline to do his investing full-time. He was averaging about two or three deals a month now, but he felt maxed out. He realized he needed coaching on how to push past this plateau and progress to the next level.

After dinner, Mark sat down in front of his computer and logged onto the Mentorship Program student web site. He spent about 15 minutes reading the new posts to the Investor Discussion Board, getting some great ideas for himself and posting encouragement to a few of his fellow students.

Once he was caught up on the new postings, he started to compose his own post to get help from one of the coaches.

Things are going really well with my investing. I feel like I have a strong handle on all five of the Core Investor Skills. I'm consistently doing deals and I feel great about my progress. I just need some help on how to leverage my time better.

I find myself rushing through the day, dealing with one part of my business, then another. I know I could be doing more deals, it's just that I need help. I've thought about starting to hire some help to leverage my time, but I'm not sure where to start with that.

I guess the bottom line is that I am ready to step into Middle Stage Level Two investing and I'm not sure who to hire and how to best use them once I hire them! Any coaching would sure be appreciated.

Mark

Mark turned off his computer and checked his voice mail. He smiled when he heard the two calls he'd gotten in response to his postcard mailing to owners who were in early stage foreclosure. He dutifully logged in the calls on his tracking form, then called them both back. It turned out one of the two was not only home, but eager to get his call. Mark set up an appointment to go visit with this owner the next afternoon. With that, Mark called it a night. He planned to get an early start the next day.

The next morning Mark prepared his next bunch of postcards for sending that day. When he finished this up at around 10:00 A.M. he went online to check for any answers to his post on the Mentorship discussion board. He was thrilled to get Stephen's response:

Mark,

I can totally understand where you are. I remember the days of running the whole show myself without any help. You are in a really good place with your investing because you're starting to build some great momentum that you can harness to take you to the next level.

Here are my suggestions for you:

First, I think you are exactly right. For you to progress you need to leverage yourself by starting to build an investing business around you. The first step for you will be to hire some full- or part-time team members that can leverage your time. Where you are now, the very best use of your time is meeting with motivated sellers, signing up more deals, and sitting down at real estate closings and collecting big checks. Anything that takes you away from that is costing you money. Over time you'll want to make sure you build in the time for you to step back out of your business so you can look at it as a whole, from a fresh perspective, to make sure your business is going down the right path, but for the next three to six months your focus needs to be on taking some tentative steps to branch out in your business.

The first four team members to hire, and the order I'd recommend to you about who to look for first, are as follows:

1. A **full- or part-time assistant**—someone who you will have do anything that saves you time (hire ASAP):
   - Screen your calls.
   - Prequalify sellers and buyers for you.
   - Organize your office files.
   - Schedule showings for your property.
   - Anything else that takes your time that they could do.

2. **Property prep team**—the person(s) who will do all the cleaning and preparation to have your houses ready for each of your showings. They are the ones who can also hang all the "For Sale" or "Rent to Own" signs you need around the neighborhood to promote the property (hire ASAP).

3. **Handyman/all-around repair person**—I think you already have this person or people. I just want to make sure you are not picking up a hammer or paintbrush, or worse yet . . . a plunger! I think you should train your assistant to organize and check on this work to free up more of your time.

4. **Bookkeeper**—If you're like a lot of investors you're probably just letting this area slide. Don't! It will come back to haunt you. I recommend you find a local bookkeeper who you can work with to get your financial house in order right from the very beginning.

Later on, depending on the direction of your business, you'll want to add on people like these:

- A **marketing assistant** to help you find more motivated sellers and qualified renters or buyers.

- A **property manager/office manager** to help you oversee your portfolio of rental and rent-to-own homes. This will be very important if you are holding a portion of the properties you are buying, which I hope you are. Also, when you start to do larger properties, like a 12-plex, the experience your team has on how to manage properties will become very valuable. (And even more so if you ever buy an even larger multiunit property.) If your business buys and sells lots of properties you can train this person to manage the closing process. She could do all the necessary due diligence and monitor the financing and closing process to keep everything on track. This would free up a ton of your time.

- A **general contractor** to help oversee any and all rehab projects you have going, if you are doing a number of them. This will depend on the direction of your business. We do about 10 to 15 rehab projects a year, so this type of person is helpful. If you are only doing one or two a year, then you may not need this person.

- A **leasing/selling agent** to help you fill empty properties and sell the properties you want. Your leasing agent will probably work for you while your selling agent will be a licensed real estate agent or broker who lists and sells all your properties. Again, exactly who you'll need depends on what type of business you are building. Ideally you would pay this person on a commission so that you are paying only for results.

Good luck with this Mark, and remember, it's a great challenge to have. Feel free to get on any of the coaching calls and get other coaches' input on this. They will all have valuable insights to share with you.

Stephen
Mentorship Coach

CHAPTER SIXTEEN

Month 8—Leon and Mary Learn Tenant Management Systems and Secrets

Leon and Mary made sure to get back home in plenty of time for the 3:00 P.M. conference call Stephen was leading. They had some important questions about how to build one very critical part of their investing business.

At the appointed time they called into the conference line and joined seven other investors who were on the call with Stephen.

"Welcome to the coaching call," Stephen greeted everybody. "What are you all working on that I can help you with?"

Leon and Mary listened as two other students described deals they were working on. Leon was always thrilled when he got to listen to the coaching feedback and brainstorming on other people's deals. Sometimes he found it easier to pick up new ideas when he could be a third party just listening. Today was sure one of those times, because he took a full page of notes on ideas he planned to use in his investing business.

When it was their turn, Leon said to Stephen, "Stephen, Mary and I are doing great. We're up to 12 properties in our portfolio. Ten of them are houses or condos and two of them are triplexes. We have all but two of the houses on a rent-to-own basis and our tenant buyers for the most part are paying on time and taking care of all the property upkeep."

"That's great, congratulations!" Stephen said. "How can I help you? What coaching are you looking for from me to day?"

"Well, Mary and I are starting to see how the more properties we add to our portfolio as long-term keepers, the more of a need we have to build better systems around our tenant management. Right now we have only eight tenant buyers and eight renters in all the units, and we're finding that babysitting them is taking on more and more of our time. Can you give us any coaching as to how to make sure we keep our focus on intelligently buying more properties and not just on staying even with what we currently have?"

"What a great question. In fact, if it's okay with everyone else on the call today, I'd like to spend a while focusing on how you create a winning tenant management system so that you make more money with a lot less effort. Is that okay with everyone?" Stephen asked. All the students on the call were quick to agree that they wanted to learn everything Stephen had to share with them on this topic.

"First, I want to share with you the big picture. I want you all to commit that you are going to build a tenant management system that includes pieces to handle signing up a new tenant the right way; managing the relationship over time, including collecting rents; dealing with evictions; dealing with tenant retention; and finally transitioning through the move-out and lease-up process smoothly if you have a resident leave you.

"It's my belief," Stephen continued, "that there are two master systems you need to create once you reach Middle Stage Level Two in your investing. The first is your personal leveraging system, how you get the most from your personal time. The second depends on what the focus of your real estate business is. If you are doing a lot of rehabbing then you need a system to quickly take a property you just purchased, fix it up, and get it back on the market as quickly as possible. For this type of business it is the time between purchase and resale, along with how you control the repair costs, that largely determines the size of your profit. If you are buying and holding, using either the rental or rent-to-own exit strategy, then the second system you need is a tenant management system. The key for you is that the longer you can keep your property filled with high-quality occupants, the more money you will make. Turnover is one of the greatest expenses you will have.

"With all that said, let's talk about some of the key components of your tenant management system. First, let's talk about how you get paid. How easy do you make it for your tenants and tenant buyers to pay you each month? How secure do you make it for your investing business that you'll get paid? I think you have to do everything in your power to dramatically increase your rent collection percentages. If you stay on top of this, then most other things take care of themselves."

BRIGHT IDEA

How to Make Sure You Get Paid Your Rent Each Month— On Time!

The key is to make it easy for your tenants and tenant buyers to pay you rent each month. The easier it is for them, the more certain you are of getting your rent. Here are four ways to make it easier for you to get paid your rent each month.

1. **Payroll Deduction/Direct Deposit.** Why wait for your tenants to get their money, deposit their paycheck, and then pay you? Cut out the middle man! If your tenant works for a company that will allow it, set them up on payroll deduction/direct deposit for their monthly rent.

2. **Auto Debit.** Next in line is an automatic transfer from their checking or savings account to your bank account. Not only does this mean that you'll get your rent on time—automatically—but it also will instantly let you know if there is a problem. No waiting for a week or longer to have your bank notify you that a check bounced. You can go online and make sure the transfer happened and take immediate corrective action if it didn't.

3. **Preaddressed Monthly Rent Envelopes and Payment Coupons.** Make it easy for your renters to send you the rent each month. Give them preprinted envelopes and payment coupons to include with their check each month that lists the rent amount and clearly states who to make the check out to. While this seems obvious or overkill, my experience has shown that it significantly increases getting your rent on a timely basis.

4. **Have a backup plan.** If your tenant doesn't pay you by 5:00 P.M. on the first when the rent is due, I suggest you have an automated process in place to quickly take action to get your money. I call this process your "Late Payment Policy and Process." This process should spell out a timeline of what actions you or your staff will take, on which day, all the way through the eviction process. If your tenant doesn't pay, immediately work with your tenant to get your money. Help them problem-solve to get your rent.

(continued)

> **How to Make Sure You Get Paid Your Rent Each Month—**
> **On Time!** (continued)
>
> And at the *same time*, your company must proceed with the eviction process. Sympathize all you want, but the eviction process must run its course until you either get paid or regain possession of your property.
>
> The bottom line is that if your business is on top of the rent collection process, most other parts of your tenant relationship will go much more smoothly.

"I think that all of you should be building a tenant management procedures manual for your team so that the key knowledge of your tenant management process is not just in your head, but in a system that someone else can work. It took Susan and me about 12 months to really fine-tune our tenant management system, but it was worth every effort. Now when we buy a 40-unit apartment building I know exactly how much we can make it cash flow, and our team gets right on the process of taking over the property and integrating it with our systems and portfolio.

"For the level at which you all are, there are **five lessons that you have to learn first before you build your tenant management system**. Some of you may already know them, but all I can say is, are you living them?" Stephen paused and let his question sink in.

"**First, you've got to be fair and firm with your tenants.** The key word to managing the tenant relationship is *consistency*. You are *always* training your tenants as to how to treat you and your property. I only hope that you are teaching them that you will live up to all your promises and will hold them completely and unmovably accountable for all their commitments and behavior. Understand that if your tenants choose a behavior, they are also choosing the consequence. You must be unwavering in your consistency with them. I hated this idea when I first got started. David and Peter used to get all over me about it. I wanted to be my tenants' friends. I wanted to care for them. I've come to learn that I have to be a tough-love parent with very clear boundaries and consistently applied consequences.

"**Second, you've got to document everything.** I hated this one even more! I'm the original ADD kid. I hate all the detail work of papering the file. But I've learned it's a discipline you need to develop. Now I have staff members that do all this, and they do it about a thousand times better than I ever could. You need to keep a phone log of all your conversations with tenants, noting date and time of conversation, what you discussed, and any follow-up you or they agreed to. You need to send official letters detailing your understanding of key conversations. You need to keep the envelopes they sent their rent payments in if the postmark shows that the rental payment was late. Are you getting the idea here?

"**Third, you've got to have the 'No Pay, No Stay' policy integrated into the core of your business.** You are not helping your tenants by allowing them to break their word to you. You hold yourself to the same standard. You pay your lenders their monthly payment. You pay the utilities. You pay your staff. And you should expect your tenants to pay you too. Of course, for some of them life will happen and they'll be in tough financial situations. Be compassionate, be thoughtful, but be firm. The only way they can stay is if they pay. Period.

"This leads right into the **fourth key lesson—you aren't the owner, you are simply the manager**. You are just the powerless little guy who has it even worse than they do, who is caught between the big wheels of the 'company' that owns the property and the tenant who has always been so nice to you. You have 'no choice' but to follow the company's policies, and that means that if they don't pay you have to follow the eviction procedures. If it was up to you, heck, you'd let them stay there for as long as they wanted for free. But alas, it's not. The company ties your hands and forces you to follow its guidelines or you'll get fired. Does it make sense why you never want to tell the tenant you are the owner?" Stephen asked.

Leon answered, "It does, but what do I do with the tenants I have who I already told I was the owner?"

"Great question," Stephen responded. "First, with any new tenants make sure you follow this guideline. As for what to do with the ones you told you were the owner, make sure you start to talk about 'your partner' whenever you can with them. For example, the next time you see them, say your partner was thinking about getting some small thing fixed. Just start to include your partner in conversations with your tenants so they get used to the fact that you have a 'partner.' That way, if you need to get firm with your tenants for any reason, you can let your partner be the bad guy and you can maintain your good-guy reputation. Got it, Leon?"

"Got it."

"Good. **The fifth and final lesson for you all is that the real enemy is turnover.** Every time you have a unit turn you have the costs of fixing up the unit, repainting, cleaning, advertising, and paying someone to re-lease it. And this doesn't even count the cost of any lost rent. In our company our goal is to keep our residents with us for a minimum of three years, and longer is better. Understanding how important resident retention is, one of the systems you will eventually need to build is your resident retention plan. This will include things like gently breaking any rent increases to them, and creating an incentive plan that makes staying in the property long-term even more attractive to them."

Stephen went on talking about his tenant management systems and answering questions for the next 30 minutes. When the call ended, Leon and Mary compared notes and realized they had a lot of things to incorporate into their investing business right away. They spent about an hour creating a written action plan of the most important ideas that they were going to implement first, and even scheduled in an appointment with each other in 30 days to sit down together and evaluate their progress. As they looked through their calendars, they saw another date that really motivated them to stay focused. In four weeks they were having a "mastermind reunion" at their house and Mark, Tim and Nancy, and Vicki had all committed to being there. The plan was to spend one full day on their investing businesses and one full day just having fun. It would mark the one-year anniversary from the date they had all attended that first Intensive Training at the start of their investing. So much had happened to all of them over the past year, and they had grown to be so close. They still met twice a month for their regular 90-minute conference call mastermind sessions, not to mention all the e-mails, phone calls, and instant messages they traded back and forth.

CHAPTER SEVENTEEN

Month 12—Final Mastermind Meeting on Their One-Year Investing Anniversary

The four weeks sped past in a blur of last-minute phone calls and e-mails organizing travel. When the day finally arrived Mary could hardly sit still, and she practically drove Leon crazy with her last-minute preparations. But it was all worth it when, by noon on Saturday, all six of them were sitting down in the family room laughing together like kids.

"Vicki," Mary asked, "Who is looking after your kids this weekend?"

"My mom drove down and is spending the next five days looking after them."

They talked and laughed for an hour as they ate. Then Nancy, ever the one to keep to a schedule, prompted them to begin their mastermind meeting.

"I know we each said we'd prepare a 'Hot Sheet' of what we'd accomplished in the past year since we got started with our investing. Let's go around the circle and share our Hot Sheets, especially the part where we listed where we plan to focus our growing investing businesses," Nancy said. "Leon and Mary, why don't we start with you, and then we can just continue around the room?"

"Okay," Mary said with a smile as Leon handed out the single-sheet homework assignment they had all agreed to.

Results of Year One

- We purchased 9 properties to add to the 3 we already owned:
  - 6 houses
  - 4 condos
  - 2 triplexes
- From these 16 units we are generating $3,200 a month positive cash flow (includes option payments collected on rent-to-own houses).
- We have one of the condos in escrow to sell for $38,000 profit (closes next week).
- Our cash flow when we factor in *all* cash profits from rents, option money, and selling the condo is $63,600 in 12 months, or **$5,300 per month**.
- Total equity in 12 properties in portfolio is $320,000.

Focus for Coming Year

- Add 10 more quality properties to our portfolio (strong rental and rent-to-own areas, needing very little fix-up).
- Sell 1 or 2 properties in portfolio.

Goal: Over the next 12 months, generate a $6,000 a month positive cash flow so that we can use $3,500 (plus Leon's pension) to pay for our lifestyle and invest $2,500 per month for our grandchildren's college funds.

"Leon and I have really felt blessed by all that's gone on," said Mary. "We've come to recognize that we really don't want to deal with any properties that need a lot of fix-up. We like working with homes in nice areas that need at most paint and carpet."

She continued, "As you can see, our goals are pretty modest, and we're on track to hit them. It just makes us feel so good to think that we can make sure our four grandkids can go to any college they want and they'll have the money to pay for it."

"That's great Mary," Mark said. "What was the biggest lesson you learned over the past year?"

Leon answered, "For us the lesson has been on the need and the process to build a strong tenant management system. We are actually interviewing a few people to work part-time for us as we start to build that. We don't want to spend our retirement rushing around looking after properties, so we've decided to build the systems and business to manage this without us doing the day-to-day part of it. It may take us a few more years to get to that place, but we're confident that we'll be able to do it in the end."

Everyone congratulated Mary and Leon on their success. Then it was Tim and Nancy's turn. Tim handed out their one-page Hot Sheet to everyone.

Results of Year One

11 Deals:
- 3 flips—earned $22,000
- 1 rehab—earned $34,000
- 7 long-term keepers:
  - Option money: $39,000
  - Monthly rental cash flow: $985/month
  - Back-end profits: $290,000

Total cash profits for year (after *all* expenses, including educational cost for workshops, home-study courses, and Mentorship Program): $78,000

Effective cash flow ($78,000 divided by 12 months): **$6,500 per month**

Focus for Coming Year

- Flip one deal a month and add one long-term keeper to our portfolio each month.
- Put tenant buyers into all long-term keepers.
- Build a "Buyers List" of 15 or more investors to easily flip deals to.

Goal: Over next 18 months, reach a total of 25 properties in our rent-to-own portfolio. Also flip 15 properties over this time and generate a minimum of $100,000 from these flips.

After giving everyone a chance to look over the Hot Sheet, Tim explained, "As you all know, Nancy and I had a really rough start for the first five months. But we are so thrilled we stayed that course because around month five things really started to change for us. We got most of our deals from networking with local real estate agents or from our 'I Buy Houses' signs. As for our biggest lessons from the year, Nancy and I couldn't choose just one, but here are our top three. First, we realize that rehabbing is not for us. After that one house ate up so much of my mental and emotional energy for less money than we made on the three houses we flipped, we realized that any property that needs more than a simple cosmetic face-lift we'll flip to another investor for a quick payday. Second, we learned that we really can do our investing in our home area even though the property values are so high. Now that we have our deals, we hope our tenant buyers don't buy because the houses are appreciating so well. We'd rather not get cashed out in 24 months but get the houses back to put new tenant buyers in at a higher rent, price, and option payment."

"The biggest lesson for us though," Nancy shared, "is that it is essential to keep taking the small steps forward each day in our investing, even when things look bleak. We almost threw in the towel at month two but we are so glad we didn't. I still plan to keep working for another 12 months at least, but after that I think I'll give my notice and join Tim full-time in our investing business."

Again everyone congratulated Tim and Nancy. Then it was Mark's turn and he passed out his Hot Sheet.

Results of Year One

22 Deals: I flipped 6 of them, retailed 4, and kept 12.

Generated:
- Cash from flips, option money, and resold properties: $194,000
- Cash flow each month from rents: $1,350 (and growing)
- Total cash flow over 12 months (from rents, option money, resold property, and flips): $202,575
- Effective monthly cash flow: **$16,881 per month**
- Back-end profits in my 12 keepers: $325,000

Focus for Coming Year

Move into commercial real estate and start buying apartment buildings and self storage units so I build my residual rental cash flow.

Goal: Within the next 24 months, build a passive, residual rental cash flow of $10,000 per month plus to increase my net worth to $2 million.

"I've figured out that for me, commercial real estate is where I want to go," said Mark. "I never thought I would be able to earn so much so quickly, but now that I have, I want to use this as a stepping stone to get into bigger deals. The way I look at it is that these larger deals will be easier to outsource the management to. Plus, the residual monthly rents attract me more than having to keep finding more properties to buy and sell. I know it will take some effort to make this shift, but I feel ready to take on the challenge.

"I already have an 8-unit building under contract that I'm going to close on in two weeks, plus there is a 36-unit building close to it that I am talking with the owner about buying. I've got a small surprise for you all, but I'll tell you about it after Vicki gets her turn."

Everyone was curious, but they turned to Vicki, who handed out her Hot Sheet.

Results of Year One

- 3 flips ($18,000 cash)
- 6 rehabs
  - 4 retailed ($148,000 cash)
  - 1 rent-to-owned ($4,000 option money plus $42,000 back-end profit and $212 per month cash flow)
  - 1 in progress
- 3 subject-to deals (I have tenant buyers in all three)
  - Option payments: $12,000
  - Monthly cash flow: $475
  - Back-end profits: $65,000

Total Profits for Year

Cash profits	$178,000
Back-end profits	$107,000
Effective cash flow for year	**$14,833 per month**

Focus for Coming Year

Focus on foreclosures, pre-foreclosure market, and tired landlords. I'm looking to find mostly houses that need to be rehabbed. I plan to do about six to eight of them and flip the rest. Of the ones I fix up, I plan to sell half and keep half for the long term.

Goal: To find two deals a month, each month, over the next year. Pick the best six or eight to fix up, and resell half of these to retail cash buyers and the other half to tenant buyers. The remainder of the deals I will flip for added cash flow.

Vicki began, "I think the biggest lesson for me was the importance of creating a support structure for myself. You've all been such an important part of that, and I'm grateful to you all." She paused because her eyes were filling with tears. She wasn't the only one in the room reaching for a tissue at that moment.

"You know how Mark mentioned his surprise? Well, it kind of impacts me too . . ." Vicki hesitated and looked at Mark. "Over the past year Mark and I have gotten very close and, well . . ." Vicki held up her left hand, which had a sparkle on the third finger. "We're engaged!"

The room exploded into hugs and tears and shouts of joy. They carried this connection through the rest of their mastermind meeting, where they spent one hour focused on each of their investing businesses in turn. But the real highlight was the love they shared and friendships they enjoyed together.

In the end they all planned to get together for their next reunion in six months. Of course, they also planned to continue their biweekly telephone mastermind sessions too.

PART THREE

YOUR TURN—TURNING THIS BOOK INTO CASH FLOW

CHAPTER EIGHTEEN

Six Success Stories to Light Your Path

I hope you've found the first two parts of the book both informational and inspirational. In this final part of the book, the focus will shift onto you. But first I do need to remind you that the successes of Tim, Nancy, Leon, Mary, Mark, and Vicki weren't a fluke. Their stories are based on a compilation of many of the successful Mentorship students I have worked with over the past decade.

In fact, about two months before the final manuscript for this book was due to the publisher, I sent a quick e-mail to the 100,000 readers of my regular e-letter. I asked for any Level Two or Level Three investors to answer a detailed survey and questionnaire to share their investor stories with me. Within five days I had over 96 responses from all across the United States and Canada.

In just a moment I will share six of these inspiring stories, but first I want to share some of the insights I gained about successful investing by studying their responses back to back.

First, it became obvious that the single greatest obstacle they had to overcome was fear. Almost every respondent shared how, in the early days of their investing, they were scared. They shared how they had to face the naysayers who said it couldn't be done, and who said that even if it could be done, then it certainly couldn't be done by them.

It is said that the best revenge isn't to get even, but to get ahead. All of the people submitting their stories had a strong element of gratitude for all they had received because they took the plunge and began building their investing business.

They spoke of the hope their early successes gave them that they could earn their financial freedom and live life on *their* terms. They shared their joy that they could not only provide the material things for their family, but that they had the time and flexibility to be there for their kids and community. It was amazing how important it was to all of them to know that they would never be financially dependent on anyone else ever again.

One thing I saw in all the Level Two stories submitted was how close these intermediate level investors were to going passive in their investing. Almost without exception, these determined individuals were just a short 12 to 36 months away from earning their financial freedom forever and stepping into a Level Three life. It was obvious that they drew a tremendous amount of joy and satisfaction from their certainty about their path on the real estate fast track. As for the Level Three stories that were submitted, there was a strong theme of gratitude and a desire to give back and help others.

Now I'd like to share six of their stories with you in the hope that they will inspire you to do what it takes on your end to get into action and go after your investing dreams. I think when you read about what they were able to accomplish, you'll realize that the stars of this book have a great group of peers in past and present Mentorship students. As you read their stories, know that you are close to experiencing the same success and freedom that they have created, if you just go after your dreams with a firm commitment and mind open to learn along the way.

Laura

Imagine what it would be like to be 19 years old and be bedridden with a broken back. That's how Laura got her start investing. While convalescing, she listened to a home-study course on no-money-down investing that her father lent her.

Two months later Laura bought her first rental property—she couldn't even walk up the steps to look at the second story! She used that property to pay for her college education by renting out rooms in the house.

When she met her husband, they actually went out on their second date and bought a fourplex together! This was the start of her investing, not to mention a happy marriage.

Laura is now an Advanced Stage Level Two investor with a real estate portfolio that generates $40,000 per month in gross rents. Over the past five years she and her husband, who quit the police force two years ago, have built a net worth of over $1.5 million.

We all have so-called *reasons* why we can't make our investing work. Things like being too young, or too old, or not educated enough, or too educated. The fact is that anyone with the drive and determination can make this work, even if they start their investing while recovering from a broken back, or if they are in a wheelchair (like an investor acquaintance of mine who has bought tens of millions of dollars of real estate), or if they are blind, like two of my students who bought six properties their first year.

The real question is, are you going to buy your excuses or your possibilities? The choice and the rewards are both up to you.

Bob

Bob is a Mentorship student who got started in the program about 12 months ago. He came from the telecom industry, an industry that has gone through some major changes in recent years. For the first 20 years he worked in a stable environment for the same company. In his next four years he worked for four different companies! He knew he wanted to get out and take control of his life, so he finally made the leap into real estate.

His first deal was a rehab project he did on a condo. He rented it out and got $400 per month positive cash flow until he sold it a year later for a $79,657 profit. His second deal, a short sale that he held for less than 90 days, made him $66,000. And his third deal has over $100,000 in locked-in profits and counting. In fact, all said, Bob made more money in his first six months of investing than in any other full year of his life. Not bad considering that he also had time to play a whopping total of 57 rounds of golf during those six months too!

Matt

The next story is about a doctor named Matt. Like many physicians, Matt worked hard, typically 70 to 80 hours a week, to earn his healthy six-figure income. Each year, though, it seemed that he had to work longer and harder to earn the same income. Insurance companies paid less and less for each unit of his work, yet his expenses and insurance costs kept climbing.

It was at this time that his son brought a book home from college called *Rich Dad, Poor Dad.** When Matt read it, it totally changed how he thought about money and wealth. It sparked him to learn the tangible, how-to side of how to break out of the rat race he was so mired in. He found one of Peter's and my books in his local bookstore and loved it. From there he went on to attend one of our workshops and invest in some of our home-study materials. His first few deals were small lease option deals near his home. Since then he's gone on to other larger deals, such as a commercial horse ranch he purchased in Montana with estimated profits of $150,000.

Given the rapid growth in his single family house business, he retired from medicine to invest full-time. It was an easy decision for him, considering that not only did he earn $70,000 on a recent transaction, but his son and daughter are involved in his business with him. For those of you with kids, can you imagine what a powerful role model you could be for them when you go after your investing dreams?

Matt's 16-year-old son has formed his own rehab company to handle the lighter rehab work for his dad, and when he comes of age he'll become a full partner in the family investing business.

Brian and Angela

Brian and Angela always knew they wanted to be financially free. Their first attempts at building their fortune involved starting up several businesses. But in the end they just spread themselves too thin and ended up losing everything—their businesses, their three properties, even their car.

---

*I get asked all the time what books on money, wealth, and success I recommend. Would you like to get my list of the top 10 books you must read to be successful and wealthy? Just go to **www.InvestorFasttrack.com** and click on the "Investor Resources" tab.

They scraped together $400 and bought an old beat-up car, which was their home for over three months while they were homeless. Unlike the average person who would use all of it as an excuse to give up, Brian and Angela used it as fuel to prove to themselves and everyone else they knew that they could in fact do it. With the last bit of their money from a remodeling job they had just completed, Brian and Angela moved to Montgomery, Alabama.

After reading one of my and Peter's earlier books they did their first creative real estate transaction, a lease option, and sold it to a tenant buyer 10 days later. Fast-forward two years. Brian and Angela have now done **50 deals**, created a six-figure income, and built up a $1 million net worth!

Sean

Sean is a Mentorship student who first found out about these ideas from reading one of our earlier books. On July 4 one year ago Sean did his first real estate deal. He still calls this day his "personal independence day."

Over the past 12 months Sean and his business partner Rick have purchased over **40 houses** worth $5 million and built up $600,000 of equity.

As you can imagine, that kind of growth brings with it challenges of its own. As Middle Stage Level Two investors, Sean and Rick are working on building the systems they need to handle that volume of business. Some months they buy six houses and they have to quickly scramble to find tenants and tenant buyers for all of the homes. But for them, succeeding in real estate is about tuning out the conventional wisdom of settling for mediocrity and stepping out on faith. It's about knowing that they have a higher purpose and must learn to trust in that purpose and direction.

Michael

Three years ago Michael's company told him they would be laying him off. With a wife who was pregnant with their first child, this was a major wake-up call to him. Even though his company didn't end up letting him go, Michael decided then and there that he wasn't going to ever be put in that position again. He would be the one in control.

He started reading real estate book after real estate book. Late one night, he was praying to God to give him direction about how to get started. At the time he was reading our book *Making Big Money Investing in Foreclosures Without Cash or Credit*, and he turned to the back of the book and read that we had a Mentorship Program. He immediately got out of bed, went downstairs, got online, and read more about the program. The next day he signed up for it. It was February 12, the birthday of his late brother, Brian J., who was a Navy Seal who was killed in action in Afghanistan.

I remember meeting Michael at the Intensive Training he attended in Baltimore. I was so moved as he poured out the story of how he felt that he had to do more in his life as a way to honor his departed brother, and to honor the other men and women of the armed forces who died while serving this country. For him, this was a sacred commitment and it pushed him to get into instant action with his investing.

One month after leaving the training he did his first deal, a lease option with $300 per month in cash flow and a $60,000 back-end profit. During his first year investing, Michael did eight deals and made **$405,000 in cash profits**, plus several hundred thousand dollars more of back-end profits he'll reap in the years to come.

This success has allowed his wife to be a full-time mom. They had their second child last October. As you can imagine, Michael got to fire his company! (Can you imagine how good that must have felt?) But the thing he is most grateful for is not the material success, but rather the lives he has been able to touch and the people he's been able to help. It has felt very rewarding to him.

What was the secret to Michael's and these other investors' success? Simple: They took action, learned from the best, and kept committed to their real estate dreams when things got hard. This same simple formula will work for you.

In fact, in the next chapter I'll lay out a straightforward game plan for you to learn what you need to learn to start earning what you want to earn in your investing. Just turn the page and let's get to work!

CHAPTER NINETEEN

Creating Your Wealth Learning Map™

As a Level Two investor, it's time for you to focus on mastering the Core Investor Skills and building your knowledge base. This chapter gives you your Wealth Learning Map™ to take you from where you are to where you want to go.

This is your action plan to grow and develop into a wealthy investor who builds a profitable investing business. Your Wealth Learning Map™ includes a checklist of all the areas you need to learn. It also gives you a step-by-step game plan to master these areas as fast as possible. Because space in this book is limited, your Wealth Learning Map™ ties directly in with the Investor Fast Track Program™ that you get for free as a reader of this book.* Make sure you carefully read Appendix A for complete details on this free $2,495 gift.

The first part of your Wealth Learning Map™ covers the information you need to master, including skills, techniques, and investor information.

The second part of your Wealth Learning Map™ gives you a structure to integrate all this information by using it in the real world. Its focus is on training you

---

*To get immediate access to the Investor Fast Track Program™ go to **www.InvestorFasttrack .com**.

to follow a powerful action plan as you develop as an investor so that you maximize both your learning and your results.

Finally, in the third part you'll learn about the 11 Success Accelerators™. These key strategies and ideas will help you succeed faster, with less effort along the way.

The goal is to help you learn what you need to learn so that you can build a $5,000 to $50,000 per month real estate cash flow as fast as possible. Let's begin!

ACTION STEP

Your Wealth Learning Map™

Part One: Mastering the Five Core Investor Skills

Core Skill One: Creating a Deal Finding Machine

- Ability to quickly qualify sellers over the phone to quickly determine motivation level.
- Ability to quickly determine the seller's situation to see if the financial aspects of putting a deal together exist.
- Mastering at least three of the following basic deal finding marketing techniques:
  - Calling "For Sale" or "For Rent" classified ads
  - Placing "I Buy Houses" classified ads
  - Using "I Buy Houses" signs
  - Direct mail campaigns
  - Referral campaigns with your personal network
  - Referral campaigns with professionals (e.g., mortgage brokers, real estate agents, attorneys, CPAs, etc.)
  - Bird dogs to refer you deals (e.g., landscapers, delivery people, movers, etc.)
  - Cultivating a farm area
  - Door hangers and flyers
  - Calling expired listings
  - Outdoor advertising (billboards, bench ads, etc.)

Core Skill Two: Structuring Highly Profitable Win-Win Deals

- Mastering the Cash Deal Track™.
- Mastering the three main Acquisition Strategies of the Terms Deal Track™:
  - Lease options
  - Subject-to purchases
  - Owner-carry purchases

(continued)

Your Wealth Learning Map™ *(continued)*

- Mastering the five main Exit Strategies:
  - Flipping a deal
  - Selling a property to a retail cash buyer
  - Selling rent-to-own
  - Renting
  - Selling with owner financing

- Layering in knowledge of the following deal structuring techniques and tools over 24 months:
  - Preselling your purchases before you close on them
  - Joint venturing
  - Equity splits (especially using the "hybrid equity split" technique I shared with you in Chapter 4)
  - Using hard money lenders
  - Cultivating private money lenders
  - Intelligently tapping into conventional lenders when needed
  - Using graduated payments, graduated prices, and reverse credits
  - Combining purchase strategies and techniques
  - Advanced owner-carry techniques:
    - No-interest, no-payment loans
    - No-payment, interest-accruing loans
    - Interest-only loans
    - Using "thank you" payments
    - Prenegotiated extension and renewal terms
    - Cross collateralization
    - Seller subordination

Core Skill Three: Negotiating Win-Win Deals
- Mastering the Instant Offer System.
- Learning to effectively use negative phrasing.
- Understanding how to always be a reluctant buyer.
- Learning to build the other party's motivation.
- Layering in the advanced negotiating strategies over 24 months:
  - Tapping into the other party's emotional brain to get the decision you want.
  - Mastering the use of labels.
  - Learning to always create competition in any negotiation.
  - How to use friction to get the deal to stick.
  - How to use the principle of momentum to incrementally ease the other party to your way of thinking.

(continued)

Your Wealth Learning Map™ *(continued)*

- ° How to let the other party feel smarter and sharper, and why this will make you more money in the end.
- ° How to effectively use concessions in your negotiations.
- ° The Hypnotic Negotiating Patterns™.
- ° Tapping into the other party's imagination to help get them to see things your way.
- ° The Hypnotic Negotiating Markers™.
- ° How to negotiate through and with real estate agents.
- ° How to negotiate with lenders and keep the power.
- ° How to deal with the pressure in the closing room.

Core Skill Four: Analyzing the Deal Fast
- ■ Mastering the Deal Evaluation Wizard™:
  - ° The Deal Quick View™
  - ° The Due Diligence View™
  - ° The Closing View™
- ■ Learning to pull the trigger on a good deal *fast*.

Core Skill Five: Understanding the Language of Real Estate
- ■ Mastering the 10 main real estate concepts and terms*.
- ■ Mastering the seven essential contract basics.
- ■ Gaining a basic understanding of how to use LLCs and corporations to protect yourself.
- ■ Knowing how to use the main investor contracts in your "Contracts Library."
- ■ Learning to avoid the nine paperwork pitfalls.
- ■ Overcoming your shyness and asking questions at any real estate closing so you can learn more.

*For immediate access to the online class on the language of real estate which will teach you all 10 of the most essential real estate terms, go to **www.InvestorFasttrack.com** right now.

(continued)

Your Wealth Learning Map™ *(continued)*

Part Two: Integrating and Learning to *Use* the Information in Your Investing

Level Two Early Stage Investors
Here is your weekly plan of action.

At the start of your week:

Focus Session: What are the top five "bottom lines" you have for your investing business this week? What are the five things that, if you did them this week and did only them, would have the greatest long-term, positive impact on your investing business?

Item	Estimated Time to Complete	Day You'll Do It
1. _____		
2. _____		
3. _____		
4. _____		
5. _____		

Skill Focus for the Week: _____

Drill Sessions: Commit to a minimum of two "drill sessions" where for 15 minutes or longer you'll practice the above skill. You can practice by role-playing with someone, teaching the skill to a fellow investor, or—gulp—using the skill in the real world of your investing.

Session One Scheduled: _____
Session Two Scheduled: _____
Session Three Scheduled: _____ (optional)
Session Four Scheduled: _____ (optional)

Drill Debriefs: Take five minutes immediately after any drill session to answer the following questions.

- What went well? What did you feel best about during the session?
- What will you do differently next time you use this skill?
- What questions do you need to find the answers to in order to improve in this skill?

(continued)

Your Wealth Learning Map™ *(continued)*

Weekly Review: Take 30 minutes at the end of each week to reflect on your week of investing and to mine as much profit as you can from the wealth of experience.

Quick-list your top five accomplishments for the week:

1. _____
2. _____
3. _____
4. _____
5. _____

What did you do during the week that worked well? What things did you do that you want to repeat and build on next week?

What one or two specific things will you do differently next week as a result of what you learned this week?

What two questions will you learn the answers to next week to layer in another key coat of knowledge?

1. _____
2. _____

Middle Stage Level Two Investors

While your weekly format will be the same, you'll now make the following shifts:

- Rather than just choosing new skills to learn, you'll focus more of your efforts on refining the large skill base you have already developed.
- Each week, find one new way to leverage your time as an investor. This could be adding caller ID to your office phone line. Or it could be to delegate part of your projects to your assistant. Or it could be to find a piece of your business to outsource to an outside provider who can do a better job for less money.
- Each week, find one part of your business that you can wholly or partially systematize. This could be to create a "deposit worksheet" that your assistant fills out each time he deposits rent checks to give to your bookkeeper. Or this could be a checklist you follow when you are hiring a new handyman. The key is to capture the expertise of that process into a system so that later you can hand that system to someone else in your business and free up more of your time.

(continued)

Your Wealth Learning Map™ *(continued)*

Advanced Stage Level Two Investors
You are going to build on the format from the earlier two stages. The key difference is that you will let go of the drill sessions. Your skills are solid now. You will shift your focus to your investing business so that *each week* you do the following:

- Spend at least two hours on building one *big* system. Big systems are the core processes that run your company. For example, this could be your "tenant management system," or this could be your "due diligence system." These systems may take weeks to rough out and months to fine-tune. But when you're done, the result will be to stabilize your investing business and leverage your expertise so that it's now part of your business and not dependent on you.
- Create two small systems.
- Get each full-time team member to do the above two steps each week (focus on one big system for at least two hours, and build two small systems).

Trial Separations: There is no better way to help your business learn to thrive without you there than to incrementally give it longer and longer stretches of time to operate without you there.

At first this will mean you being out of the office for the afternoon. Later you will stretch this to a full day. Then two days. Then a full week. Then two weeks. When your business can thrive for a full two weeks without you there, then you know your business is on the verge of going to Level Three.

Trial separations give your team and systems the chance to stretch and grow. They also give you the chance to see where the weak spots are that need attention, and where the strong links are that need rewarding.

(continued)

Your Wealth Learning Map™ (continued)

Part Three: The 11 Success Accelerators™

Accelerator 1: Mentors

There is no better way to learn than by modeling someone who has succeeded in this area before you. Ideally you will cultivate several powerful mentoring relationships over the years.

Accelerator 2: Mastermind Group

A mastermind group is a select group of people who get together to help each other achieve specific chief aims. Your mastermind group can support and encourage you in your investing. They can give you straight and valuable feedback from their outside perspective. The group also brings to bear the positive aspects of peer pressure as it gives you a place to be accountable for your actions and to work hard to earn the respect of your peers.

Accelerator 3: Drill Partner

Especially in Early and Middle Stage Level Two, it is helpful to have another investor at your level to practice, role-play, and observe each other in the real world. You can teach each other and give feedback to each other. A drill partner is like your gym partner. Even when you don't feel like working out you know that he or she will be waiting at the gym, so you force yourself to show up even when you don't feel like it. After 10 years of teaching investors how to be wealthy I am convinced that getting yourself to show up, even when you don't feel like it, is one of the most important qualities of those people who make it.

Accelerator 4: Home-Study Courses

There are so many powerful courses out there that can add layers of knowledge to your foundation that you'd be foolish to ignore them. When you feel like watching television, put in a DVD from one of your courses. When you are in your car, listen to educational CDs as you drive. I started this habit over 10 years ago and it has made a huge difference in my life. Over the years I've listened to literally *thousands* of CDs (and audiocassettes when they existed, and now downloadable audio files). The average American spends nine working weeks each year in their car. Use this almost *three months* of working time to accelerate your learning by getting and listening to home-study courses while you drive.

(continued)

Your Wealth Learning Map™ *(continued)*

Accelerator 5: Quality Investor Workshops

There is something so potent in getting away from the world for two or three days at a time and throwing yourself full-out into a learning environment. Think about it. It takes me over three full years to perfect a workshop where I can teach the group in an accelerated fashion such that they get a full five years of my experience in just two or three days. It is one of the best forms of leverage. I take my own advice on this one. Each year I still attend at least two high-quality workshops myself.

Accelerator 6: Repetition

We learn best when we can reinforce that learning over time through repetition. This is why home-study courses are so valuable, because you can listen and watch the same material over and over. This is why doing regular drill sessions each week is so valuable. It's been said that repetition is the mother of all skills.

Accelerator 7: Immersion

The only thing better than repetition is immersion. By diving fully into the subject you will learn with more intensity and speed than you ever could imagine. This is why workshops are so effective, because for those two or three days you enter into that world fully. What is the best way to learn a language? By living in a country where you are forced to interact in only that language. Tap into this powerful learning accelerator wherever you can.

Accelerator 8: Feedback

I've always believed that feedback is the breakfast of champions. Heck, it's the lunch, dinner, and snacks too! This is why your mentor, mastermind group, practice partner, drill debrief sessions, and weekly review sessions are so critical. Each gives you another layer of feedback to fine-tune your learning. I also suggest you use technology to get feedback. Audiotape yourself on the phone (just your half of the conversation please, unless you get permission from the other person). Videotape your role-playing with your practice partner. At first this is almost painful as you see yourself under a microscope. But with a little time you sand off the rough edges and get excited by your growth and progress. In the end you'll succeed 10 to 100 times faster with all this feedback than if you choose the common path of least resistance which the average investor takes by default.

(continued)

Your Wealth Learning Map™ *(continued)*

Accelerator 9: Learn Right the First Time

There is nothing harder than unlearning a habitual way of doing a skill. This is why I urge you to do whatever it takes to learn from the best teachers so that you learn the right way the first time. In today's wired world you have so much access to the best teachers, there is no need for you to settle for anything less.*

Accelerator 10: Use Smaller Learning Sessions More Frequently

Spaced repetition is a powerful force in learning fast. More sessions done more frequently will always lead to greater learning and integration. Rather than read once a week for three hours, break it up into three one-hour sessions. More and smaller bits are better and easier to digest, just like with food. Rather than eating a huge meal one time each day, it's much healthier to eat several smaller meals spaced throughout the day.

Accelerator 11: Practice the Way You Want to Play

I had an old school coach back in the days I played for the U.S. National team. He forced us to practice all our drills and scrimmages at "game tempo." Why? Because under the stress of the real world you will revert to the ingrained habits you have formed. The hours you spend practicing your investing skills are only valuable if you have used that time to practice at game tempo.

*For a list of my favorite teachers on various real estate and wealth topics—from books to home-study courses to workshops to mentoring programs—just go to **www.InvestorFasttrack.com**.

CHAPTER TWENTY

Closing Thoughts on Your Wealth Building

Everybody Can Win!

There is a rumor in the world that the only way to make money investing in real estate is to take advantage of other people—to wait until people are vulnerable and then pounce. Sadly, I can understand why this rumor exists with such persistence, because it fits with the average person's worldview.

Most people see the world as a zero-sum game. That means that if they win, somebody else must be losing. They see a fixed pie and believe they must scramble and scrape to claim a bigger piece of it. In order for them to be wealthy, someone else must lose.

But this just isn't how the world really works. In truth there are infinite ways to create wealth that help and respect other people. In fact, it's my belief that the only way to build enduring wealth is by creating value and offering positive service to the world. The more value and service you create, the more wealth you will be rewarded with.

But the belief that wealth is severely limited still poisons many good people who otherwise could enjoy the wealth that is available to them. For example, take the case of Susan. She and her husband were two of our earliest Mentorship students. I remember how Susan struggled with her comfort over the money she and her husband were earning, fearing that it would all come crashing down, worried that they wouldn't have enough. At one of the wealth trainings she attended, we did a powerful exercise that helped her shift this limiting belief. Within 36 months, she and her husband had created a million-dollar net worth. But even more important than this money was the dramatic difference I saw in her as she came back to other workshops we held over the next few years. She seemed lighter and much happier. When I asked her what the difference was she told me that she had finally stopped worrying about money. She realized that she and her husband had the tools to create as much wealth as they needed. With this realization came a sense of peace of mind and trust.

Truly there is unlimited wealth out there waiting for you. The only thing you need to do is to put the investing strategies you've been learning into practice. When you apply the ideas in this book, you will be creating both cash flow and net worth. At first the cash flow you build will be active cash flow—money you work for each time you earn it by flipping, selling, optioning, and leasing your properties. Over time, as you grow your real estate portfolio, more and more of your cash flow will come from residual rents that automatically flow to you month after month. Eventually, as you build your investing business, you'll shift these income streams into passive cash flow.

Imagine for a moment how good it will feel to go out to your mailbox and know that every month $5,000 to $50,000 of net cash flow will be waiting for you when you pull down the flap of the box. Or better yet, imagine how much simpler and freer it will feel when you have all that money automatically deposited into your bank account each and every month—year after year. Think about the lives that you will be able to bless with your financial wealth. What are the expressions on their faces when they accept your gifts with joy and gratitude? What do you hear when they thank you? How does all this make you feel?

Think about the freedom your cash flow and net worth will buy you. Time to spend playing with your children and grandchildren . . . time to spend on vacation with your loved ones . . . time to sit and watch a sunset and feel closer to your Creator . . .

Real estate has proven itself to be one of the most powerful wealth creation vehicles. And now you have the Real Estate Fast Track to speed you on your journey.

Always remember that the wealth you have is a gift to you. How you put your wealth to use to bless the lives of other people is your gift back to the world.

In life, it's not the money you earn that counts—it's the lives you touch that truly matter. It's not a question of what you earn, but rather what you do with what you earn, that matters most.

Still, if you don't get out there and earn those dollars, you are limiting the gifts of time, freedom, and security that you are able to share with the world. I think you owe it to yourself, your family, your community, and to the world as a whole to create massive wealth and find creative, healthy ways to share a huge chunk of it.

In the end it is all up to you. You no longer have any excuse to settle for financial mediocrity. You have the knowledge to create great wealth, and now it's up to you to put these ideas and strategies into action.

It's Decision Time

It's been said that in times of adversity you don't have a problem to face, you have a decision to make. What is your decision going to be? Are you going to choose to give in to your fears and keep "thinking" about getting started with your investing? Or are you going to do whatever it takes to make your financial dreams your finan cial reality?

When you make the commitment to go after your dreams, a world of opportunities will open up to you and guides will appear in your life to help direct you on your journey. In some small way, I'm hoping that this book and the *Creating Cash Flow* series are just such a guide. I feel blessed that you chose me to be your mentor on your journey to building a profitable real estate investing business. I *know* you can do it. If all my years of working with investors just like you to build their cash flows and net worths has taught me anything, it's that it is totally doable for you to succeed. In fact, you can do it faster than you ever dreamed. Will you do it in a year or two? Probably not. But over the course of the next five years you can build the real estate portfolio and business that you need to generate a lifetime of cash flow to provide for you and your family forever.

Thank you for joining me through the pages of this book. I wish you success and joy in your journey.

The Investor Fast Track Program™— Your FREE $2,495 Gift from the Author

Dear Reader,

Do you truly want to turn the ideas and strategies in this book into a consistent stream of real estate cash flow so that you can enjoy the time and freedom you've always dreamed of having?

If you answered yes then I urge you to take the next step and claim your free $2,495 bonus for reading this book.

To register, all you'll need to do is go online to **www.InvestorFasttrack.com** and use the access code: "**cashflow777**."

When you register online you'll get immediate access to this comprehensive 90-day online investor business start-up system. It's designed to help investors like you master the ideas in this book and to quickly and easily put your investing on the fast track. It's like a rocket booster to help you launch your investing to the next level so that you can enjoy the freedom that a $5,000 to $50,000 per month real estate cash flow will bring you.

A Surprising Secret That Few Readers Know

You may not know this, but every time I write a book I'm left with thousands of words that must be cut or the book would just be too long. In this book the original manuscript had dozens of sections that I had to edit out for space! It was heartbreaking to cut out so many powerful investor strategies and techniques, but I had to do it anyway.

But I found a compromise solution that worked (in fact, it's one that I used on the last book, too, and everyone agreed it was the perfect solution!). I simply put all the extra content up on the Web as part of this valuable bonus!

Actually, I took it 10 steps further and turned much of that extra content into online investor training workshops that you get for free. Here are the details of what you'll get *free* for a limited time as part of this special gift to readers like yourself:

What You Get as Part of This Valuable *Free* Bonus:

- Powerful online **investor workshops** that will make building your investing business easier and faster!

- **Exclusive interview** with the top tax strategist in the country as she lays out the seven biggest real estate tax loopholes!

- **Private access** to a sample marketing "Master Mailing Calendar," including the word-for-word scripts to use to get mailing lists of sellers for FREE!

- State-by-state listings of which form of deeds and key documents to use!

- And much, much more!

You'll Also Get Instant Access to 10 Free Online Investor Workshops:

Workshop One: How to Build an Investing Business That Works So You Don't Have To!

Workshop Two: 22 Ways to Find Motivated Sellers!

Workshop Three: The 3 Keys to Structuring Deals Without Cash or Credit!

Workshop Four: Insider Secrets to Negotiating Profitable Deals!

Workshop Five: How to Avoid the 9 Deal Pitfalls!

Workshop Six: The 10 Most Important Real Estate Terms and Concepts!

Workshop Seven: 6 Ways to Leverage Yourself as an Investor!

Workshop Eight: The Biggest Secret to Creating Wealth with Real Estate!

Workshop Nine: The 7 Most Powerful Real Estate Tax Loopholes!

Workshop Ten: The 5 Most Important Asset Protection Strategies for Investors!

Best of all, you'll be able to attend all these workshops from the comfort and convenience of your own home!

Who Is the Investor Fast Track Program™ Right For?

It was designed for three groups of people:

Group One—Brand-New Investors

People who have always wanted to get started investing in real estate but in the past lacked the tools and support to make their investing dreams happen. For those of you in this group, I urge you to register immediately. This is the single most important thing you can do to make sure you will succeed with your investing. You'll get immediate access to hours and hours of cutting-edge investor training that just isn't available anywhere else.

Group Two—Intermediate-Level Investors

Intermediate-level investors who've already gotten started with their investing but need more clarity and direction on exactly what steps to take and how to avoid the costly mistakes other investors have made in the past as you grow your investing business. For those of you in this group the biggest thing you'll get by registering right now is the certainty and assurance of *knowing* that you now have a definite, concrete, and winning real estate business plan to follow so that your success is *guaranteed*!

Group Three—Experienced Pros

Experienced investors who want to take their existing investing businesses to the next level. You'll get a powerful framework to help fine-tune and turbo-charge your existing investing business and make it 10 times more profitable. The biggest danger you face is getting trapped working at your investing business instead of building the business that lets you enjoy the real estate cash flow *and* the freedom you deserve. That's why it's critical for you to break past these common barriers and use the Investor Fast Track Program™ as the spark to help your success skyrocket to the next level and beyond.

The bottom line is that this valuable bonus is for readers like you who want to build huge real estate cash flows as fast as possible and are willing to take action.

Whether you're completely new to investing and this is the first real estate book you've ever read or you're an experienced investor with dozens of properties in your real estate portfolio, the Investor Fast Track Program™ will help you take your investing to the next level.

The Real Reason I Can Give You This $2,495 Bonus for <u>FREE</u>

Let's face it. We live in a cynical world. Some skeptics are wondering how I can give every reader such a valuable bonus for the price of this book. It just sounds too good to be true . . . unless of course you understand my three motivations for giving you this $2,495 package for free.

First, I know that I am enjoying the lifestyle I am today because of the people who helped me along the way. I feel a calling to share my good fortune with other people so that you can reach your dreams and highest aspirations. Remember, I was once an amateur athlete living on $6,000 a year of income! I feel compelled to share this gift with as many people as I can.

Second, I know that when I share my knowledge and insights as openly and freely as possible, those of you who are meant to will choose to do other business with me. Whether you choose to attend one of the workshops I'm holding or just to recommend my books to other people that you know, I strongly believe that the more value a person gives to the world, the more will ultimately come back to them.

Third, when you register and go through the Investor Fast Track Program™ you'll notice that there is a strong element woven throughout the program of giving back. I believe that you cannot be wealthy without finding ways to openly and generously give to groups and causes that are bigger than yourself. Part of my mission in life is to help a generation of investors become massively wealthy, and to inspire and educate these investors on how to intelligently give away a large portion of that wealth in ways that bless the world. (Don't worry, not only will you be making so much money that you'll joyfully write checks to your favorite charities, but more importantly I'll help you build your investing business in such a way that you'll have the time to personally volunteer in the areas in which you feel most called to contribute.)

Here's How the Investor Fast Track Program™ Works!

Step 1: Go online to **www.InvestorFasttrack.com** to register using the password "**cashflow777.**"

Step 2: Take the Fast Track Intro Class™ that will share with you exactly how you can use the Investor Fast Track Program™ to grow your real estate investing business. It will give you the specific steps to take to leverage your investing efforts so that you immediately begin to grow your real estate cash flow.

Step 3: Follow the 90-day action plan and take all of the FREE online investor workshops. You'll literally get access to the same insider secrets and advanced investor strategies that I used to charge tens of thousands of dollars to share!

Step 4: Tap into the other powerful investor tools and resources that are available to you on this private web site, including downloading five FREE investor books.

Warning! If you don't think it's worth all the hard work and effort in the first few years of your investing so that you can enjoy a **lifetime** of financial freedom, then please do *not* register for this bonus. The powerful information and clear action-oriented strategies and tools would only frustrate you.

Only *register right now* if you understand that to make money investing in real estate takes energy and action, especially during the start-up phase.

If you want to make millions with zero work and zero effort I suggest you buy a lottery ticket. If, however, you are willing to invest the time and energy in the early years to build an investing business that will pump out consistent cash flow and create windfall profits for you for years to come, then *register right now*.

10 Reasons to Go Online and Register Now!

1. This special bonus offer is available for only a limited time and may be withdrawn at any time. You'll kick yourself if you miss out on this opportunity!

2. The sooner you log on and get access to all the powerful information and investor tools, the sooner you'll start making money investing!

3. Real estate is one of the most certain paths to financial freedom!

4. The Investor Fast Track Program™ will help you get out of the rat race and become financially free!

5. I just may come to my senses and start making people pay for this valuable bonus! (In fact, I reserve the right at any time to start charging for what this valuable bonus is really worth.)

6. The sooner you start making money investing, the sooner you can start sharing your good fortune with other people!

7. It will help you take your investing to the next level!

8. It will inspire you to take instant action!

9. It will help hold you accountable so that you make money, not excuses!

10. You'll build so much momentum by reading the book and logging on now you'll literally be propelled to your next real estate success!

Register Right Now and Get the Following Five eBooks—FREE!

When you register right now you'll also get my five most popular ebooks—absolutely free! These books are:

- *Seven Simple Steps to Sell Your Property on a Rent-to-Own Basis*
- *The Hidden Secrets of Seller Financing*
- *Three Simple Steps to Flip a Deal for Fast Cash Profits*
- *Short Sales—Making Money on Foreclosure Deals with Little or No Equity*
- *The Nine Essential Contract Clauses When Buying Real Estate*

How You Get This Powerful Bonus—Free!

To claim your free bonus package simply go online to **www.InvestorFasttrack.com** right now and complete the enrollment form. When prompted for your pass code simply enter "**cashflow777**." It's literally that easy!

Again I thank you for reading this book. I wish you a lifetime of success and happiness and know real estate will help you achieve this. Enjoy your "graduation gift" of the Investor Fast Track Program™!

My very best to you,

David Finkel

P.S. To get your free Investor Fast Track Program™ ($2,495 value), simply go to **www.InvestorFasttrack.com** and register using the password "**cashflow777**."

P.P.S. I urge you to register right now because this offer is for a very limited time only and I'd hate for you to miss out!

Ambassador Number: _____

The *Creating Cash Flow* Series!

We hope you've enjoyed Book Two of the *Creating Cash Flow* series. As you've learned in the book, there are three investor levels.

Level One investors are just getting started and need to prove to themselves that real estate can and does work for them.

Level Two investors work not only to develop and fine-tune their investor skills, but also to begin to build a real estate investing *business* instead of just settling for being a real estate investor.

Level Three investors have transitioned out of the day-to-day operations of their investing business and have the freedom to enjoy the incredible Level Three lifestyle that setting up their investing business the right way has provided for them.

The series is designed to teach you how to start as a Level One investor and grow to become a financially free Level Three investor as fast as possible.

Available in Bookstores and Online Now!

Learning to get started making money investing in real estate has never been easier or more certain. In Book One of the wildly popular *Creating Cash Flow* series you'll learn the fastest ways for you to launch your real estate investing business.

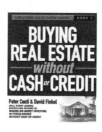

You'll learn:

- The 6 best sources to fund your "nothing down" deals!
- The 5 fastest ways to find your first deal in 30 days or less!
- 7 ways to maximize your cash when investing!
- 21 scripts to negotiate profitable real estate deals!

This book will show you the fastest way to get started investing in real estate—step-by-step, action-by-action, strategy-by-strategy.

To be released Spring 2007!

Are you ready to "go passive" with your investing? Level Three investors have learned to transition into passive profits with their investing business so that they can enjoy the freedom and security of a Level Three lifestyle.

In Book Three of the smash success *Creating Cash Flow* series you'll learn how to super-size your profits by investing in commercial real estate.

You'll learn:

- How to master the 7 Critical Wealth Skills of Super Successful Investors!
- The 4 pathways to passive real estate cash flow!
- The 9 deadly investor mistakes that could cause you to lose everything!
- 25 "must do" action steps to leverage your time and money as a Level Three investor!

Ex-Olympic-level athlete turned real estate multimillionaire **David Finkel** is one of the nation's leading real estate and wealth building experts. Over the past 10 years his more than 100,000 clients have literally bought and sold over $1 *billion* worth of real estate and made hundreds of millions of dollars in profits.

Finkel has co-authored 17 real estate and wealth creation courses and four other real estate bestsellers, including the *Wall Street Journal* and *BusinessWeek* bestseller, *Making Big Money Investing in Foreclosures Without Cash or Credit*. Two of his earlier books were selected as among the top 10 real estate books of the year by syndicated real estate columnist Robert Bruss. His first book, *How to Create Multiple Streams of Income Buying Homes in Nice Areas with Nothing Down*, was selected as one of the all-time top three investing books by the American Real Estate Investors Association. His most recent book, *Buying Real Estate without Cash or Credit*, was an instant bestseller upon its release.

Finkel has had a hand in thousands of real estate deals and is still an active investor with investment companies that buy residential and commercial real estate across the United States.

Finkel co-founded Mentor Financial Group, LLC, a real estate training company with more than 100,000 clients across North America. While Finkel is retired from the business, he still guest teaches or hosts a handful of high-end wealth workshops each year, including the Maui Mastermind event.

For several years Finkel was the co-host of the nationally broadcast *Real Estate Radio Show*, one of the most popular investing shows of all time. His how-to investor articles have been featured in over 4,000 newspapers and periodicals across the country, including the *Wall Street Journal* Online and the *Miami Herald*.

His real estate and wealth blogs at www.wealthshortcuts.com are two of the most popular wealth creation blogs on the Web.

To find out more about Finkel, or any of his wealth creation programs or resources, simply visit him on the Web at www.wealthshortcuts.com.